THE BACK YARD
A Bermuda Childhood

Ann Zuill Williams

**MACMILLAN
CARIBBEAN**

With love to my children,
Tana, Julie, Nicky and Frank.

First published 1988

Published by *Macmillan Publishers Ltd*
London and Basingstoke
*Associated companies and representatives in Accra,
Auckland, Delhi, Dublin, Gaborone, Hamburg, Harare,
Hong Kong, Kuala Lumpur, Lagos, Manzini, Melbourne,
Mexico City, Nairobi, New York, Singapore, Tokyo*

Printed in Hong Kong

British Library Cataloguing in Publication Data
Williams, Ann Zuill
    The back yard : a Bermuda childhood.
    1. Bermuda. Social life, 1939–1945.
    Biographies
    I. Title
    972.99′009′94

ISBN 0-333-48333-2

CONTENTS

Foreword iv

Introduction vii

1. Orange Grove 1

2. The Family 10

3. From The Peak 18

4. Ducks 21

5. Harvey 24

6. Friends and Goings-on at Home 27

7. Christmas and Easter 37

8. Treasured Possessions 41

9. Kindergarten 43

10. Camping 45

11. Wartime 50

12. Rationing 54

13. The Train 58

14. Horses 61

15. Dogs 70

16. Cats 78

17. Review 82

FOREWORD

I have had it in mind for some years to write down what I remember of my childhood in the War years. We in Bermuda, as children, were extraordinarily lucky to have a happy and safe upbringing, while across the Atlantic and stretching far beyond Europe into the Pacific, life for other children was bewildering, shattering and intolerable. Our days were spent in the normal way, school, holidays and an orderly home life. Apart from the fact we knew war was happening somewhere, our lives were carefree and casual.

Unlike today, it was quite safe for us to run down Flatts Hill and dive off the rocks into Harrington Sound, or join the other children on Flatts Bridge to dive into the tide, swim like demons to get out of the current, clamber up the rocks and back on to the bridge to do it all over again. We didn't have to worry about cars, motorbikes or speed-boats mowing us down—there weren't any. We knew everyone so if by chance someone was in trouble or hurt, word was soon carried home for help to be sent.

My only regret is that I did not start to write this some years ago before my Mother died. She would have been an enormous help prompting my memory for so much that I have forgotten. I hope she will approve from her place far away. My husband has been more encouraging than I ever dreamed of, for which I am truly grateful. I think our children will find interest, amusement and thoughtfulness for an era gone by. They read and listened to the beginnings of these remembrances and asked me to continue. There are no letters to remind me. This little book is purely a record of what a child knew and understood then. However, I have come forward in time in some chapters, and in Chapter 17 have brought up-to-date some of the people I have talked

INTRODUCTION

Britain declared War on Germany in September 1939 when I was four years old. I was too young to understand what it all meant, but was aware of a tension and fear in the grown-ups who saw their world turning topsy-turvy and were helpless to do much about it. As I grew up, I realised how lucky we were. The stories from those of my age who experienced awesome traumas sent chills up my spine; stories, like that of the girl aged six, who didn't know which way to run when a German plane flew low over her garden, the pilot peppering the lawn with bullets, laughing at her terror, my husband's account of the day a bomb exploded in his school playground, and that of the Jewish French girl and her mother who were horribly tortured to try to make them give away her father's whereabouts. Our life on a little island in the middle of the Atlantic was safe and idyllic. I had no idea of my good fortune, nor did I appreciate the beauty of our life until years later.

We spent that summer in North America. My elder brother, William, travelled by train with my parents across the United States to San Francisco. My other brother, Jim, and I went to Canada to stay with our Canadian nurse and her family. They had a summer house on Lake Huron a few yards from the beach. There was Cossie, our nurse, Doris and Betty, her sisters, their mother and Pop, their father. Pop was best. He took us to town every morning in his huge car, and would say, 'Waddya want today?'

We sang out, '*Chips*!' We had never had crispy potatoes before.

'*Rats*!' said Pop, and bought us a packet each. We ate them on the kitchen doorstep out of cereal dishes. In the evenings, Doris sat at the harmonium banging at the keys tunelessly,

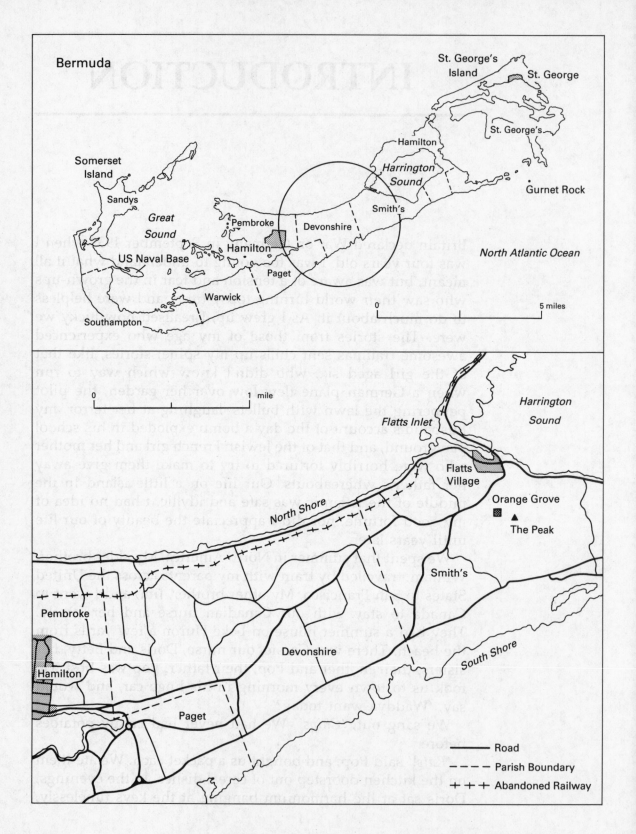

Bermuda

St. George's Island

St. George

St. George's

Hamilton

Harrington Sound

Gurnet Rock

Somerset Island

Sandys

Great Sound

Pembroke

Devonshire

Smith's

Hamilton

North Atlantic Ocean

US Naval Base

Paget

Warwick

Southampton

5 miles

Harrington Sound

Flatts Inlet

Flatts Village

Orange Grove

The Peak

North Shore

Smith's

Pembroke

Devonshire

South Shore

Hamilton

Paget

0   1 mile

Road

Parish Boundary

+ + + Abandoned Railway

and singing at the top of her voice for unknown reasons, 'Lettuce for supper, lettuce for supper.' We loved it and cheered her on.

I wasn't impressed with the beach as the sand looked dirty and had a funny texture. There were ugly sand dunes with spiky grasses growing from them. Between the dunes ran water coming from somewhere and there we were allowed to play. I do not remember going into what I thought was the sea. It was probably too cold, or maybe Cossie couldn't swim. I never saw her in the water, even in Bermuda.

I had not seen motor vehicles until that time and was terrified one night when a truck crashed all by itself outside the house as a tyre went hurtling off into the darkness. In the moonlight I could see the driver vainly trying to save himself. It must have been the sand dunes and the wheel that gave me the nightmare which recurs when I'm very ill. Everything is like a black and white movie. First an enormous black tyre, looms into vision spinning towards me through the sky. I try to run from it, but the sand dunes are in the way. Among them are telephone poles leaning in the wind, their wires flapping. I can't get away and I finally wake in a sweat, cowering behind a dune.

The carriage was the everyday mode of travel. Ours was unusual and looked more like a hearse. When it rained, the blinds were rolled down and snapped to the carriage frame. Here the family were about to set off for Hamilton to board the *Queen of Bermuda* for our trip to America and Canada in 1939.

Summer came to an end and we returned to New York to sail home on the *Queen of Bermuda*. She was a beautiful liner. I remember her better in later years, but that year, I remember that apart from throwing up in my bunk when it got rough, I loved being in the playroom because in it was a wooden rocking horse several times bigger than me, and all I wanted to do was ride on it. A few days later, we sailed majestically into Hamilton Harbour.

It was exciting because so many people were on the dock calling out messages of welcome to all those on deck. People were mingling everywhere as we got off the ship, collecting luggage and calling for carriages. My aunt gathered me into her arms, holding me tightly against her chest, almost groaning with emotion. 'Oh... thank God you're home safe and sound!' Only later did I realise the significance of her greeting. We were on the brink of War.

The *Queen of Bermuda* being docked at Hamilton. In recent years the men of the Royal Navy did diving practice at the docks and to their delight came up with dozens of plates and other pieces of china that go to make up dinner services. The ship's turn around time for the return trip to New York was so quick, the kitchen hands had no time to wash the dishes, so jettisoned them through the port-holes. One of my husband's Naval friends went home to England with a complete set of *Furness Lines* china, enough to set a dinner table for a dozen people.

1 ORANGE GROVE

Orange Grove has been the family home for ten generations and is difficult for me to describe as I took it for granted, not realising the influence it was having on my development. My son came up with the line. 'To describe *Orange Grove* as it was in the War would be to describe it as it is today!'

He's not wrong. As an eight year old, if asked to describe it, I might have said something like, 'Well, it's a big house at the top of Flatts Hill. When you get there you'll see a drive with a big rubber tree in the middle opposite The Whitney School playing-field. You turn in there, follow the carriage drive up and round 'til you come to the top, an' you'll see a big white house with green blinds...that's *Orange Grove*.'

There is a lot of land around *Orange Grove*, about 40 acres. Its boundaries join other lands, so there were many houses we could go to without being on the road. In those days, no one minded you taking a 'short cut' through their back yard on your way to someone else's house, or down to the bottom of the hill to go swimming. You just called out, 'Morning', or 'How you today?'

It is an impressive house built about two-thirds up the highest hill of the Island. It faces North. From there, views of Harrington Sound and the North Shore make a lovely panorama to watch ships sail up the channel making their way to Hamilton Harbour or the Dockyard. It is easy to tell how the weather will be each day by the ever-changing colours of the waters in the Sound. The colonades across the middle supporting the verandah above, give a dignified impression to the front of this old house, some of it dating back to about 1650. By contrast, the back has a ramshackle appearance with its large stone-roofed wooden verandah jutting from the top floor, supported by wooden pillars underneath and with a

The imposing front of *Orange Grove* is known as the front yard. The date-palm blew over in a hurricane and grew in that postion until it died long after my parents became grandparents. Now its baby grows straight at its base. For many years Father tied the old tree to a post when hurricanes blew in case it crashed through the library windows.

staircase leading up and round to it. Big flat-roofed additions to the kitchen and laundry areas seem to lean on the house at both ends.

All houses must have their own water-tanks as there is no central supply, the only source being rain. Unusual for a house, there are three water-tanks at *Orange Grove*. One is built against the side of the house next to the back verandah, the other two are large with 'catches', one by the clothes-lines to the East, the other at the top of the hill just below The Peak. Catches are few on the Island as land is scarce. They were made on sloping ground leading down to the tank for perhaps 50 or 100 feet. First it was necessary to scrape away the top-soil exposing the rock. A low retaining wall was built all round and then the area was covered with cement and lime-washed making a smooth undulating, brilliantly white bumpy terrain for rain to rush down filling the tank fast. All roof tops and catches were lime-washed to purify the water, but to make quite sure the water was kept in good condition, a goldfish swam a lonely dark life for years in a tank. Occasionally when a tank had to be cleaned or repaired, a fish skeleton was found in the silt giving rise to worries of contamination, but we suffered no ill effects.

Inside *Orange Grove* the rooms are large, the drawing-room and front hall giving an air of formality. Off the hall is the library, the important room in the house where everyone congregates to talk and drink. Downstairs the ceilings make it look dark as they are the floorboards of upstairs and made of cedar. When company downstairs caused us to be banished upstairs, or we were supposed to be tucked in bed, we wrote

The drawing-room. Clearly seen are the heavy beams that support the bedroom floors above. The family resemblance to our ancestor in the portrait over the mantelpiece has come through in my brother Jim, his youngest son and our son.

saucy notes and pushed them between the floorboards. The guests were treated to little scraps of paper fluttering to the floor below. There would be a moment's silence as the note was read, followed by artificial titters from the guests and *trouble* for us. Upstairs, the bedrooms are large too, especially the one over the front hall which was occupied by my parents who enjoyed two double four-poster beds. It has five doors opening from it, two to the landing, one to the top front verandah and two to other bedrooms. No wonder my Father was exasperated while dressing. He vainly tried to cover his manhood with his undervest as we marched through, ignoring his indignant shouts of, 'This is a Goddamn goldfish bowl. *Get Out!*'

Once inside the front hall the first item to attract one's attention is unexpectedly mounted on the opposite wall. The stuffed head of an enormous male elk with antlers like tree

The front hall taken from the drawing-room. The elk's head is directly opposite the front door, a smaller one hangs over the door to the library. The thickness of the arch wall is about 18 inches. We are watched by more ancestors.

branches watches attentively with arched neck. Another head of a smaller variety graces the door into the library. These, plus one other in the back hall over the dining-room door, were the prizes of my grandfather, who shot them in Idaho and brought them proudly home. A handsome wide arch between the front hall and the old fashioned drawing-room makes one room, excellent for large parties.

When we entertained in the drawing-room we were on our best behaviour. As a little girl I would be ushered in to speak to special guests. My Mother was entertaining a dignified American lady to tea one afternoon and I was taken to be introduced. She was wearing a white cotton hat, starched stiff, finishing in a high point. It looked exactly like the black one my Mother wore on Hallowe'en when she dressed as a witch for our fancy dress parties. I was intrigued by the hat and in a piping voice said, 'You look like a witch.'

Like all mothers when their children say such things, she could have wished me anywhere but there, but the lady took it well and said, 'Well. . .I suppose I do!'

On another day, the author, Helen Keller who was blind was there. She was also stone deaf and spoke in an odd voice. I had to stand against her knees so she could feel my hair, face, shoulders and dress. It was explained to me that in that way she could 'see' and would recognise me again as long as she could feel me. I was unsure of this kind of greeting, but by then had learned to hold my tongue when the warning lights gleamed like laser beams from Mother's eyes.

The kitchen is as old-fashioned as any you might see in a museum. In those days, as well as an *Aga* stove, we had a big kerosene range with enamel chimneys and mica windows under the cooking grills. A seven foot pine table stood in the middle and was scrubbed daily. I learned to scrub a table until it was almost white. The old Welsh dresser, filling one wall, was crammed with china of all descriptions, enormous mixing bowls, pots, pans, glass bowled kerosene lamps, and utensils hung or sat on shelves all over the room. There was a small icebox, painted pale green, which had a block of ice about a foot square placed in the top. The ice gradually melted into a pan at the bottom, cooling the contents as it did so. We had an ice-cream making machine which we churned and churned the same way as in making butter. Ice was delivered by horse and cart from the *Hygeia Ice Company* four miles away in the City of Hamilton. The cubes were covered with old sisal feed bags full of dust and bits of grain to protect them from the sun, but the ice cart still left a tell-tale line of water as it slowly progressed along the road making its deliveries. Cubes were specially ordered for parties, one for the galvanised tub, usually used to bath the dogs, but on those occasions to keep the bottled drinks cold, and one for the punch bowl, to chill and dilute the potent rum punch. The Company also stored winter clothes and carpets during the hot months for a modest fee, to protect them from moths.

The laundry is at the other end of the house and still has the old slate sinks taking up the length of one wall. There is only a small window for light and ventilation, so on wash and iron days the heat there is stifling. We became proud owners of a *big* washing machine with a mangle about 35 years ago. It's still going today...just!

Most of the bedrooms have four-poster beds that are so high, each has a stool of appropriate height to help one climb aboard. My bed, the oldest and finest, made of West Indian mahogany with heavily turned posts, has a handsome step ladder made of cedar which took me to the top when I was small. An array of large cumbersome furniture fills the house, some very good, some not, mostly Victorian but a few pieces are very old. Everywhere hang pictures. In the drawing-room our great-great-grandfather looks benignly down, and in various parts other long-gone members hang on the walls or reside on bureaux. There are nice paintings, interesting and dull photographs, pictures of favourite animals and places. The mantelpieces and furniture are covered with ornaments crowding one another, with no particular connections.

Everything went on from the back of the house. The carriage drive finishes in a circle around a garden of orange trees and flowers, the stables and horse trough on the other side. We kept a goldfish in the trough too. I wondered how it managed to escape being sucked up into the horses' mouths, but it did, swimming seductively just under the surface.

People came to the back door and walked in, calling for whoever they had come to see. If anyone came to the front door, we knew they didn't know us well. 'Who can that be?' we asked in hushed tones, as we went to see, wearing our formal faces.

The back garden, known as the *Back Yard,* has huge trees of allspice and avocado, and is wonderfully shady. From a branch of the allspice tree still hangs the swing. A Surinam cherry tree grows by the verandah, producing delicious cherries, and attracting bees and flies as they ripen. We, and the birds, gorged ourselves, dropping the seeds and sour ones, helping to make a terrible mess, as they fell on the untidy patchwork of slate pieces. My Father had brought the slates home from the Cathedral which was being refurbished. He decided a good use for them was in front of the verandah so had them cemented in place to make the ugliest patio possible. But he was clever with another item he brought

The back of the house shows a complete contrast to the front. The shaded garden is to the left of the hedge, the circle drive on the right. The whole area is the Back Yard.

The Wheel Gate under a half-moon Bermuda stone arch. Perhaps this little monument was erected by Father to leave a significant mark on the land as his father did with The Peak.

home. A ship's steering wheel with a diameter of about five feet had lain in the back of *Pearman Watlington & Company* for many years, a relic from the *Pollickshield* which was wrecked off the South Shore, its bridge still visible at low tide, I believe. Father decided to erect the wheel to swing on a pivot under an arch of Bermuda limestone to make a handsome gate.

By and large, everything is the same today as yesterday, except perhaps the kitchen, which has graduated to a gas stove and two refrigerators. The plumbing was old and erratic when I was child. It's more erratic now. The electric wiring has been patched and added to over the years making it spark more than ever. The fuse boxes hang naked on the wall above the draining-board near the stove. All the wires run visibly along the ceiling before disappearing through the opposite end, dispersing themselves through the house. We were used to all these things and quite happy in our unusual surroundings, never concerning ourselves about bad wiring, blown fuses, a broken-down water pump, or, when the lower tank by the clothes-lines was empty, having to switch over to the tank on the hill to get water by gravity, thus making the pressure only one better than a dribble. It was common practice to drag a heavy chair to the sink, clamber on that and the draining-board to go through the laborious task of finding a dead fuse. We *still* do it, for Heaven's sake, only now there are more fuses upstairs in a *bathroom*!

2 THE FAMILY

My parents married in their middle thirties several years after the First World War. Father had fought in France with the American Army. He came out unscathed, with an enduring love for France and her people. Mother had been in love with a Naval officer who was killed in a bicycle accident in Scotland. Afterwards, her mother was ill with cancer for some time and Mother nursed her to the end. Father had asked her to marry him several times, but Mother was evasive, until two years after her mother's death. Father, exasperated with her hesitations, gave her an ultimatum, 'Your Mother has been dead for two years. I want a wife and children. I want you, but if you don't say you'll marry me now, I'll find another woman.'

She agreed. They were married at seven in the morning. People rose early to be at the Church including Mother's Brownies. Late morning, they took ship for a honeymoon in Europe.

Their first child died tragically at birth. Not long afterwards they were rewarded with William, and two years later, Jim. By the time it was my turn, Mother was 40 and Father 43. There was no such term as 'generation gap' in those days, but we were the subjects of this. My parents were born in the 1890s when the Victorian era had been well established for over 50 years. Our up-bringing in the 1930s and 1940s was based on that theme.

I cannot say how my brothers felt about it, but I fought for my emancipation from an early age, particularly where my Father was concerned. He in his turn respected me in many ways but could not give me credit for my own intelligence or accept that I could do things properly...more to the point, his way. He never let go the restraining rein for fear I would run loose and bolt. Consequently, I grew up with a certain lack of confidence, but with a bravado I did not quite know how to handle, rushing ahead and retreating in the same breath. I *did* bolt, in as much as I married an Englishman and went to live abroad. *Then* I ran home to them at each opportunity, partly because of my dependence, partly because perhaps emancipation was not so great after all, and I was scared, and partly for the love of my Island. In my late forties, and a grandmother, I suggested to Father he must surely have a bad opinion of himself if that is how he thought of me! To be fair, his criticisms did nothing to deter my love for him, for when I was troubled, or in trouble, it was Father who listened and helped. Mother felt everyone should sort out their problems for themselves and did not change her attitude until after I married. We then became each other's confidante, our relationship turning to the closest trust and love a mother and daughter could have. She was not just Mother, she was my best friend and we thoroughly enjoyed each other.

Apart from the plain old discipline of bringing up children, the most difficult time came when I reached puberty. I think Mother was at a loss how to deal with it. She gave me a book titled *The Birds and Bees*. It was exactly that, except for the last page. It illustrated a mother breast-feeding her baby! It confused me for a long time. I wasn't much interested in birds and bees, but the mother looked like The Virgin Mary. How could The Virgin Mary connect with the birds and bees? By the time I was 13, girls fraternised with boys more closely than when Mother was a girl and it made her job more difficult.

Of course, I could have done a complete bunk when I grew up, but there was a veiled threat from Father, that if I did, I might well dip out of my inheritance. The inheritance would be substantial and I certainly was not going to lose that. Also, I loved my Mother dearly and needed her guidance. He had the effrontery to say that if I did not name our first daughter with my Mother's name I would not inherit a particular property. It was Mother's property, *not* his. I did not object to the name, and it is tradition in my Mother's family to give the eldest daughter in every other generation her grandmother's name. I like tradition, but not threats. I knew my Mother would not dream of 'cutting me off', in that most of what was coming to me was from her estate, but such were the powers of my Father, he might have forced her to do his bidding. At this point it does not matter for which reason my daughter is named Christiana, she likes tradition too, and I am sure will try to persuade her own daughter to do the same.

It wasn't all 'stiff upper lip' and 'children should be seen, but not heard'. People arrived on their bicycles, or in carriages, dressed in the appropriate white for tennis parties that were more social than accomplished, followed by tea in the front yard. They were fun and informal. Grand tea parties were held in the front hall, the ladies smartly dressed with hats and gloves, the enormous silver tea-urn at one end of the table and dozens of cups and saucers spread round. Mother delegated someone to work the urn while she circulated amongst her guests. At Hallowe'en, the fancy dress parties were a huge success. There may have been as many as 30 weird and wonderful looking children. A Grand Parade was held in the front hall and prizes given for the various categories, the funniest, ugliest, cleverest and prettiest. After tea we prepared ourselves for the terrifying climax... The Witches' Room! Ushered one by one into the darkened back hall, we shook the dripping wet hand of the Witch. She sat on a throne looking horrible, lit by a dim green light from a paper lamp shade with a skull and crossbones on it. I knew it was Mother, but never got over being horrified at the sight of her. We went through various antics, tasting things we could not see, walking the gang-plank and touching things. We recoiled in revulsion, then were freed back to the front hall. The other children, still waiting were full of questions, but we had been sworn to secrecy and for those few minutes were superior over the others.

From time to time Father taught us to act out small skits or poetry and the neighbourhood were invited to the show. I was not happy acting. My first stage-fright was making my entrance through the dining-room door to the drawing-room, seeing the rows of people filling the front hall. Sometimes these heroics were acted out on the school stage with other people of the Parish doing their party pieces too, some being very funny. I think we were making money for the War.

In spite of some of the previous remarks, my parents were as fair as parents can be, but strict. By the time I was about

11, I had seen two movies, while my friends had seen many. I created such a din, Father eventually agreed to take me to the movies once a month. We sat through some dreadful ones until he could bear it no longer. I was allowed to go with my friends on a Saturday afternoon.

Our horse riding took us down to the race-track and the jockeys. We got so many good tips on the horse betting that I begged Father to take me to the race meetings. I was not allowed to go alone, so, accompanied by confidence in his betting luck, he took me. We won lots of money. The track wasn't large, but on the far side was a high bank that hid

The library. Mother resting on the *chaise-longue* and Father at his favourite pastime, banging away at his typewriter with his habitual cigarette. He stopped smoking in his 70s. Sandy is sleeping near him. Notice the old radio on Father's left. It was switched on only for news bulletins. I remember it being used only on one other occasion. The maids said it was my Mother talking. It didn't sound like her and I have no idea what she talked about, but I believe it was true. She was speaking at the Island's embryo wireless station.

mysterious happenings. The riders disappeared out of sight for a minute, and as they came out from behind, those who had been the leaders before, had strangely fallen behind. He was amazed at his good fortune and my predictions.

Father developed a stomach like a bay-window soon after I remember him. He was not tall so the stomach did not suit and heralded his arrival wherever he went. Cigarettes protruded incessantly from the centre of his lips when he sat at the typewriter, the smoke making his eyes squint as he exhaled, but he never removed the cigarette until it was finished.

He missed the loving parental touch. His mother died when he was nine and as far as I can gather, he and his father were incompatible. In all the years I can remember, he rarely spoke of him, but he did of his mother. It is a sorrowful tale he told of being taken to his mother's death-bed to say good-bye. Those things made him vulnerable on the one hand, aggressive on the other. He could charm almost anyone, especially ladies. Equally, he had violent fall-outs with people to the extent no speech would pass between the parties concerned for years, sometimes forever. He loved books and history. It was no hobby, but a preoccupation. Our house was cram-jammed with books. Some say, 'Oh, we've got so many books.'

They don't know what they are talking about. When I say 'books', I literally mean thousands. He loved them and was an author of repute on the Island's history.

An aunt left him her genealogical collection of Bermuda families in her will. He took the legacy seriously and made it a life's work, collecting letters and information, recording births, marriages and deaths. The work is known over the world. If a person had a Bermuda ancestor and wanted to know more about it, he was referred to my Father. Many times letters arrived from abroad with requests for information on a family tree. Often, when a person visited the Island, a telephone call was greeted with an invitation to come to the house, and in the comfort of his library to do their own research.

Mother's character was a complete contrast. Her father died intestate when she was six, the only child of his second marriage. He was not a young man when he married my grandmother as the children of his first marriage were a generation older than Mother. She was lucky to grow up with the devotion and guidance of her mother who was 42 when she was born. Mother might have done many things if she had been a child of today, for she was highly intelligent and well educated, but she devoted her life to marriage and children. Her extensive knowledge of the botanical world surpassed many others. Her glass-house held a rare collection of ferns. Guests were enthralled when taken on conducted tours through the gardens which she and Father worked hard to bring to the charm they have today. Her conduct amongst the rich and famous was as natural as it was to us.

I realised how the marriage worked between these two different people when they were nearly seventy. Father needed the tenderness of a mother. Mother needed the strength of a father. She spoiled and babied him...he made the major decisions. People said what a beautiful woman Mother was. Naturally, I thought so. She was a lovely woman, the special kind one rarely meets, the epitome of a gentlewoman. She remained so even as age took over. Her figure was short and plump with sturdy hips and legs. My daughters and I have inherited them. In order to help my self-consciousness over my fat legs, she pointed out paintings by Rubens explaining that he liked his women amply endowed. She enjoyed helping my friends and me with our play. We had a trunk under my bed full of old clothes for costumes. On rainy days we pulled it out and turned ourselves into all kinds of people. A few favourite garments still exist. One is a gold embroidered blue velvet cape, and another is a blue and red plaid evening dress of Mother's. I loved it and wore it to fancy dress parties when grown-up. My daughters also wore it to parties when in their teens, even to Sandhurst! My daughters still ask to borrow a pair of red silk pantaloons. When I wanted my hair to look special or have it 'put' up at the back like Mother's, she went to great pains arranging it to suit the purpose. At boarding school, I was told to let it down by my music teacher as it looked too grown-up. I was furious as Mother liked it and had taught me how to do it.

My birthdays were events. Our lush gardens were a haven for games. Most were played in the Back Yard but a favourite wartime game called *Blockade*, was played by Harvey's House. Treasure hunts went on all over the land.

Whenever tiresome guests did not know when to leave or

had not the panache to know how to say, 'We must be going now,' Mother eased them out with such tact, the unsuspecting guests never realised how they found themselves on the door-step. In later years when faced with the same dilemma, we have been delighted when we managed to 'do a Granny Kitty'! Her gentle generosity was endearing. Yet, she could be stubborn, especially when Father was being his most dictatorial or demanding. I marvelled at how she handled him, and said so. Mother's dear friend, Agnes, from her boarding school days in America and a godmother to me, wrote a poem that sums her up.

> But where is Kitty? Never ask.
> She's busy with some useful task.
> She is feeding a cat,
> She is trimming a hat,
> She is cooking a cake,
> Or an elderly drake.
> She is plucking bananas
> That won't wait for mananas.
> She is cleaning a closet, arranging a shelf,
> Whatever she's doing it's not for herself.
> She is giving advice
> On how to be nice.
> To wretched J Ds who were headed for vice.
> She's crocheting or knitting
> The while babysitting.
> She's preparing to speak
> At a meeting next week.
> She's darning a sock,
> She is mending a lock.
> She is planning a party
> For thirty or forty.
> If a friend is to be buried or married today,
> She is making a wreath or a bridal bouquet.
> So what if she is just a few minutes late,
> Let us love her, admire her, and patiently wait.

Five years separate William and me and as a result I played more with Jim. William was the Boss and felt he got lumbered with the blame or too much responsibility. I felt I was always in trouble and often *he* was the cause of my punishment. Jim had frightening bouts of bronchitis every year. Mother kept vigil, as a kettle of *Friar's Balsam* steamed with moisture on top of the old kerosene stove by his bed. The boys looked like brothers with their dark hair, but William was robust and fearless, Jim the reverse. I came between and was blonde. William was good at sports, Jim hated them. Both were envious of the other, the elder because he thought the younger had too much attention, the younger because he could not keep up. Yet, they did many things together, playing with their tin soldiers, their clock-work train and ganging up on me. We all went to boarding school at 14. Up to that time, I was the bratty sister who got in the way, but then came a great day. They invited me to spend the day at Harvard. To my astonishment, instead of being referred to as a 'pain in the neck', they searched me out to meet their friends, saying, with what sounded surprisingly like pride in their voices, 'I want you to meet my sister, Ann.'

Well! I preened, and for the first time felt like a woman. After that, we had great times with our respective friends. I am inclined to forget the things we did together like picnicing, sailing, canoeing, building sandcastles and playing in the rain. The traditions and *Orange Grove* are old, but they carry on with the new generations.

3 FROM THE PEAK

In the middle of the Island are many acres of unspoiled land and that is where the highest hill rises above Flatts Village. My grandfather built a stone tower that seems to burst from the top of the hill and called it The Peak. From that spot is a spectacular view the length and breadth of the Island. Getting to the top of the tower was a major feat of courage because for some reason bees made their nests there. The door was kept padlocked and we knew that as we undid the lock the bees would come out at us in droves. The stairs wound round the walls to the top and the game was to dash up with the swarm buzzing about your head, reach the little door in the turret and burst out into the sunshine, slamming the door behind you before you were stung. The reward was stunning, the view was magnificent. To those who had never been 'up to The Peak' it was truly gratifying in spite of the bee run.

Behind The Peak is the boundary wall of the next property. The US Army wanted to occupy our land around The Peak and the tower was perfect for them. My parents stood with the Army's envoy wondering how they would wangle their way out of the proposal. Father, with inspiration in his voice, pointed over the boundary to a house in the distance and said, 'Why don't you ask that man if you can rent his land? You see the highest point of the hill is over there. He indicated a craggy rock just over the wall. That is what happened. They took the other land and a large number of American Army personnel camped there in dark green tents. They built another tower on metal legs with a radar machine that scanned the horizon in its constant movements making a continuous low whining noise as it did so. Sometimes the soldiers did manoeuvres through the land dressed in their

Aerial view of *Orange Grove* and The Peak with the catch below. On the right are US Military aerials, the middle one was the first. More recently a satellite tracking station was installed. To the left of *Orange Grove* is the carriage house and feed room. Sloping behind is the lower catch and tank. The clothes-lines are behind that. To the right of the house can be seen the flat roof of the laundry. Behind are the roof tops of the stables on the left, John and Harvey's houses on the right.

camouflage uniforms, tin helmets protecting their heads and guns held ready. From the back verandah we could see figures crouching and running through the growth. Jim used to leap up and down gleefully crying out, 'The Germans are coming! The Germans are coming!'

It was all in fun until the day I was resting in my room and a part of the ceiling collapsed, crashing down with a thunderous noise. I sprang from my bed, with feet flying out behind me and terror in my heart. I scrambled through the house diving over the furniture, yelling for my Mother. 'The Germans have come! The Germans have come!'

My grandfather built The Peak for the spectacular view. Nowadays a radio aerial replaces the turret and is used by a taxi firm and sometimes by the Police.

When we saw a line of ships sailing up the North Shore, we chased up the hill to The Peak where we could see for miles and watch the cruisers, frigates or destroyers, submarines or aircraft carriers moving slowly into the Dockyard. Several in a line was an impressive sight.

In later years The Peak was a good place to go with a boyfriend. No one could see if you sat on the floor as the retaining wall was about 3½ feet high and no one could climb the stairs without being heard. One girl came with a friend and borrowed the key from me one day, and did not come back for a long time. When they did, she said, 'Don't tell Mama where I've been.' The reason was obvious nine months later.

4   DUCKS

Growing vegetables and fruit and raising livestock to feed each household was commonplace. In our case, it was decided ducks were the thing to have. I do not know why ducks rather than chickens. Perhaps they are more prolific and better layers, but anyway, a flock of large white ducks appeared.

Their home was to be where the long rows of clothes-lines have always been. A small pond was dug against the side of the catch and lined with cement, with a slipway at one end for the ducks to waddle down and for the water to be easily swept out. A large wire cage was erected nearby where they slept at night. During the day they were allowed free to peck at the grass under the lines and wash themselves in the pond. Ducks are messy creatures, so it made the job of hanging out the laundry precarious, trying to avoid the excrement under foot and at the same time trying not to drop the garments. There were plenty of other places the ducks could have lived, but such were the eccentricities of our family. Everything was arranged to be the most tedious or inconvenient. The laundry is as far from the clothes-lines as possible, the refrigerators are in the pantry and quite as far from the stove or the kitchen table as they can be. The most used room, the library, is farthest from the kitchen and so on.

The ducks thrived well, laid dozens of eggs and sometimes a couple appeared stuffed and roasted for Sunday lunch. The quacking and croaking noises were pleasant to hear when I woke in the early mornings and watched the sunrise come up over the hills at the East end of the Island. One winter's morning, two babies were hatched to everyone's surprise and my delight. They had been ignored by their mother so were brought to the kitchen to live in a cardboard box beside the *Aga* stove. One poor little creature died next day, but the other was strong and we named it Donald Duck regardless of course, as to what sex it might turn out to be. He greeted us every morning from his box with excited cheeping and chirping. It seemed impossible such noise could come from a creature so small. His down was soft and yellow, his little beak flat and strong. When he was taken from his snug bed he followed whoever was in the kitchen, cheep-cheeping all the time, back and forth, waddle waddle. He was in danger of being stepped on, or worse, attacked by the cats and dogs, but he escaped all that and was a charming little companion. He was fascinated by bright objects. I had a ring from a Christmas cracker that had a stone as brilliant as a diamond. Whenever he saw it he pecked and pecked, and I was surprised at the strength of his beak. If he got my finger instead of the stone, it hurt.

Jim and I watched intently when Donald had his swim in the dogs' bath.

On nice days we took him out to learn what goes on in the great outdoors. We decided eventually he was old enough to learn about water, so the big old galvanised tub used for bathing the dogs was dragged into the garden and with Jim's help we filled it to the brim with warm water. I did not think Donald would know how to swim, but was assured ducks knew these things, so we slipped him over the edge. He loved this new sensation, and excitedly flapped his inadequate wings, as he cheeped and splashed, spinning in circles, thoroughly enjoying himself. Abruptly, he disappeared below the surface and stayed so long beneath the, by now murky, waters, I was sure he had drowned, but up he popped, still telling the world what it was all about. Sometimes the flock would come on to the back verandah, perhaps looking for tasty morsels from the kitchen or merely for an excursion after it had rained as puddles collected over the uneven slates. Donald was gradually allowed to join his relatives to get used to the grown-ups and they to him. His beautiful downy coat was being replaced with stronger growth and proper white feathers were beginning to appear. Too soon he grew too big to live in the kitchen and permanently joined the flock as a precocious teenager. His tail feathers curled as he matured into a handsome drake, so we were right to name him Donald.

For a long time he came back to the kitchen door and enjoyed the privilege of being a special person, chatting and pecking at our fingers to encourage titbits. The call to be with his own kind took over eventually and he rarely came to us for attention. He did not come when he was called and it was impossible to differentiate him from the others, so on a particular Sunday when we had duck for lunch, I couldn't swallow it. I don't enjoy duck even today, and now my children will understand why 'Mummy likes ducks'.

5 HARVEY

Harvey and my Father had a strong and healthy dislike for each other. Harvey looked after the horses and was a highly important factor in the yard. His relationship with my Father worked because both loved my Mother. Every once in a while something Harvey said, did or did not do, made Father so angry he fired Harvey, who then went home in a huff.

Immediately, the running of the stable-yard was thrown into chaos, because who was going to put the horses to bed, feed them and clean them out next day? I have no idea how it worked, but come evening one of Harvey's young sons, or both of them, would turn up to do their father's job. Whether my Mother had an arrangement with the Harvey family or not, I do not know. There was no question of Father doing the job. This went on for about three days, then Harvey would be back doing his work with the horses, driving the carriage as usual and no more was said.

When it was raining, the horse was hitched to the big carriage and Father was driven to town by Harvey. As a little girl I was allowed to drive with them. I don't remember the drive to town as much as the return journey. Sometimes I fell asleep on the front seat, resting my head against my old friend, sometimes we talked. I learned a lot about the horses, their temperaments, why they liked this or that and generally how to look after them. Harvey said to me one morning as we neared home again, 'You know somethin'?'

'No, Harvey, what?'

'Vell...yah Deddy, he's a Davil but yah Mama...oh... she's a *Angel*.'

I believed him, and then understood how it was when Harvey was fired he always came back.

I loved his black face, yellow teeth and short grey hair of

tight little curls under an old flat felt cap. He rarely changed his trousers except for events like weddings and funerals. Under his trousers he wore, winter and summer, long white drawers to his ankles. I knew he did because when he sat down they showed above his shabby old ankle boots. I wondered how he could stand so many clothes in summer.

It was fascinating to watch him get his worn tobacco pouch and his little cigarette papers out of his trousers, slowly fashion a flimsy, ill-packed cigarette, then, deliberately running his kinked tongue along the gummed edge until it was truly damp, roll the small packet carefully between his fingers, thus turning the white paper a gruesome brown, dyed by the tobacco inside. Sometimes I was allowed to lick the paper while he held the untidy little parcel, making me feel privileged for this treat.

There was a special little stone building (just a room really) which was called *Harvey's House*. It wasn't for living in, but for keeping his personal things and partitioned off was his bathroom. The bathtub had seen better days. Made of concrete, it was pitted brown and grimy, I doubt ever used. The toilet was black at the bottom, not white like those in our house, and the whole place had a distinctive smell, a sour tangy odour mixed with stale tobacco, and to this day if I smell that smell, it's Harvey's. It was not a good smell, but to me, a childhood one and at the time I thought no more of it.

Just before I travelled to England to be married, it was arranged that I should have my photograph formally taken in my wedding-dress standing in front of the fireplace in the drawing-room. Harvey was invited to come in and watch. Invited to join him was Olivia, who in her long life played many roles in our family from as early as my Father's youth. You will read about her later. These two had a wonderful morning watching all the excitement of me trying to look elegant in my specially designed dress, holding a bouquet of flowers carefully put together by my Mother. Between the two of them the whole session took forever because of the never ending commentary going on about how they were 'Goin' to gat into a rowboat, an' gat some awers and row all de vay across de beeg Atlantic Ocean and go to de vaddin'!'

'Yah gotta do de rowin' Bi, cawse I shuwer cahn't.'

'Oh, gurl, yah gotta be de nawigate-tah.' All the time the laughter and cackling was ringing round the house. Harvey sounded like he was enjoying a brawl, Olivia, like an over-excited old hen.

Not long after that, a few months, I returned from England to visit my parents, and Harvey started complaining of pains in his stomach. He would go into the kitchen, sit on the high stool near the *Aga* stove and say to me, pointing to the decanter on the sideboard in the dining-room, 'Gimme a liddle tot of yah Mama's bes' rum to help de pain.'

Of course I gave it to him, to the disapproval of Ella, the cook. 'A-yunn, vhat's yah Mama gonna say when she sees de rum's gawn down?'

I didn't realise he was really ill. In fact for a long time I don't think he did himself, and I was troubled later as to whether I should have given him the rum, because he died of his tummy pains.

6 FRIENDS AND GOINGS-ON AT HOME

Orange Grove from the earliest times had servants. At first they were slaves, and later, long serving valued friends.

OLIVIA lived in a small cottage at the foot of the drive across the road with a verandah that met the road. She never married but bred six children each with their very own Daddy. When she wasn't washing, ironing or cooking, her leisure was to sit on the verandah and talk to people as they passed by. She was fat and flabby, her face round and wrinkled with a nose almost too flat for such big nostrils.

'Listen to Livia. She's laughin,' we would say from up on the hill, for her laugh was full-blooded and loud. With her mouth wide open, raucous infectious noises emitted from her heaving belly, reverberating half-way round the Parish and all who heard laughed too.

She was as much a mother to my Father as one could be because his mother died when he was so young. So he, his two younger brothers and sister were very dependent on Olivia for her warmth and love, and her discipline too, I guess. She was boss of the laundry and still working for our family as an old woman. When my parents needed her for babysitting, Harvey drove down in the carriage to collect her, and drove her home again late in the evening before he unhitched the horse, put it to bed, and made his lonely way home by bike. We loved her waddling figure moving through the house. In the evenings, she used to make us scrambled eggs. We finished every scrap, even though they were the worst scrambled eggs I ever ate! On Christmas mornings after Church we called on her, taking presents. She was ready with fruit cake and bottles of sherry or rum on her kitchen table, and we all had to have a taste. She took my

Olivia posing with her devilish smile in The Back Yard.

Father in her arms and old as she was, with painfully swollen legs and feet, she danced him round the kitchen table laughing and joking all the time.

Her skirts were long, covered with an even longer apron and she was rarely without her old black felt hat. Poor swollen legs stretched her thick stockings beyond their capacity, so they looked tight and strained. Her warmth and affection we lapped up, sitting on the floor of her verandah with our feet in the road, listening to her nonsense and making her laugh. I always took new friends to meet her, and when I began to take boyfriends, she would look up with a coy twinkle in her eye, and whisper, 'Is dat de vawn you gon' take?'

She was disappointed when I shook my head, until the day I took the one I had chosen. She was overjoyed and clapped her hands in glee at the thought of what I had coming. To make sure I got it, she was on hand when my wedding cake was being made and stirred it round three times for *Luck, Joy...and a Boy*!

I never saw her angry, though she had a wild temper when riled. A woman who lived on Flatts Hill made her so mad after an argument she dared her to walk by her house ever again. The unfortunate woman did not take her seriously for next day she came up the road to be confronted by Olivia swinging a carving knife. She was so terrified she leapt up on to the bank of my uncle's land and ran to his house screaming and yelling, 'Save me, save me, Livia's comin' and she's gotta knife!'

She too was up the bank, struggling, and reached the kitchen door gasping venomously, 'Vere is she? Ahm gonna kill 'er! Lemme gat 'er!'

It happened my aunt was spring cleaning, so the living-room had all the furniture in the middle as Olivia's enemy rushed through the house. The description of Olivia on one side of the furniture, her foe on the other, the one screaming her fear, the other hell-bent on destruction, had us helpless with laughter. All was saved when the poor woman managed to get out of the front of the house and run away up the road, Olivia still yelling. 'Ahm gonna gat 'er, ahm gonna, you vait!'

DOT came to us every Tuesday to sew. She could not have been more of a contrast to Olivia for she was a gentlewoman of the highest degree. We looked forward to Tuesdays when she came with her quiet charm and lady-like manners. She had sewed for my Mother's family from the time she was a young woman. The patterns were made by herself out of brown paper, everything from bathing-suits to chair-covers. Her name was Olivia too, but she said because she was so small when she was born, they called her Dot. Thunderstorms terrified her and when the lightning began to flash, she hid behind the laundry door and shook. I was sent to fetch her

Dot was reluctant to have her photograph taken, but showed grace and charm on her 90th birthday.

into the kitchen where Mother kept everyone busy making cake or cleaning the kerosene lamps in case the lights went out.

My Mother was Brown Owl and the Brownies met at our house on Tuesdays. I think it was arranged on purpose so Dot could help teach us how to sew on buttons, make tea, set the table, and learn the womanly things about housekeeping. Dot's domain was the playroom behind the library at the back of the house. The piano was next to the sewing machine and like it or not, she had to be a good audience for our practice and crazy chopsticks. We had our fittings in the playroom, but in order to see how a dress was progressing it was necessary to go to the back hall where a long mirror hung. It never occurred to anyone it would be better to have a mirror in the playroom, not that there was room anyway. If you wanted privacy while trying a dress in the hall, too bad, the hall was the route to all the rooms in the house.

Dot promised to make my negligée when I married. She was an old lady by that time, but with our combined design and her home-made paper patterns, she devised a lovely flowing gown of pale blue. I wore and wore it until many years later it fell to bits. She retired at about 90 and we longed for the great day when she would be 100 and have a message from the Queen. Sadly she didn't make it. She taught me most of what I know about sewing and I never thread a needle without thinking of our dear Dot.

LOUISE came to us when my Mother was expecting me. She was 17 and came as nurse-maid. She is one of my first memories and I loved her as dearly as my Mother and called her *Weez*. Her friends down the road used to tease me and say, 'Ah'm gonna take Weez from you.'

I cried and clung on to her with my arms wrapped round her neck as she held me and I would cry out, 'No, no, no, you can't take Weez!'

One afternoon when Mother was out, she and the other maids rushed round the house pretending to run away, and then Louise collapsed on the kitchen floor. I thought she was dead and pounced on her, screaming for her to wake up. The weight of me on her stomach was too much and she giggled.

I spent a lot of time at Louise's house. I loved her father, Jack. He drove a carriage that was available for hire. He had a raucous laugh and must have enjoyed us, because I remember that laugh so well. Friends and I loved being around his stable-yard with its poinciana tree growing in the middle. Once, on our way there, idly walking along the old cart road in the land, we saw one of Jack's cows in obvious distress. She was grunting and heaving and we did not know what was the matter with her. Then, from her back-end began to appear something awful. We stood with gaping mouths as a dreadful mess dropped to the ground in a bloody heap. We were galvanised into motion all at once. With flying hair and

Louise holding my hand and *Little Pillow* under her arm. We are
dressed in our 'Sunday go to Meetings' for my Uncle's wedding.

feet we scampered helter-skelter across the field, over the
wall and into the yard, yelling for Jack at the top of our
voices, 'Jack, Jack, come quick! De cow's sick, somethin'
dradful is happenin'!'

Jack bent over, clapping his hands on his knees, rocking
with uproarious laughter. 'Oh, de cow ain' sick, she's only
caahvin'!'

There were ten children in that house. How they all went
to bed I do not know because the house was not big, but
everybody was happy. Inside the back door was the dining-
room, a lace cloth on the table and a big plant growing in a
tall stand. Off that was the kitchen with an old brick oven

over which Louise's mother continuously toiled. At the front was a stone verandah with assorted chairs and oddments, and inside a long corridor with rooms off met the dining-room at the other end. The first room was small but used as the living-room and had an upright piano. Everyone seemed to be able to play tunes on it. Louise played best. Her favourite song was *In the Gloaming* and I loved her to play and sing it, especially when later she taught me to play. They all had good voices and sang in Church. Thirty years later I listened to one of her brothers reading the lesson. His voice was supreme in its understanding of the words and the sonorous tones echoed round the nave.

LU was our cook during the War. She was a large person with an ample bosom and a warm heart inside. I do not remember her ever being annoyed. She was a cheerful person to have about the house and an excellent cook. The dishes she produced, even with rationing, were attractive and mouth-watering. She took a pride in her work but enjoyed her jokes as well. One April Fool's day, she cooked fresh bread for breakfast and made a big thing of giving me a special bun she had made especially for me. It was as hard as rock! When Donald, the duck, was a baby and living in the kitchen, he loved to follow her large feet as she moved with purposeful strides back and forth between the kitchen and pantry. Lu loved Donald as much as the rest of us and always promised it wasn't Donald we were eating when we had duck for Sunday lunch. I wonder if she believed that herself?

The maids came and went over the years, but most stayed on until they married or had babies, not necessarily in that order. Often sister followed sister so we knew whole families. On Mondays, three maids came to wash the clothes in the three slate sinks. One scrubbed with the scrubbing board, the next rinsed and the third starched. Then they carried the heavy loads in wicker baskets out to the clothes-lines to dry. Sheets, towels, pillow-cases, dresses and shirts billowed like signals in the breeze. The shirts on the line numbered 40 or more in a week's wash. Everything went on the line including the whitened shoe-laces that disappeared every once in a while, to the fury of someone or accusations to another, only to be found later as part of a bird's nest in the eves of the back verandah. We had a goat named Jillian who caused plenty of trouble at the clothes-lines. I do not know why we had Jillian in the first place, except she amused us and frustrated the rest. She stood on her back legs and boxed us when we got on her nerves, and when she had kids she had to be milked. Nobody liked goats milk, not even the cats. For reasons best known to someone else when she was tethered down by the clothes-lines, not only did she drop her pellets all over the grass, she stole the clothes from the line and ate them. Between her, the birds and the ducks, it's a wonder we had clean laundry, or any at all, for that matter.

A large population of Portuguese emigrated from the Azores over the years to be farmers and gardeners. At *Orange Grove* the only white people employed were Portuguese men to farm the land and tend the gardens. They lived on the property and the wives rarely worked outside their own homes.

JOHN was our gardener and lived in the cottage behind the Back Yard, next to Harvey's House. He was a sweet man and went about his daily tasks in a steady unhurried way. He taught me to saw wood. I would sit on the other side of a tree trunk from him and with an enormous double-handled saw we gnawed through it, he doing the pushing and heaving, me, the grunting. He kept a pig near some orange trees, a safe distance from the house, as my Mother said, 'Pigs smell.'

Every so often the pig had piglets. I was rather afraid of the pig, but John taught me how to handle the babies and convinced me that she wouldn't hurt. The piglets could walk as soon as they were born and squealed enough to waken the dead when picked up. Pigs are the only creatures I know that look adult even in their baby stage. He loved his pigs, but sold them to market all the same. His favourite dog was the tiniest puppy I had ever seen, a little fox terrier, so small it curled up in his old boot. The puppy stayed small and was his faithful and constant companion.

Poor John developed throat cancer and refused any sort of operation because, 'Nobody's goin' to cut me with a knife!'

They didn't and he died, still the gentle kind man we loved.

ELLA has been the cook and mainstay of our house for the past 35 years or more. As I write this story she is in her 70s

Ella on the back verandah as she is today in her middle 70s.

and still working for the family. She told me she used to look after us when Louise had her days off. I don't remember her then, but I do as a teenager when she came to do housework. She soon showed us she was a woman of character, with a heart full of kindness and generosity, plenty of humour, but God help you if she was crossed. Best to clear out of the way when she gets mad. She married one of Olivia's sons. The two strong minded women were not the best of friends but managed to remain civil to each other for the most part. Not long after she came to work on a permanent basis she took over as cook and over the years has done us proud with her fine meals. She has been delighted when a guest has wanted to know her recipe because she was always unable to give it! Her method was a bit here and a bit there until it looked or felt right. Birthdays were an excuse for cakes, the more special the birthday, the more special the cake. My parents have had wonderful cakes over the years, and important anniversaries got the works too!

She soon learned the ways of *Orange Grove* and could 'welcome in' or 'see off' the right and wrong people. All who knew us headed for the kitchen first, to say 'hello' to Ella, and it might be some time before the person got further into the house, the conversation in the kitchen being much too interesting. She has kept us in line, telling us frankly if we weren't dressed properly or what we just said, 'ain' nice'. Her remarkable ability to confuse her words has taken on an extra special meaning. Her cocker spaniel was greatly endeared when she referred to her as 'my cockle Spaniard'. Hysterics became 'historics', and coming from Ella that could mean either one, if you get my drift. 'Gurl, I vas historical!'

She carries an ample body supported by slim ankles and legs, but even at her age after long years of hard work her complaints are few, except for, 'The Arthur Ritis in my knees, you know.' She became quite agitated when she heard about 'that Neutral Bomb'.

She stayed with my family and me in England for a month. The first morning she came downstairs saying. 'A-yunn, somethin' dradful is happened to me, look at my legs gurl, Ah'm gawn all vhite!' The drier atmosphere and hard water had made her legs go scaly. We giggled and gave her hand lotion to rub on. Driving her over Salisbury Plain she became visibly uncomfortable watching the wide expanses of fields and wild land flashing by, and eventually bleated out her fear, 'Gurl, I vun like to valk down dis road all by myself at night!'

She is not one to show affection. If I want a kiss I have to go and get it, but her love of giving has showered me, my family and grandchildren with presents we treasure. 'Ella, you mustn't gurl, it's too expensive!'

'Yah bin good to me, so that's vhat Ah'm done.'

Everyone roared with laughter when our grandson, aged four months, burst into little chortles when he first clapped eyes on her, 'Yah nava seen such a ogly black ole face as dis, hav you chil'?'

You can't help loving such a woman. There will never be another like her.

7 CHRISTMAS AND EASTER

In spite of the War, Christmas and Easter were exciting and fun. In the weeks before Christmas, Mother painted ferns and screwpines in silver, gold and red. We helped paint them in the Back Yard on a big table covered with newspaper. In the last week she spent hours wrapping presents for all our relations, her bed covered with paper, cards and string. We had to be sparing as it was scarce and what stayed good was saved for the next year and so was the fern. Two days before Christmas we trudged up the hill in search of a cedar tree to decorate and stand in the front hall. We strung lights between the antlers of the elk and Mother made a handsome centre-piece for the hall table.

Then came Christmas Eve. Harvey hitched up one of the horses, the carriage was filled with the presents, fruit from the garden in baskets, fudge and cakes from the kitchen, and we set off to deliver round the neighbourhood stopping to 'sup' and wish Merry Christmas to our elders.

In the meantime, in the kitchen, the great 'Cassava Pie' making was in progress. Cassava is a root that grows long and strong with a tough brown skin. A day or two before Christmas the roots were brought to the back verandah by Harvey and John, who washed and scrubbed them until the skin was off, revealing the whiteness of the meat. The long job of grating the roots into the galvanised tub commenced. Our grater was home-made from a thick plank of wood, large tin cans opened down the sides with holes hammered all over and nailed on either side of the plank to form an arc. It was a 'hammish' grater but did the job perfectly, and is still used today. When all was done, the cassava had to be washed and squeezed through cheese-cloth to get rid of the juice which was said to be poisonous. Lu and Mother had prepared a stew of beef, chicken and salt pork. The cassava was put into my grandmother's two huge old brown pottery mixing bowls to be dressed with lots of eggs, spices, sugar and butter. Everybody who was around had to have a 'stir' for good luck. Using fingers was best. The feel of the starchy dough gave the hands a clean smooth texture and the earthy smell was as characteristic as the smell of a horse being shod. The mixture was spread on the bottom and up the sides of large deep roasting pans, the stew ladled in the middle and covered with the rest of the cassava, then into the oven for hours of cooking and basting from the stew stock. Cassava Pie is the traditional Bermuda Christmas fare. No two families make it exactly the same, and people often do not like other people's pie.

'It don't taste right, I don't like all that allspice in it,' or 'It's got no spice at all and taste like nothing.' It was hard to be polite about pie you didn't like because everywhere you went you were proudly offered a 'piece of our pie'.

(Arrowroot was treated in much the same way except when washed and squeezed through the cheese-cloth, the liquid was saved and poured into large meat platters, and left on the tank to dry out in the sun. After drying, the baked starch left on the plates was broken into pieces and stored in bottles on top of the Welsh Dresser in the kitchen. There is still some there, bottled in 1947! Arrowroot is good for settling the stomach as well as an excellent starch for the clothes.)

When evening came my mother tied name-tags on to three of my Father's longest socks and hung them from the fireplace in the bedroom of whoever's turn it was as we alternated each year. The nights were cool and in our dressing-gowns and slippers we followed her every move full of anticipation and excitement. She recited *The Night Before Christmas* as we went to bed, dying for morning to come.

We were awakened at dawn by the smartly uniformed Salvation Army with their brass band playing Christmas Carols outside the front door. They had played all night and walked for miles heralding the Christ Child's birth, giving pleasure to all who listened. We ran downstairs and opened the door welcoming in the sound of the music. They played our favourite tunes, while Mother went to the kitchen to make them coffee and Father rifled his wallet for a donation. If it was a nice morning we sat in the Back Yard while they had their refreshments, but if it was wet we stayed in the kitchen by the warmth of the *Aga*. Their leader, a charming man and oldest by far, did not drink coffee and Mother made him his special hot milk. No matter what the weather they came to start our Christmas Day.

On Boxing Day we waited to hear the drum beat of the *Gombeys* making their approach towards Flatts. *Gombeys* were a group of black men and boys dressed in costumes decorated with bits of mirror, shiny buttons, ribbons and anything that glittered, with magnificently tall head-dresses made of peacock feathers. As soon as we heard the drums, whistles and instruments making their music, we hurried down the drive to be ready as they arrived to perform for those who lived around Flatts. It made an awesome sight, for their faces were painted in terrifying designs, and as they began to stamp out their African derived rhythms, the music became more frenzied and exciting, the drums thumped and the whistles shrilled. Everyone began to move with the rhythm as they made their erratic leaping movements, never missing the beat as they grabbed up the pennies people threw into the middle of their circle. It was thrilling and exhilerating and if I looked forward to Christmas, Boxing Day and the *Gombeys* were a major part of it.

Easter was just as nice and quite different. Flowers were in abundance, the sun warm, promising the long hot days to follow. Kites are flown on Good Friday, so on Maunday Thursday we made our kite of tissue paper, a cross of wooden battens, string, glue and rags for the tail. Next day, before we were allowed to fly it, we had to go to Church for part of the three hour service. I loathed it. It was boring, but I wanted to fly a kite in the afternoon so Church it had to be. Sometimes we took the kite up to The Peak and launched it from the top where it usually caught up in a cedar tree. Other times we took it down to the school playing-field where lots of others were flying theirs too. I think we spent more time retrieving the kite from trees, mending it with extra paper, lengthening or shortening the tail than we actually did flying it. After Good Friday the Island was littered with crashed kites in trees, electricity cables, chimneys, boats and overboard.

On Saturday, flowers and foliage of all kinds were cut and taken in our bicycle baskets round to Church to decorate it for Easter. After weeks of no flowers, the place suddenly came alive with the smell and prettiness of decorations everywhere, the Altar, the rails, the choir screen, pulpit and each pew down to the Font at the back. The chattering and laughter of busy women making it festive after the drabness of the Sundays before, somehow came as a surprise because at any other time you 'shut up' in Church unless to sing or pray reverently.

We went home to boil eggs and paint them colours ready for next day. Mother made a secret Easter Basket and hid it in the land. She then wrote clues and hid them round the garden. Our cousins and any children living on the property came for the Treasure Hunt...I do not remember finding the basket myself, but once it was found, we sat in the long grass to eat the candy and eggs the Easter Bunny had so kindly brought us. By that time we were probably getting late for Church so hurried through the land and over the hill to get there on time. 'Have you cleaned your teeth?' Of course we hadn't, so we picked the rough sage bush leaves to rub on them and make them shine.

TREASURED POSSESSIONS

My little pillow. My aunt gave me a baby pillow when I was born that I clutched on to like others do a teddy bear. *Pilla* went everywhere with me, and if I lost it in the four-poster bed at night I created a howl that woke the house until it was found and I could stuff it back into my mouth to suck. In later years people looked somewhat bothered when I said, 'Oh yes, my pillow goes everywhere with me, it even went on my honeymoon.' When asked once what I would rescue first if my house caught fire, the person's face expressed bewilderment when I said without hesitation, 'My little pillow.' Never mind the silver, the jewelry, furniture or anything else, my little pillow, what's left of it, still gets out first.

Baby. There were lots of toys to play with, but Baby, my rubber doll, was the only one I gave all my devotion to. She was small with a pretty little face, her wavy hair moulded in the rubber of her head. Dot and Mother made her clothes. Sometimes she was a baby, sometimes a little girl. Bonnet, dress, petticoat, pants, and socks I changed constantly. Sometimes, I made her a patient in hospital and covered all her wounds with bandages. When I once swabbed her with peroxide to clean her bad places, a dribble ran down her forehead leaving a clean scar to the tip of her nose that she kept forever. All that practice was useless for when I had a real baby, I had no idea what to do. Before I went away to school I wrapped her in a cloth and put her in the drawer where my mother kept her 'show' dolls. She was worse for wear by then but dear to me and there she would be safe. From time to time I took her out, gave her an airing and covered her with talcum powder to stop the rubber going sticky. She lived in the drawer for about 20 years until one summer while we were visiting I unwrapped her to see how she was as she had not been aired for a very long time. Her little face was crumpled and wrinkled, her fingers were coming away, and her round little knees had gone spongy. She was a pitiful sight. With tears in my eyes I folded her in a new cloth and buried her on the hill.

9 KINDERGARTEN

I cried and cried on my first day at school. I was a week late starting because I had been sick in bed. As we walked into the classroom, I held Mother's hand tightly. The room was full of chattering children. They had all settled down and had made friends. I stood miserable, feeling afraid and lonely. I clutched at Mother begging not to be left there, but she went away leaving me in the care of Miss Fleming.

Miss Fleming came from Canada, had short dark wavy hair and a pretty face. I buried my head in her lap as she tried to soothe me.

Like all children, I settled down too and enjoyed Miss Fleming's class. She was affectionate and warm hearted, she taught us to read and kept us busy. No one knew of dyslexia in those days, but I remember having difficulty with 'was' and 'saw' and my 'd' and 'b' seemed to get mixed up. We had to stand at our desks when it was our turn to read, hold the book out straight with both hands and look smart. I had total blanks on occasions and would be unable to figure out what words like 'that' spelt. My hands went cold and damp and I breathed so deeply I felt faint all because I was terrified of making a fool of myself. But Miss Fleming was always kind and helped me through.

Her intellect was put to a difficult test one day when a rumour went round school. 'Charlie Swift has broke out ove de asylum an' he's loose!' Suddenly she had a bunch of hysterical children all terrified to go home. 'But, Miss, they say he's comin' down Middle Road and gonna pass this vay!' Poor Charlie Swift was harmless. He had beautiful long waving red-blonde hair and thought he was Jesus Christ.

Our classroom looked straight out of the front of the building to the gate on the road and we all strained in our seats to look out. Miss Fleming gathered us in a circle round her knees with her back to the door, wisely realising there was no point in making us sit with *our* backs to it, and began to explain he wouldn't hurt us. One girl wept with fear, 'Cuz, I gotta to go down Flatts Heel and he weel too!'

Then he came. An eerie quiet followed as we watched the unfortunate man walk slowly passed the gate and on down the road. We stared and trembled. School was just down the hill from our house and I walked there everyday through the land meeting up with my cousins as I passed their house. That day, I ran home like the wind, panting and stumbling in my hurry to find Mother who was quietly showing a group of guests unusual trees and flowers in the garden. I had been taught not to interrupt when others were speaking, but not this time. I grabbed Mother's skirts, breathless with running, fright and excitement and I spilled out what had happened and stunned the company into silence as I gabbled my way through the event. I don't think Mother had heard of Charlie Swift, but she certainly knew who he was after that day.

At the end of the year we moved up to Form I and the serious side of life began. We had to learn. The year was spoiled when I found out the difference between good and bad teachers, and their idea of truth and untruth. I had been given a handsome volume of *Uncle Remus* stories for Christmas. I loved *Brer Rabbit* and the others and took the book to school at the request of my teacher who said she would read some of the stories to us. At the end of the day she said she would keep the book for a while and read us more another day. I never saw the book again, and everytime I asked for it back, promises were made but it never appeared. I think with hindsight she lost it and did not know how to admit it, but I never forgot, nor forgave.

10 CAMPING

People were not allowed to go abroad for pleasure during the War years. Instead, my parents rented a house at the East end on the South Shore each summer for the holidays. Our Uncle Hal and Aunt Winnie joined us with their boat and tents, pitching camp on a couple of grassy acres adjoining the last beach of the Island. My Mother and Father weren't fond of camping and only spent a token night under canvas, but my brothers and I spent many nights there. We had pup tents just big enough to crawl into and lie on a camp cot while the grown-ups had two big tents for living and sleeping. There were no sleeping-bags in those days. Instead, we folded an old cotton blanket the size of the cot, then folded a sheet crossways to make a top and bottom tucking the end under the blanket. On cool nights we tucked another blanket carefully round, because if anything was left trailing on the ground it made a ladder for ants. In the morning we made it up and rolled the whole thing into a sausage 'to look neat', but it always looked like a bundle of rags. I was scared on moonlit nights because I could see armies of cockroaches crawling over the canvas outside so I tied my flaps down tight to keep them out. There were no toilet arrangements. When the need arose, we took a shovel in one hand and a roll of paper in the other and found a spot as far from camp as possible and dug a good hole for the purpose. 'Don't forget to fill it in well afterwards,' echoed after us. The shovel was big and heavy but I learned to stamp on it hard.

Uncle Hal and Aunt Winnie had a little black and white dog called Mick who always went in the boat and stood in the bow sniffing all the smells as they breezed passed his nose. He loved that just as much as digging a crab out of its hole on the beach. He dug and dug, scattering sand in all directions until the wretched creature emerged with its claws raised high in defiance. Then he chased it unmercifully down to the sea and barked triumphantly as it was swallowed up by the waves.

The boat, called *Docea*, was painted blue with a long open cockpit and an engine in a box in the middle. First job after camp was made was to drop the lobster pot. Anybody else would have taken the boat a little way down the shore and dropped the pot near some likely looking rocks, but not Uncle Hal. We had to motor from his safe mooring in the calm waters all the way out to the South Shore and the open sea, bouncing through the waves until we reached Gurnet Rock, a huge ominous eruption rearing from the sea with not a blade of grass or a place to climb on to it. I was afraid of the Rock and frankly, still am. It is a lonely place far from shore. The sea rises and falls against the shining surface ejecting hissing noises in splashing bursts from the rock crevices. It was highly dangerous to my mind, as the boat rose and fell making popping noises and the bow threatened to crash against the slippery black rock. What if the engine failed? We would be doomed! I cannot imagine why I went with him unless I was told to, but I learned to be brave. Anyway, I had my brothers to compete with. Nothing gave them more satisfaction than to put me down a point. Not only were there lobsters, but barracuda and green morays, and I knew in a day or two we would have to go back to fetch the pot up again. Sometimes the pot came up containing other things like big squirming eels which were not easy to get rid of from the wire cage. If the catch was numerous the creatures wounded each other or bit at one another in their bid to free themselves from their prison.

Once we had the prized lobster Uncle Hal took it back to the house to cook for lunch. I hated the spiny creatures with their wavy feelers trying to catch my legs. At the kitchen door I was confronted by a great lobster on the floor barring my way. With yelps I ran to the other door only to find one there too. Uncle Hal loved to tease me. His favourite prattle to infuriate me was an advertising slogan for *Lucky Strike* cigarettes he said was just like me.

> So round, so firm,
> So fully packed,
> So free and easy on the draw.

It was guaranteed to cause the desired effect.

He had an old diving helmet made of solid brass with long hose-pipes dangling from it. The other ends of these were attached to a hand pump. I was six or seven at the time and the thing stood nearly as tall as me. It was so heavy the only way to wear it was to stand in deep water and as the helmet was lowered from the boat over your head, sink down so the water took the weight. On board someone had to pump the air down the pipes as you walked on the bottom. It was as lonely as Hell. I hated it because I was scared of what might come out to meet me from the rocks, and I didn't trust them to keep pumping from above, especially my brothers. We took turns going down. I wouldn't have minded so much had there been two helmets, then Mother could have gone with me, though, if the truth were known, I don't think she was that keen when her turn came. There was an emergency rope attached to the person and the boat. If you were all right you tugged once and above knew to give more play on the rope for further exploration. When you wanted to come up you pulled twice, and above slowly pulled in the rope, guiding you back to the boat. I was ready to pull twice as soon as I got down there. Most of the time they took pity on me and pulled the whole affair off and I could float gratefully to the top.

I learned at that early age how to cope with the hard of hearing for both aunt and uncle were exceedingly deaf and had complicated hearing aids. Aunt Winnie's was the better one but the amplifier was burdensome. Uncle Hal wore earphones with wires leading to a black box the size of an old *Brownie* camera which he carried in his hand. In the boat he took it off, so without it and with the noise from the engine, when you shouted things like, 'Take me home, I don't like it out here,' they went unheard if he was so minded, but if you shouted you were going to be sick, he heard then. Listening to the BBC news was of daily importance. It came at 1pm. The volume had to be turned to its maximum, they had their sets tuned high and sat as close as possible to the old radio straining to hear through the crackles of static while we heard it best sitting in the garden.

At night after supper, sitting with the camp fire burning down, Aunt Winnie taught us songs of a disgraceful nature like,

So they built the ship *Titanic*
And when they had her built,
They said, 'Here's a ship the water will never come through',
But God with his mighty hand
Said 'This great ship shall not stand'.
It was sad when that great ship went down.
It was sad, it was sad, it was sad when that great ship went down,
To the bottom of the...husbands and wives, little children
Lost their lives, it was sad when that great ship went down.

We sang merrily with two more verses reiterating her demise, and everytime we sang the chorus and got to 'little children' we raised our voices to screams to emulate the children drowning.
Then there was,

My wife has a fever now then
My wife has a fever now then,
My wife has a fever
I hope it don't leave her,
I long to be single again.

She died of course and he married another, far worse than the other, so we started from the beginning because that one got a fever too.
We sang all ten verses of,

My ole man, he played one, he played knick knack on my thumb,
Knick knack scally wack, give a dog a bone,
My ole man came rollin' home.

All the songs had rollicking tunes and rhythms, so we sang them loudly and irreverently.
We sang an old sea shanty of which I never understood the meaning until I grew up. I've sung it as I learned it all my life even so,

In Amsterdam there lived a maid,
Mark well what I do say,
In Amsterdam there lived a maid,
And she was Mistress Offertrade,
I'll go no more a-roving with thee fair maid.

It came as a shock when I learned Mistress Offertrade was a bad lady!

11 WARTIME

The War brought the blackout. The curtains had to have heavy linings to keep in the light. 'So the Germans can't see us,' said Jim. We were in trouble if we put the lights on before we pulled the curtains.

Driving home after dark in the carriage was difficult. The carriage lamps could not be lit and the only way of knowing if a carriage was coming in the other direction was to listen for hoof beats or wheels on the road, tune the eyes to the darkness and sound the carriage bell which was an oversized bicycle bell attached under the floor and stamped on by the driver. Painted white on the back of each carriage was an eight inch square that glowed in the dark.

Horses liked to take themselves down the middle of the road, and if they had to move over for an on-coming horse, they forgot they were pulling something wider than themselves, so unless guided further over, there was a collision, followed by over-reacting horses and swearing drivers. The horses knew their way home, and often, day or night, a cozy picture came into view of the faithful creature taking his slumbering master home. Many a sleepy man woke to find himself safely home in his own back yard and the horse, head bowed, dozing as he patiently waited to be unhitched, and quite likely still wearing his straw hat with ears falling slack as they protruded from the roughly cut holes in his sunshade.

The buildings where the army lived, the corrugated buildings where they kept equipment, were painted in crazy black and brown zigzagging stripes to camouflage them from enemy aircraft. I was told it made them look like trees, but I could never understand that. Standing on a hilltop it was quite clear to me what were trees and what was camouflage, so how was that going to confound the Germans?

On warm nights we had canvas cots on the front verandah off my parents' bedroom and slept there in the cool. Before I settled for sleep Mother would lie down with me and point out the important stars in the galaxy. We found the Big Dipper, the Little Dipper that guided us to the North Star, Orion and his belt of three stars and the Heavenly Twins holding open the doors of the Milky Way. At night on that latitude the sky is brilliant with stars against the midnight black.

Our evenings changed from star hunting, to plane hunting. The sky was crazily criss-crossed with search lights beaming up in all directions. They waved over the sky apparently at random, when suddenly two beams trapped an aeroplane like a spider catches a fly. The tiny moving speck tried to dart away, but was lit up and imprisoned for all the world to see.

As time progressed there was more and more activity around our shore. Strategically this tiny Island had become very important. There already was the well established American Navy base in the Great Sound and the Royal Naval Dockyard at the Western end of the Island. It was a safe anchorage and a 'bolt hole' for warships in need of rest or repair. Many ships limped to the safety of Bermuda having been torpedoed and badly damaged. Captured ships were brought in. Merchandise of any worth was sold through a set-up called *The Prize Court*. Many Bermudians augmented their possessions with booty from the Prize Ships.

Britain was desperate for warships, so in 1940 Sir Winston Churchill and President Roosevelt made an agreement that America would provide ships and Britain would lease lands in parts of the world for American bases. Bermuda was one, and a US Air Force base was built at the Eastern end. The advent of this changed the face of Bermuda and its position in the Atlantic forever. It became like an extra appendage of the American mainland. We went down to see how it was all happening. It was almost a pilgrimage for my parents, seeing for the last time the disappearing familiar contours. The inland waters were churned up to fill in land between islands. Great diggers and shovelling machines rose up and over sand mountains like huge crabs to terrify the onlooker. It was as if some Almighty Hand had come and swept up our pretty tranquil land and turned it upside down to appease the Devil. The only nice thing I remember was finding fossil shells in the heaps of sand. After that, Bermuda seemed to fill up with almost as many Americans as resident population.

When the ships came in, some of the men had to be found places to live while repairs were carried out or passage on some other vessel was available. I remember some who came to us. One was a Petty Officer from the Royal Navy. He was plump and rode a bike that he leaned up against the kitchen wall. He ate breakfast with me, and I think might have had a child my age, or a niece perhaps, because he spent a lot of time amusing me and I enjoyed his company. A Frenchman came. He was young, blonde and courteous. My Mother liked him particularly and he enjoyed staying at our house. Before he left I asked him to sign my autograph book which he did, in French. I had no idea what it said, but Mother did and translated it for me, I can't remember now what it was, but it was nice and for some time afterwards Mother had letters from him. There was a pretty young woman too, who spent most of her time sitting upstairs on the back verandah. I think she may have been wounded. Somehow, she seemed to be convalescing. An eccentric middle-aged man spent time with us at one point. My Father was impatient with him and couldn't wait to get rid of him.

There were also the days when we went down the hill into Flatts Village to the Frascati Hotel which was used for the USO and to feed and help the forces. The ladies of the Parish made mountains of sandwiches. I don't know what went into them, I just saw piles and piles of white bread in towers higher than I, and the hungry boys devoured them in a trice. Some of them had been through bad experiences, and often owned only what they stood up in. A friend of my Mother's whose own son was away fighting the War gave his best jacket to a young man going home to the cold weather with nothing warm to wear. When her son came home after five years and asked where his jacket was, she told him what she had done with it.

At Christmas 1944, I was ill with an ear infection. Instead of improving with treatment it became worse and by the New Year I had a mastoid. Our doctor seemed unable to cope with the condition, but as luck would have it, an ENT specialist had been torpedoed from his ship and was marooned on the Island waiting for passage home. He went to the Hospital to offer his services and I was one of his first patients. He was kind and gentle, with a good-looking face. I remember being driven by Harvey to the Hospital and Mother saying I would probably have mustard poultices put on my ear to draw out the infection, but I didn't and was allowed home. It had been arranged that I should go back in two days for treatment in Hospital, but I became very ill over night. The following day I was taken to Hospital by ambulance. When we arrived the 'special' doctor from London examined me and told my Mother he must operate immediately, otherwise I would not live until the next morning. It must have been terrible for her at the thought her child was dying. She sat outside the operating room for the three hours it took to save my life. I spent two months recovering in the Children's Ward and was given more presents than at any Christmas. The mastoid left me deaf but this never bothered me nearly as much as those who get exasperated when I don't hear. After the War, I think the doctor became a well-known Harley Street surgeon.

12 RATIONING

We soon learned what the word 'rationing' meant as the War raged on. I understood when it touched me personally, particularly in the matter of shoes, butter and sugar. I cannot remember how many ounces of butter and sugar we were allowed each week, but it was about two of each I think. Mother had little jars that were either screw top bottles or her empty face cream jars from *Yardley*. Each person had two jars and each had a piece of adhesive tape stuck to it with the person's name printed clearly on it. We were five in the family so that meant 10 jars, plus those for the live-in staff. On Fridays the new rations arrived on the delivery cart and the sharing out procedure began for the following week. All the spare butter and sugar was emptied from the jars and put to one side to be used up. The old scales were put on the kitchen table and the measuring commenced, intently watched by me to make sure I got my full whack! Each was weighed with precision then gently poured or scraped into the jars not wasting anyone's fair share. Mother said if we were very sparing with our rations during the week she would make fudge with what was left over. Everyone liked chocolate fudge except Jim. He liked peanut butter and that made me *mad* as a separate amount had to be saved for *him*. Sometimes I used more than I intended in the week, or more to the point was just greedy, and to my undying shame stole scrapings of butter from someone else's jar. Louise caught me at it and I was thoroughly punished for such a shocking display of dishonesty. Naturally, I learned not to be so greedy and it is surprising how far butter will spread if you work at it. In those days butter didn't keep as it does today. Our children probably have no idea what rancid butter is like. It could not be eaten or used for cooking, it had to be thrown out, preferably burned so the animals couldn't forage it from the pit, where the horse dung and waste food unsuitable for pigs was thrown to make compost.

We were sent food parcels from time to time from friends in America, and in one parcel was a tin of butter. My mother locked it away in the store cupboard 'for Christmas'. When Christmas came she opened the tin. Tears of dismay and frustration assailed her for being frugal, the butter was rancid. It is a dreadful smell and a worse taste.

We had three buckets for trash. One was for paper and anything that would burn. The second was for tins and bottles that eventually found their way to the dump. The third was called 'the peeg's meat bucket'. All waste food went in there and every evening one of Louise's brothers came to fetch the bucket and take it home to feed their pigs. The pig in my grandmother's time was named 'Miss Manners', so if there was an extra piece of meat on the platter or food on the table, Mother said, 'That's for Miss Manners.'

The ships carrying flour were delayed like those carrying any other commodity trying to reach our harbour. Sometimes when a bag of flour was opened horrified shrieks of, 'O Gawd blass me, de flour's got veewils!' echoed round the kitchen. Weevils are nasty little creatures that thrive on grain of any sort. The sight of the miniature black beetles crawling through a bag of flour was disaster and it had to be thrown out too, like the butter. The bakery sold day-old bread in the hope people would eat less which didn't help their questionable reputation, for when your rationed loaf produced a dead cockroach, rusty nail, or went mouldy after half had been eaten, complaints were rife. Flour was shipped in hundred-weight bags made of white cotton, often with a flower print, so even if the flour was full of weevils, the bags were good for making underpants and petticoats. Some bags only had the name of the company stamped on them and if the print happened to turn up emblazoned across your bottom it was obvious you were wearing 'flowah bags' and good sport for teasing!

Being islanders everything was saved and put to use for something. 'I'll just keep that, it might come in handy one day,' came from anyone's lips. Years and years later I was clearing out my parents' garage while they were away. All round the sides were old lamp-shade frames, frail with rust, bent saucepans with no handles, bottles by the score, kitchen utensils rusty and broken, an old toilet without a seat, dozens of wooden knobs for the ends of wooden curtain rails, picture frames, the odd broken chair, bicycle wheels, and I can't remember what else. I began to fill the car with items destined for the dump. 'A-yunn,' said Ella, always on hand to keep an eye on things, 'You badda not throw thet avay, yah Mama might vant it for one of de rented howzes.' She grabbed from the car a broken colander or splintered rolling-pin.

'Ella, if my Mama put that into yah house, you'd say, "Mis Zool vhat you think Ah'm gonna do vith dat?"'

Every person had ration-books for food and clothing. For the growing children it must have been difficult because we outgrew our shoes faster than the ration-books allowed. Shoes were passed on from child to child which caused foot trouble for some in later years I am sure. Once I was taken to the shoe-shop for a new pair of shoes. A friend had a beautiful black patent leather pair from abroad with thin straps and little buckles. I did so want a pair like that, but school was about to start and sensible shoes it had to be. I made a huge fuss, begging Mother to let me have pretty ones, not caring it was the only pair of shoes I could have, and I think she nearly used her own ration-book to spoil her selfish child. In the end, I'm glad to say, she refrained. I had a sensible lace-up pair of shoes. I've hated lace-ups all my life. When I was away at boarding school and we were 16, we manufactured all sorts of excuses to wear our moccasins instead, Plantar warts, sprained ankles or toes, blisters, in-growing toenails, anything, until the teachers wore down and agreed we need not wear lace-up shoes anymore. Mine went out of the window to God knows where, for they were gone in the morning and I didn't care.

Our clothes were passed on round the neighbourhood. That was good because it meant we had more to choose from, and like the grass on the other side, other girls' dresses were sometimes nicer than yours. Of course, clothes were always 'made over' and Dot, who was so clever with her patterns from scraps of paper, could make up anything, in cotton, silk, or heavy wool, turn curtains into chair-covers, and chair-covers into skirts. She had a way of making gathering stitches, and with the material held taut and the needle flat, she wove it up and down fast and neatly. I loved the clothes she made except the school uniforms and she would say, 'You don't like this dress do you Ann?' Then I would be embarrassed for fear of upsetting her because I knew she wouldn't enjoy making it if I didn't like it. Materials, like everything else, were scarce and we had to be satisfied with what was available. It taught me to be careful with my possessions knowing that if I ruined something, I would have to go without. I never saw anything made of patchwork except for the crocheted rugs my mother made out of rags with a large wooden hook. Perhaps it was carrying shortages too far. Soon after the War we made up for it because new materials arrived with pretty colours and patterns and what was called the 'New Look'. I was old enough to be fashion conscious and join in with the delight it gave the women.

We kept a round pewter bowl on the sideboard in the front hall and into that went all the silver paper from chocolate candies. We had to smooth it out and fold it up small. When the bowl was overflowing, Mother took the contents to someone in Hamilton where it was added to more and shipped to Europe to help with the war effort. I am told now that those collections were not worth 'a drop in the ocean'.

Those are the important things I remember that affected my life. We were constantly told, 'You finish what's on your plate. Think of those children in England who haven't got what you've got.'

The reaction was, 'So what? I don't like Quaker oats, or sugar apples, or fish with bones in it, or duck, and if they wannit they can *come and geddit*!' We didn't know those children. We were all right and although we probably complained a lot about why we couldn't have this or that, we never went hungry or short of anything to cause us hardship. I hadn't really known any other sort of life, so as far as I was concerned, such trivia as not seeing mangoes or plums until after the War came as a nice surprise. I had occasionally seen those beautiful red table apples with their four bumps on the end that stand up straight on a plate. I might have complained about not having more of those, I can't remember. We had plenty of clothes and were warm in winter. The fact I was disciplined over the shoes was no worse than being disciplined for any other reason. I thought the worst thing of all was the failure of the oats and bran to get through in the cargo ships to provide the horses and cows with their essential food. I was very upset when lack of it caused a horse to become ill.

13 THE TRAIN

In the early 1930s a train service commenced travelling the length of the Island from Somerset to St George. It was a useful mode of travel for many, but my memories were of it constantly breaking down. When I was 10, I went to the High School in Hamilton. The train stopped near school and it made sense to use it when the weather was bad. We rode our bikes to the station, which was not much more than a shed as I remember, and sometimes left our bikes there to pick up on the return journey. Other times we took them on the train to ride home in the afternoon if we had errands, extra duties or thought the weather would have improved by then. It seems to me the train broke down usually about halfway along and it was a wonderful excuse for being late for school. In the afternoons, after fruitless efforts to get it going, we were fed up, jumped off the train and clambered down the bank to walk home. That was often more adventurous because we would try to persuade a passing livery carriage to give us a lift. When asked if we had any money, and we didn't, we were told to 'hoof' it. Looking sulky, we hung back as the carriage went on down the road and when the driver wasn't looking, we ran up behind, grabbed a part of the chassis and swung our feet over to get a bumpy, but free ride. Many a carriage carried unpaying passengers that way...all the children loved doing it even if they only wanted to go a few yards. Jack was the only one to let us get away with it.

In bed I listened for the train coming into earshot from a long way off. The tune changed to noisy rattling as it trundled over the high bridge at Flatts Inlet, and the sound gradually died away. It was easy to tell which way it was going just by the noise. I tried to be asleep by the time the noise had gone, but when you're trying to do that, you're listening as well, so it never worked.

My Father was asked to give away an elderly spinster at her wedding in St George, half the length of the Island away. The train was the obvious way to get there, the only trouble was the ceremony was to be at 7am. Mechanical things didn't function very well in our house, likewise, the clocks. The evening before the wedding, each told a different time and one with a working alarm could not be found. As a result my Mother spent most of the night awake so as not to be late for the early rise and six o'clock train. Of course, at a crucial hour she dozed off into a deep sleep. I woke to hear a great commotion in their room. They had woken in the nick of time and were flapping about the room in chaotic confusion trying to dress. I heard my mother's agitated voice shouting, 'You go on ahead and I'll catch you up.'

'You'll miss the train, you're always late!' came the irritable reply.

More snappy remarks followed as my Father rushed from the house, and I watched him fly down the drive on his bicycle yelling over his shoulder, 'I'll get the train at Store Hill and tell them to wait for you at the Aquarium!'

Soon Mother was flying off down the hill too, holding on to her floppy hat with one hand, guiding the bike with the other. I don't remember where she got the train but all was well and they made St George in time for the ceremony. Afterwards, the octogenarian newly-weds and my parents came all the way back to *Orange Grove* for a wedding lunch.

The train tracks ran flush in the middle of the road the entire length of Front Street in Hamilton. It was a homely sight, the ships tied up at the docks on one side, the train rumbling along in the middle, the carts and carriages moving along either side of the track, the shops across the road with their varied verandahs and the people on their bicycles going about their daily business. We collected crown caps from mineral and Coca Cola bottles and just as the train approached, ran from my Father's shop to lay the caps on the track to watch them flattened into pennies by the iron wheels.

On wet days riding the bike diagonally across the tracks took some care and attention for carelessness caught the wheel between the rails and threw you to the ground in a thoroughly hurtful way. It usually happened because you were in a hurry to get across before the train went by, so it was a mad scramble to drag the bike and yourself out of the way, oblivious to how grazed or bruised you were. It only happened to me once.

The train was never a money spinner, quite the reverse. At the end of the War as buses and cars filled the streets, its economy was worse, but what to do with it? The problem was solved when it was learned that British Guiana wanted to buy a train. It was sold to them, lock, stock and barrel. I wonder if it worked better for them?

14   HORSES

Almost every household had a horse. That noble beast was of enormous importance as it was the prime method of transporting everything from people to cargo. Each horse was a family pet, treasured, carefully tended and loved. In return he did the bidding of his master. From the 1800s until after the Second World War, the horse was one of the most important members of the household.

There were carriages of all descriptions, landaus, buggies, hackneys, gigs and so on. We had two carriages, a cart and a pony trap. The small carriage was a two-seater buggy with arms and back made of cane, a Surrey fringe canopy that folded up like an umbrella, and behind was a small seat hanging over the back for an occasional passenger who had to hang on precariously as there was no proper back rest. The big carriage was like a big black box and the only one like it on the Island. In fact, I have never seen another like it except in some parts of the world, where the horse-drawn hearses have a similar appearance. The roof was flat and rigid, but the black canvas sides could be rolled up in fine weather to let the breeze blow through. In bad weather with the sides down, it did look funereal. When it rained, a black waterproof cover was snapped on. It was made especially to fit over the foot guard and right up to the driver's chin with a slit for the reins to pass through. The only way to see out from the back seat when it was all shut down, was through a small mica window in the back cover, or to stand up and peer over the top of the tarpaulin cover at the front.

Apart from opening and shutting, the carriages only changed in appearance for weddings and funerals. Every carriage had a horsewhip that stood straight up in a pocket beside the driver. On wedding days, clean white ribbons

61

Father about to set off for Hamilton with Prince hitched to the buggy. Sandy ready to chase alongside until told, 'Go home!'

were criss-crossed carefully up the whip finishing with a flourishing bow and streamers. On funeral days, a sombre black ribbon was wound down the whip. Processions for both occasions were invariably long, carriage after carriage followed one another. You clapped and cheered as a happy wedding party clattered by, or stood with quiet respectful dignity in deference to the bereaved as a cortège moved slowly past.

At *Orange Grove* we were indeed fortunate to have two large dark coated horses named Prince and Potter. Prince was a fine highly strung fellow, who had been a Sulky racer in his time and loved to go as fast as possible. He hated processions. At weddings when all the guests assembled in their carriages after the marriage ceremony, and fell into line behind each other for the journey to the bride's home for the reception, he was frustrated to the point of madness. The noise of the carriage wheels and the horses' hooves clattering along the road was too exhilarating for him. The horses pulled their carriages at such a fast and excited pace that Prince thought he was on the race-track and wanted to win.

62

Harvey had a hard time restraining him behind the carriage in front, as it would never do for a horse to break rank and race on ahead of the bridal party. Funeral processions were punishing, the carriages went at walking pace and he knew he could win if *only* he could get that bit between his teeth. Potter, on the other hand, was a placid even tempered plodder. He was slow but ready to do what he was told.

When the War began to bite as far as supplies reaching the Island were concerned, one of the crucial items we needed was feed for the horses. The crab grass which grows everywhere and that all horses and cattle enjoyed, does not have enough nourishment for a proper diet, making it imperative to supplement with oats and bran. Without it a horse was liable to colic and other ailments. Of course, as with people, some horses have stonger constitutions than others and could survive without. So it was with Prince and Potter. Prince became ill without his feed, but Potter could manage.

At times when no ships were getting through to bring the much needed grain, decisions had to be made. Who should have the feed? It was decided Prince should have it, albeit rationed, and he would be the one who was worked. Potter was put to grass until more feed was available. We hoped for the best. If one of the horses was unwell, a mush of bran and molasses was cooked and fed to it, warm and soggy, from a large saucepan. I don't think the horses liked it, because it seems to me there was an enormous hoo-ha as the poor creatures were force-fed the medicine.

At that time we also had a Shetland pony named Bessy. She was primarily for us, the children. She pulled the two-wheeled trap to take us to the beach or on other little outings. Like all Shetlands she was unpredictable in her mood. She could be loving and affectionate on the one hand, irritable and snappy on the other. We knew if she laid her ears back and showed the whites of her eyes we had better look out! She liked to kick and stamp her back legs. I remember so many times my Mother getting the punishment. Just as we were about to set off with Bessy hitched to her trap, she would kick and stamp. Her little hoof would come down like a bolt from above on to Mother's foot, who then hobbled into the pantry and raised her leg up to the china sink and turned on the cold tap, to let the water wash soothingly over the poor offended foot.

One afternoon we decided it would be a good idea to introduce Bessy into the house. After all, she was small and wouldn't take up much room and it would be quite fun to have her in the house with us. So, we led her across the back verandah and into the back hall. My mother walked through at that moment and ordered us *out*! We started to make our retreat, but before we could, Bessy dropped an ample load precisely in the middle of the Persian carpet. Well...perhaps it wasn't such a good idea. Another day we found Bessy lying on her side in the garden. She was very sick and couldn't get up. She had a severe case of colic and had to be treated to the bran and molasses routine. After that she was given the supplementary diet and recovered to nip and stamp as devilishly as before.

We had been without oats and bran for a very long time and none of the horses was being fed properly. It was causing great concern, but on a small Island we were helpless to do anything until a ship came in. There was much excitement one morning when Harvey arrived early to say, 'A ship is

Posed in the front yard are Jim and myself holding David, William holding Bessy. The old slatted summer house is in the background with the lone date-palm beginning to lean.

comin' up de channel an' Ah'm goin' to hitch up Prince and go to town to see if I can get some feed!'

He was gone all morning, but came home triumphant with half a bag of oats! A bag weighed a hundred-weight, so half a bag was precious little, but what came on the ship had to be shared by all.

Towards the end of the War a friend of ours was leaving the Island and gave us her beautiful little mare named Gypsy. She was lovely, her coat a rich shining brown. She was too small to pull the big carriage but she was good in the buggy. She was high stepping, held her head up and made the four miles to town in no time. Her temperament was fine except she was terrified of the train. Some of the railroad tracks ran across the road. She hated going across the level crossings and bolted over as fast as possible. If by an unfortunate chance a train appeared, it was too much. She reared up on her hind legs and screamed her terror. The buggy was in danger of overturning, and once, she reared so violently, the shaft broke, which made it far worse as the dangling pieces struck at her legs frightening her all the more. All control was lost until the train was well away and out of earshot. Poor Gypsy had to be unhitched from the buggy and walked home while the broken vehicle was taken away for repair.

My Mother happened to answer the telephone one morning when a well-spoken woman asked politely to speak to my Father and refused to say who she was. Mother's curiosity took her to another 'phone to listen in. The lady said, 'Will, I want to give you a present.'

My Mother was incensed at the idea a *woman* should offer her husband a present like that and not say who she was. She hung up and waited to hear what Father would say. Her suspicious mind was soon allayed. The woman was a friend of both Mother and Father and the gift was to be Freda, a horse. Freda came with one condition. She was never to be sold or given away. When we no longer had need of her, she was to be put down. She had been a British Army horse at one time so was big and strong, a good carthorse, able to do hard work and pull heavy loads.

Living on a small Island inclines the inhabitants to be frugal and thrifty in many ways. At times flotsam washes up on shore, and if considered it might come in useful, the finder takes it home. It might be seaweed. A cartload of that taken home and spread beneath the citrus trees makes good fertiliser. It might be driftwood, good for burning.

This time, the find was a wooden catwalk made of teak or oak, about 25 feet long, and thought to have come from a submarine or a freighter. My parents were determined to bring it home. It was a mammoth undertaking, but somehow it would be managed. Freda was hitched to the cart and driven the five miles to the particular beach. The shore there is many feet below the level of the road and there was no way of getting the horse and cart to the object. The catwalk was semi-buried in the sand, but we managed to drag it free and haul the enormous treasure up the bank. It looked like a strange and fancy type of ladder. Getting the hulk up to the road was one thing. Getting it on to the cart was another, as it was so long and the cart was only about six feet in length. The whole family had been mustered to help and Harvey was in charge of Freda. As we managed to get one end of the ladder on to the end of the cart, Freda, who generally was well mannered and calm, began to stamp about apprehensively sensing the load that was about to come. She was right, for as the catwalk was heaved further on, the front wheels of the cart began to lift off the ground at the same time lifting her front legs. Some of us had to scramble on to the front of the cart and stand on the shafts to keep the balance, while others had to get to the other end of the burden and hold it up. If we were going to get it home, that is how we would travel. Harvey, who had been holding Freda's head, calmed her enough so he could climb back into the driving seat. Two of us stood on the shafts, the rest holding up the tail end as we set off on the precarious journey home. It must have made a comical picture, this family taking their precious cargo along the road. It took a long time and negotiating the hills was an accomplishment, uphill was hard and long for Freda, downhill we had to use the brakes, or she would have the whole load on top of her. Luck was with us and finally our prize was home. It was placed on big blocks of stone along the garden wall in the Back Yard where it became an extremely uncomfortable bench. Freda had proved her strength.

When I was about 10 years old I was loaned a Welsh pony named Perky. He was for me to look after and learn to ride. I was excited with my new charge and it didn't take long before I knew how to handle this extrovert, fat, white mischief maker. He gave us the greatest fun. Some of my friends had horses too. One was Diamond Dick who lived on grass so had what was called a 'grass belly'. When he went faster than a walk his stomach sounded as if something was flopping around inside. Another had a Palomino named Goldie who kicked while you were trying to climb into the saddle. We took him to the catwalk and used it as a mounting block. Even then he kicked and managed to get the leather belt holding up my baggy jeans, the belt snapped and I was left looking stupid as my trousers fell to my ankles. Perky was a great character, and enjoyed the antics we put him through, I think. We pretended we were cowboys and bucking broncos. We would leap on his back from behind, or throw ourselves across him while he was on the move. We stood on his back and rode him like circus trainers. I could make him rear and walk on his hind legs, or rear and buck at the same time to pretend I was breaking in a wild horse in a rodeo. He was a fine jumper and loved it, though I was not. If the jump was high, he sailed over beautifully while I was thrown over his head or left behind. At one point we went to the pony club thinking it a good idea, but it was so dull, we quit. As a result, we never learned any style or had a 'good seat', but we were fearless riders. He liked to get his own back from time to time. He had a ticklish spot just behind the place where the back of the saddle ended. If I put my hand on that place he bucked and looked mad. If I persisted he bucked until he threw me off.

Sometimes we rode to the beach to let the horses cool their legs in the balmy roll of the waves. They loved splashing about but I had to be very careful not to let the water go over Perky's knees. If I did, he flopped over and wallowed in the salt water. I fell off, the harness was soaked, and so was I. The gleam in his eye was enough for me to know he enjoyed throwing me in and he didn't care we were two miles from home, that I had to hose him down then set about saddle soaping the harness before I could go into the house. We had a lot of fun, my pony and I. When I grew too big for him he went back to his old home for a richly deserved retirement. A few years later tragedy struck. He was in his paddock when there was a thunderstorm. He was struck by lightning and killed.

The back hall. Originally the staircase ran steeply up from the left. In 1943 Father had this handsome stairway built of cedar cut from trees on *Orange Grove* property.

It was always a sad and terrible day when a horse died or had to be put down. If the horse just died, it had to be dragged or carted to a burial place. The grave was huge and had to be many feet deep. If the horse was fatally ill, or too old, it was led to its grave to stand broadside beside the gaping hole and the job was done. Some shot the poor creature in the head, but we had the vet come who injected the horse and it toppled into its grave ready to be covered up. I only watched this once. It was Potter, near The Peak, and I never want to witness such an occurrence again.

During the War, times were desperate for the livestock. We were lucky and managed to save ours, but not everyone did. A large number of horses had to be swum over to one of the islands in Hamilton Harbour to live on grass and God go with them. Of course many died. It caused great hardship. Without a horse, it could have a drastic effect on a man's livelihood.

When the War ended, life on the Island had changed dramatically, things mechanical had made an appearance. The American forces had trucks, buses and cars. Many islanders wanted cars too. After all, they got you places much quicker and you stayed dry. They didn't have to be tended everyday, didn't have to be fed, didn't get sick, didn't take fright and didn't misbehave. Eventually laws were passed after long arguments. Many restrictions were made regarding speed limits, size of vehicles, the number that would be allowed, one car per household except for doctors who could have two, etc. With cars came motorised bicycles and businesses could have trucks and vans. The tranquility which had reigned for centuries was shattered with the explosion of the combustion engine.

So ended the long and valuable era of the man and his horse. Today there are very few and life is the lesser for it.

15 DOGS

David was a bull terrier and middle-aged by the time I bawled my way into the world. He had become used to my brothers for several years so yet another creature around to abuse his dignity was not an unknown quantity. Bull terriers are not big dogs, but they are strong, so David obliged when I crawled up over the end of his tail and sat on his back. If he was sitting down as I did so, then of course I fell off, but if he was standing up, I went riding. He had big nostrils and I wanted to find the other end of them. To my shame, I pushed little sticks up his nose to see how far they would go. This type of dog is renowned for having the 'killer' instinct. If he went into the attack, the throat is what he went for. If he got it he didn't let go, but David neither hurt nor threatened us. He just moved off with an expression of hurt resignation on his face.

When he was getting old, it was decided a young dog should be brought into the family to soften the blow when David was no longer with us. Bill was his name, another bull terrier, and David would have nothing to do with him. Bill was a usurper and mental to boot. He barked at everybody and everything. He travelled all over the neighbourhood causing alarm and telephone calls from angry neighbours. Mother had a full length mirror in her bedroom fitted to the wardrobe just inside the door. Each time Bill came into the room he caught sight of his reflection and went wild with fury to find another dog in his way. He barked and snarled, attacked and beat at the mirror, but the vision beat back and would never go away, infuriating him all the more. The fight became so intense we had to tear him away for fear he would break the glass and do himself some terrible harm. In his madness he snapped at us. He disappeared and I thought

Look how upset I was when David sat down and slid me off his back to stop me riding giggity-gig.

Bill went to 'dog heaven'. My brother says he ran away several times and finally joined the American Army at their base in the Castle Harbour Hotel.

The closest dog we could get to a bull terrier after that was a bitch who was half dalmation. Harvey took my Mother in the carriage to fetch her and they drove home with the six week old puppy cradled in Mother's arms. Mother said she was a Wartime dog and so, named her Wren. We had never had a puppy before. Everybody loved her, especially David, who took on a new lease of life with this bouncing lively little female cavorting round him at every waking moment. He taught her the job she had in life, to be a watch-dog, and that meant rush out and bark at any approaching stranger. She took her job seriously, I am sure sensing her surrogate grandfather could no longer be as effective as she. She terrified various people into throwing things at her, like a whole bundle of newspapers uncontrollably released by the paperboy in his fright, or the milkman relieving himself of several bottles of milk at her aggressive greeting. She was not impressed by that kind of retaliation, so with her bull terrier instinct went into the 'kill' routine. No longer did we have a delightful creature who just gave us love and affection, and only cost her food, but one who cost us any number of pairs of trousers (usually a spare pair of my Father's, if they would fit) to replace the ones she caught hold of and tore to shreds, petrifying the wearer. Luckily in those days people didn't sue for damages as much as they do today. Money or replacement agreeable to both parties in a private transaction usually sufficed.

David was so old in the end, he went blind. It was pitiful to hear him in the upstairs hall in the night crying and confused because he had lost his way trying to find the verandah. He had to be guided everywhere or rescued from his lost state of mind. He snapped at me one morning when I went to help him. I suppose I was about six at the time, and the next day when we came home from town in the carriage, David had wandered down to the road and had been rescued by Olivia who kept him on a blanket by her feet, waiting for us. We took him home in the carriage. That afternoon we children were sent swimming at our aunt's house in Flatt's Inlet. When we came home David's basket was sunning on the verandah. We knew he had gone.

Wren was still a puppy when she contracted jaundice. Her eyes went quite yellow. She felt cold and miserable and Mother used to wrap her up tight in a blanket, she liked to be buried, head and all. That was all very well while she was ill, but for the rest of her life, on chilly nights she wanted to be wrapped up too. We didn't mind that, but when she clawed insistently at my Mother in the early hours because she had been out of bed and wanted to be wrapped up again, it was not so amusing, especially when the blanket had travelled with her as she went out, sometimes way into

Wren in her favourite place, close to Mother. The dogs were not allowed on the furniture, but at times Mother's soft heart took precedence.

the garden. She grew into a caricature of a cross-bred bull terrier *cum* dalmation. She was short, broad-chested and mean with those of whom she disapproved. Her ears were half-way between straight up and lying flat. They started off as if they would stand up but fell over half-way, so the ends flapped. She had the dalmation spots, though indistinct, giving her a mottled look. Her killer instincts were strong, and like bull terriers, when going into attack made no noise, as happened to the postman one morning in the pouring rain. He was leaning into the kitchen door handing over the mail when Wren came out of the back door. Without a sound she grabbed the poor man's ankle. Luckily he was wearing Wellington boots, for surely she would have hurt him badly. Even so, it caused such shouting and yelling everyone came at the run. She decided the ducks were enemies as they flapped away from her pursuits. Once she had caught and

73

killed one, the taste of blood was in her—killing ducks became a necessity. The only cure was to tie a dead duck round her neck, tie her to a big tree away from the house and leave her there for the day. She cried and howled and I was dared to go near her (I did) for this was a serious punishment to teach her to leave ducks alone. It taught her because she never touched another duck again. She sucked their eggs instead. We found dozens of eggs smashed and empty, and finally caught her scattering ducks from their nests destroying their produce. Harvey had the cure for that evil. He filled an egg with a solution of ammonia and water, sealed the shell together with melted candle wax (which happened to be red) and shoved the whole thing into her mouth. She learned.

There were no bull terriers for her to mate and very few dalmations. Our vet however, had a dalmation who was hyper-active and had to be kept in a kennel. Wren fell in love with him so they married and had a beautiful litter of puppies. A litter is a full-time occupation after the first few weeks, but of course, they gave us infinite fun and it was hard to part with them when they had to go to their new homes. The next time we decided to mate Wren there was a new dalmation on the Island who was thought to have a better pedigree and temperament. The dog was brought to the house and both were locked in the stable to get on with the marriage ceremony. A horrendous noise ensued of fighting, snapping, growling and yelping as they collided with the stalls. It sounded as if half a dozen dogs were trying to tear each other apart. When the door was finally unlocked, out bounced Wren like a spring, with teeth bared and hackles up. She dared the suitor to come near. He, on the other hand was desperate for her and wouldn't be told, 'No'. She had given her allegiance to Hyper-Active and never accepted another.

From the litter we kept a dog named Sandy. He looked much more like a proper dalmation, tall, well spotted and affectionate. The male in him took him down the hill to find the local talent when those alluring scents came his way. He would be gone for more than a day at a time, trailing home at last, exhausted from his battles and conquests. Many times he needed stitches to mend the wounds received from other amorous would-be lovers. He was the biggest fellow in the Parish and fathered a remarkable array of confusing looking canine species. He got it down to a fine art. John's family had a small 'Bermuda police dog', a cross between alsatian and anything else, but with a 'look' of that breed. She was pretty and named Lassie. Sandy loved her and they spent many happy times roaming the hillside together. When her season came the family were told to, 'Take her and lock her up somewhere, because we get no peace from Sandy.'

She was taken over the hill to a deserted wooden shed, tied up with a chain, and the door shut. They thought that was perfectly secure and plenty far away, about a quarter of a mile. Dogs have a sense of smell that goes for miles so it was not long before all the boyfriends assembled at the shed. Lassie whined and whimpered from the inside while the boys prowled round snarling and beating each other up. Soon they began to dig a hole against the side. The smallest one got in first. It was Puppy, who belonged to Harvey and whose puppyhood was many a long year past. With one dog in, the digging got more frantic with the scramble to be with the bride. All the time Sandy was working with the rest until about eight dogs had managed to scramble their way through the difficult hole. Poor Sandy was too big to get through. The enemy was inside, so was the prize. All he could do was sit and howl his dismay. At twilight Mother and I went to fetch the poor unfortunate dog home. It was nearly dark when we got there, and marking our track with a torch, we heard a lot of excited barking as we approached calling Sandy's name. Our astonished eyes could hardly believe what confronted them. There was Sandy, big and proud, barking his wonderful achievement, because sitting happily beside him was Lassie wagging her tail in sheer delight. But still we heard the frustrated barking of the other dogs. Mother shone the light at the hole behind the loving pair. As she did, Puppy stuck his head out and barked, only to be sent back yelping as Sandy bit him on the nose. Another tried his luck and got the same treatment. Lassie couldn't get *free* but she could get *out*. We marched Sandy off telling him how disgraceful was his behaviour. As the others realised the coast was clear, so appeared a motley lot of dogs crawling from their prison, each thinking they would now have their girl, but she told them she had made her choice, 'Don't come near me.'

My father said Sandy was a very clever dog and taught him tricks. He would say, 'Sandy, would you rather go to school, or be a *dead* dog?' Sandy rolled over and played dead. It didn't matter what you asked him he would rather do as long as you finished with 'dead dog'. He always played dead. He could give this paw and speak with a purposeful 'wuff'. His best trick was Father's *pièce de résistance* for guests at a party. Father taught him to put his paws on his knees and a tasty morsel was placed on a paw. Then Father raised his arms in the air, with hands held in supplication, he sang out in a holy tone, 'And make Sandy and good boy...A-A-men.' As soon as Sandy heard 'men', he knew he could have the morsel. It was gone in a gulp. He was patient and stayed with his paws up, watching Father's face with adoring eyes and the crumb on his foot for as long as his Master kept him waiting, knowing in the end the cue would come. One day, the Bishop and his wife came for tea. Father thought Sandy should do his trick and said, 'Come on Sandy, say your prayers.' Up came the paws and Father and Sandy did their party piece. There was a deathly hush. The Bishop was not amused.

Our hero hurt his paw badly on barbed wire which kept it bandaged for a week or more. When the bandage came off he held his foot up looking pathetic and sad, asking so miserably for sympathy and attention. Of course he got it. 'Poor Sandy, who's a poor boy then?' we would say along with anything else in a similar tone of voice. After that, when he was scolded for being naughty, up came the paw and he hobbled on three legs. If you then said, 'Oh, you're a good boy,' he would rush away, all four feet going strong.

The next litter gave us Miranda. She was mine, my very own dog. She slept in my room, preferably on my bed, which I loved, and got us both into trouble with Mother. She grew bigger than her mother but remained smaller than Sandy. She was beautiful and feminine in her ways. She was my special companion and loved to run with the horses when we went riding.

All this time Wren was teaching her offspring what David had taught her, guard the house and all who belong, see off everybody else. Three healthy dogs rushing from the house each sounding the alarm is an intimidating sight. Delivery people were the ones who came off worst. It wasn't long before the reputation, 'Saucy dawgs up at *Orange Grove*' was well known.

We got phone calls, 'Lock up de dawgs, ver gotta a massage to bring up.' The postmen refused to deliver the mail, and the reputation stayed with us long after the terrible trio had gone.

On a beautiful summer afternoon my parents had a tea party. As often happened, we took our guests for a walk to the top of the hill to The Peak. Of course the dogs went too. On the way back, with exuberant joy they jumped into the fish pond to chase a toad. They came out black, covered with silt and rotting weed, spraying water with their wagging tails—not a popular move. We were told to give them a bath. We couldn't do as we usually did because that meant bringing out the old galvanised tub and the hose, and washing them in the Back Yard. The party was being held there and was all set up for a very fine tea. We took them upstairs to Father's bathroom and put them in the bathtub. They'd never had a bath in the bathtub before and got even more excited. Because everyone was so beautifully dressed we locked them upstairs on the front verandah out of sight in the hope they would quieten down and dry off. We went back to join the party which was going well and being enjoyed by everyone, the little episode with the dogs forgotten. Just then the sound of a low rumbling, something like distant thunder, came from deep within the house. The conversation stopped, as suddenly the screen door on the back verandah flew open and out shot a dog as if catapulted. The door slammed shut and instantly flew open again with a shattering vibration as another dog was seemingly fired out, each one thrilled to be free and back at the party. There was a moment's stunned silence as everyone froze like statues, and then the reactions began. Two ladies jumped on to a bench with no thought for their flying skirts. They tipped over the bench, demolishing their dignity altogether. Another was holding a cup about to take a sip when she froze, and instead of the tea going to her mouth, it went the other way, straight into Jim's face. He reacted by knocking over a table with sandwiches, teacups and plates. All the women screamed and the men yelled. The family shouted commands which were totally ignored by the wet delighted delinquents. The party degenerated into something much more fun and Father decided we all needed drinks, not tea.

16 CATS

This book would not be complete if I left out the cats. Cats were an integral part of *Orange Grove*. My Mother loved cats, my Father did not. It was part of the bargain he had to make when he asked her to marry him. If he wanted her as a wife, then cats had to come too.

Felix was an experienced old tabby cat. Mother kept a tin of dried catnip in her wardrobe and when she thought Felix was looking a little under the weather she gave him a few leaves. What a binge he had! He rolled over them, rubbed his nose in them, purred and miaowed in abandoned tones rolling over the floor like one demented. Really drunk he raced round the room, up the curtains, over the beds and across the furniture, causing scatter-action wherever he landed. He loved milk and his favourite way of getting it was from the breakfast table. He dipped his paw into the jug then drew it carefully back to suck and lick. His friend was Misty a slate grey cat Mother said was Maltese because she had an 'M' clearly marked through the fur of her forehead. Misty was like any other healthy female and was ready for mating more often than was good for her. When those times came round other toms came to try their luck and Felix fought for his rights.

The nightly chorus was like an amateur orchestra trying to tune up, accentuated by high pitched yowls and low pitched growls, followed by continuing grumbles like a cello with a loose string. You waited for the preamble to finish as the orchestra burst into hysterical *staccato* screeches on its way to the finale, rising to such a *crescendo*, the audience could bear it no longer and rose to boo and hiss.

Misty would produce a litter some weeks later, preferably on Mother's bed. Mother preferred them produced in a box, in a cupboard, in her bathroom. Her bathroom had a permanent label on the door 'KEEP SHUT—kittens inside', so was known as the 'cat's bathroom'. We had to keep the door shut as tom-cats like to kill kittens and the dogs weren't averse either especially Sandy. The bathroom window opened on to the top verandah at the back and we kept it open just enough for the mother to get in and out, but not until the kittens had their eyes open as after that the tom-cats seemed to lose interest in killing their off-spring.

It was hard to part with the kittens and more often than not, Mother kept one. The others went to their new homes in a box with a tin of evaporated milk for company. Mother kept a black kitten with a white chest for me which we named Penguin and called Penny.

All cats like to take presents to the ones they love, but all they can think of are mice and if you are lucky, a rat. Neither Mother nor myself liked this generous attitude and did everything to discourage it. Mother was best, she screamed her head off at the sight of a cat coming in with the dreaded present in its mouth, sometimes still twitching. Penny was thoughtful, she brought me a live mouse in the dead of night when I was sick. I woke to feel something running up the side of my leg. Instinctively, I knew what it was and did a good imitation of my Mother showing her disapproval. Penny was affronted and left the room, the mouse went past my nose, over the headboard and was lost in the curtains of the four-poster. By the time my parents arrived to see what was the matter, there was no present and no cat. They thought I had had a nightmare and tried to soothe me back to sleep. They did not believe my story until Penny reappeared and sat on the end of the bed with her tail swishing and eyes flashing about the room waiting for the poor creature to venture out. When it did, she sprang, captured the petrified animal, walked haughtily out of the room and ate it noisily in the hall, making sure we heard each bone crack.

We had a terrible time when she climbed trees as she was afraid of heights. She would cry and miaow for hours until someone heard and went to help. When the dogs chased her up the Mammy apple tree she flew to the top. It stands about 30 feet high with a girth the size of an old oak tree. No amount of cajoling, encouragement or saucers of milk would budge her. Her feet were spread-eagled across the bending branches, each claw jammed in the bark. We had to persuade a tall neighbour to climb a ladder, get into the tree and drag her writhing body down.

She had her own ideas too as to where she would have kittens. We searched all over the place, in the cupboards, under the beds, in the stables but they were hard to find. I didn't find her last litter until I went out to the feed store and there they were, half a dozen kittens nestled in my bicycle basket. We kept two kittens and named them Night and Day. Night was sleek without a trace of marking while Day was as pure as driven snow. They were inseparable. When it came time for them to kitten, we knew because they began scratching around the house for a nest. It was time to put a cardboard box in the bathroom cupboard. They arranged things so they had their kittens within days of each other. It was clever, each one got time off from the eternal feeding programme. We amalgamated them into one large box. It was easy to discern their babies for they always arrived black or white. It became a study to watch these cats and their children at feeding time. There might be eight or ten in the box and suckling one mother might be six or seven of either litter, while the other only had two or three. It worked well. As the babies grew older we put them on the verandah to play and have more space. It worked most of the time, but sometimes, if we were away from the house for a length of time, Sandy managed to break through the home-made barriers and savage them. It was a dreadful sight to see dead kittens spread across the boards. It never occurred to us to tie a kitten round his neck. He was an engaging dog in the ordinary way, but until the kittens could scratch his nose, they were easy prey. I can't remember how many cats we had at one time but usually about four not including the transient procession of kittens.

Mother rose early each morning to make coffee for Father and tea for herself. While the water was heating there was time to feed the dogs and cats. Depending on their age and health, the coffee and tea process could take a considerable time. The evaporated milk had to be diluted and sometimes a raw egg was beaten in. All had a share, including me. I loved my milk and egg. If the animals needed building up, raw minced beef was provided, especially ordered from the butcher as 'cat's meat'. The dogs finished up with dog chow, then everyone followed Mother upstairs as she hooked her nightie in one hand and carried the tray in the other. I think my Father was rarely aware of the time it took to get his coffee while he was happily snoring in bed. But, there came the day when he was awakened by blood curdling screams from the kitchen. I woke to hear him scrambling out of bed. Yelling his imminent rescue, he skirted the furniture, raced through the room and down the stairs as fast as his rotund body would allow, to find Mother dancing on the kitchen table, pointing abstractedly to the floor at a large rat who was thoroughly rattled by the commotion. Another morning she put her legs over the side of her high four-poster and cried out, 'There's a dead rat on the floor, Will!' Obligingly he crawled out of his four-poster and stood on another delivered to him.

Somehow I became the owner of a life-like rubber mouse. I hid behind the kitchen door as Mother came through from the dining-room carrying the early morning tea-tray. I leapt from behind jiggling the mouse by its tail in front of her nose. The intention was to tease, but, oh dear, I was stunned by the reaction. She let out a piercing scream. The tray flew from her hands and crashed to the floor. Every single piece of china smashed to bits in a horrible mess of tea leaves, milk and sugar. After a moment's shocked silence she came to herself and started for me. I bolted and didn't go back for an hour!

Breakfast time gave guests considerable trouble. The cats roamed the table in the hope of being able to sneak a piece of bacon from a plate. We were used to it and gave a sharp whack to one lying in wait. The guests weren't sure how to deal with this and were too polite to throw the animal across the room. More than once, while reading the paper, an unsuspecting person found the bacon gone from his plate, then was confused, feeling reasonably sure he hadn't eaten it himself. Later, my husband said it was a fight between the cats on the table and the dalmations under the table coming up between his knees ready with their long tongues. Well. . . we loved our animals and delighted in shocking people.

17 REVIEW

All those precious animals are dead, of course, and sadly many of the people I have talked about, but generations go on. Some of the children have the right to say their parents and grandparents would be proud they did so well. There must be those too, who would *not* be so proud to say they had anything to do with their children! Not many people become famous or infamous, but most achieve a degree of successful recognition and can be pleased with what they did with their lives.

My brothers and I, like so many others, can trace our ancestors back for many generations, so our parents were delighted when we began to produce the new generation, their grandchildren. We raised 10 between us, five boys and five girls. Now those children are grown-up, marrying and producing their own generation...grandchildren for us.

William, my elder brother, decided to be a journalist and was Editor of the Island's only daily newspaper, *The Royal Gazette*. After many years he changed direction becoming Director of *The Bermuda National Trust*, an important body whose job is the preservation of historic buildings and the conservation of the limited areas of unspoiled land. I seem to remember some debate as to who was going to carry on in the family business. William had made his decision so Jim was left with the matter of carrying on the family tradition in the general merchant's firm of *Pearman Watlington & Company*. It wasn't considered I should take on such responsibilities ...daughters married, had children, preferably boys, with the odd girl thrown in who would marry well and keep the generations going. In retrospect, if I had used my head and had more pushing, I could have become quite good in the business, but such was my upbringing. It was considered right I should have some sort of ability, though it didn't matter what, as long as I had a good education and could conduct myself properly in adult intellectual company. The intellect eluded me, and truthfully, I wanted to marry and have a family, which I did, and have no regrets as to how my life panned out. Jim decided after some time he had been inhibited enough and was going to be his own boss. He left the family firm and bought the *Bermuda Book Store* which he has been running ever since. I have travelled extensively round the world with my husband Colin, though oddly enough not while he was in the Royal Navy, but after he too changed direction and retired from the Navy to join the big commercial world.

Dot continued to sew for us, faithfully arriving each Tuesday morning to sit in her chair in front of the same old sewing machine (which Mother had had converted to electricity with a foot pedal after Dot broke her wrist badly and found turning the sewing wheel painful) making and mending until she was nearly 90 years old. When we were going back to boarding school and said our good-byes to Dot, she would say, 'I might be pushin' up the roses by the time you get back.' 'No, no, you can't do that!' we replied. We were sure she would still be there. Through those years she proudly watched her son become a teacher, a headmaster and finally the Head of the Education Department. He was a quiet gentleman, like his gentlewoman mother.

Ella married Gerald, one of Olivia's sons. Their eldest daughter Eunice joined the household at *Orange Grove* although she was bringing up and still producing her own large family. She has stayed with our family all these years, giving an extra backbone to her mother, being our affectionate friend and taking on all kinds of other activities, like the Church, the Boy's Brigade, helping others more in need than herself and always ready to help in any way we asked. She is the one who remembers where something we have mislaid can be found, and no one can 'do up' a piece of linen more beautifully than she can. One of her daughters, Chris, went to England at the age of 19 to study nursing. As I lived in England I was asked to be her guardian. She was frightened and homesick, uprooted from her comfortable Island home. We were shocked by the cell-like room she was to live in at the nurses' quarters. She bravely stuck it out and became a highly qualified midwife specialising in premature babies. She often came to stay with us and I love her as one of my own. That love was made more endearing when years later she called me her 'other mother'.

Jack's family are a diversified lot...one son became Deputy Prime Minister and is an excellent radio commentator for cricket matches. Another served the Church devotedly for many years and drove a taxi for his living. It is beautiful indeed to listen to him read the lesson in that fine Bermudian dialect. A third son, Will, the one we knew particularly well, was the best bartender I have ever known and was much in demand for parties. Once you told him the drink you favoured he never forgot even though it might be months before he saw you again. Louise married Chauncey, a mason by trade, I think. I remember the excitement the day they married. I was about 10 years old and sang the hymns so loudly, my mother had to shut me up. I was at their house sometimes when Chauncey came home from work, and was struck by the thought that I had never seen my Father greet my Mother the way Chauncey did Louise, for no matter what she was doing he put his arm round her waist, kissed her gently on the cheek and said, 'How is Mummy?' Mummy had six boys. They all had names beginning with 'G' except the youngest who got 'D'.

'Because we couldn't think of another "G"!' they said. Chauncey's gentleness and charming humour must have helped him in his real ambition to join the ministry which culminated years later when he became a Bishop in the Pentecostal faith.

I think we had a unique upbringing in a crazy turmoiled world. I hope our children will understand a little more of what life was like and our grandchildren be aware that not so long ago life wasn't all computers, fast travel, central heating and money. It may come as a surprise for the youngest members of the family to know someone still alive can remember a time when cars were carriages and roads were not tarmacadam...Certainly, one of our daughters said, 'But Mummy, it was another world!'...It was.

Bermuda has now moved forward with the rest of the world. It is cosmopolitan and sophisticated with modern air-conditioned buildings, jumbo jets arriving and departing each day; streets bustling with cars, motorbikes and tourists, despite the speed limit of 20 mph. The days of the simple life, the slow gentle ways, the serenity, gracious manners, have partly given way to the worldly life of thriving businesses, international banking and the universal problem of drugs. The people are not truly concerned with the tremendous happenings in Europe, Africa and America, of war, famine and earthquake. They may cluck their tongues at riots in South America or the wretchedness of Ethiopia, but it has no real effect on them. They are more concerned about what happened down in St George last night, or, 'Did you know about that big fire in Town this morning? I could see the smoke from Paget!' Thus it retains a certain security for those who remember their grandparents and can tell their grandchildren about them. To me the Island is the symbol of the *Continuity of Life*. We know who we are, where we come from, where we are going.

For those of us who live away from the Island, in self-imposed exile, our sights are set on the day when we will return for good. We long for blue skies, the clear blue-green water so inviting on a summer's day, hot sand underfoot as we cross the beach and flop into the cool waves of the Atlantic as it splashes round us. We long for the cheery 'hello' and, 'Hey gurl, I haven't seen you in a long time, where you bin?'

Most of all we long for our families and friends, even those with their funny ways. We like it best in our own Back Yard.

CONTENTS

Introduction: A Well-Rounded Workout for the Brain   iv

THE EXERCISES   1

An Invitation—Keep Going!   255

Answers   257

About the Author   282

INTRODUCTION

A Well-Rounded Workout for the Brain

THE GREATEST FEAR among older adults is dementia, and as a doctor of psychology specialising in Alzheimer's disease and related dementias, I am often asked by seniors in the community, "How can I reduce my risk?"

My answer is always: Exercise your brain! Research has shown the benefits of keeping cognitive abilities strong. Those who have challenged their brains throughout their life have a lower risk of developing dementia,* and those who have mild cognitive impairment (MCI) – a large risk factor for dementia – and exercise their brains can keep their cognitive abilities stronger for longer.†

This workbook has been specifically designed to provide a variety of exercises for different cognitive abilities. Research supports that brain exercise 1) must be challenging, and 2) must target various cognitive abilities, not just one (e.g., only doing crossword puzzles).

Our brains need a well-rounded workout just like our bodies!

In this workbook, each worksheet is labeled with the cognitive ability that is being exercised. Since many of the tasks exercise multiple cognitive abilities, I have labeled the worksheet with the primary cognitive ability that the task targets.

There is no one right way to approach this book. You can start at the beginning and work your way through the exercises in order, or you can pick and choose the abilities you would like to work on each day.

I do recommend that you complete a variety of exercises targeting different cognitive abilities in each sitting, which is the best way to get a well-rounded workout. Just like our bodies, if we only lifted weights for one muscle and not all the others, it would not be a very good workout. I also recommend doing a minimum of three hours per week of cognitive exercise. The American Medical Association recommends a minimum of three hours per week of physical exercise, and I believe we should do the same for the brain.

As you work your way through this book,

---

* Verghese et al. (2003). Leisure activities and the risk of dementia in the elderly. *New England Journal of Medicine*, 348(25), 2508–16.

† Reijnders et al. (2013). Cognitive interventions in healthy older adults and people with mild cognitive impairment: A systematic review. *Aging Resources Review*, 12(1), 263–75.

you might notice that there are many more language exercises than other targeted cognitive ability tasks, such as memory. Yes, this was intentional. In case you are wondering, here's the reason why: Usually the first thing to go as we get older is our short-term memory, and I wanted to exercise memory in a simple way, without overdoing it. I didn't want anyone using this book to become discouraged and quit if they had to struggle through many of the exercises. Language, on the other hand, is an ability that tends to stay relatively strong, and while exercising it to keep it strong for as long as possible, we can also aid broader cognitive functions. You know that "tip-of-the-tongue" phenomenon when you can't think of words as quickly as before? These many language exercises will help you strengthen those neural networks and potentially increase word retrieval speed. Other cognitive abilities have even fewer exercises, such as attention and sequencing, because those abilities are being exercised in many of the other tasks, but are secondary to the one listed on the page.

Now let's have some fun!

THE
EXERCISES

GRANDCHILDREN COMPARISONS

Using the clues given, make the requested comparisons to determine the correct answer.

1. Your grandchildren are racing in the back garden. Jimmy beat Cathy, and Melanie beat Patrick. If Patrick beat Jimmy, what was the outcome of the race?

1ST PLACE	
2ND PLACE	
3RD PLACE	
4TH PLACE	

2. Your grandchildren are measuring their heights. Tom is taller than Sally, but he is not taller than Lucy. Amber is not as tall as Sally. What is their order of height from tallest to shortest?

1ST (TALLEST)	
2ND	
3RD	
4TH (SHORTEST)	

3. Your grandchildren are comparing their allowances. Kate earns more than Henry, who earns the least. Joe does not make as much as Kate. What is their order from the highest allowance to the least?

1ST (HIGHEST)	
2ND	
3RD (LEAST)	

4. Your grandchildren are comparing their grades. Yvonne earned a higher grade than Albert, but she did not earn as high of a grade as Neil. Marie earned a higher grade than Neil. What is their order from highest grade to lowest grade?

1ST (HIGHEST)	
2ND	
3RD	
4TH (LOWEST)	

5. Your grandchildren are comparing how many toys they have at your house. Louie has less than Tamra, who has less than Olivia. Robert has more toys than Olivia. What is their order from the most toys to the least?

1ST (MOST)	
2ND	
3RD	
4TH (LEAST)	

6. Your grandchildren are playing a board game. Eva has 4 more points than William, but she has 8 less points than Vivian. If William has 32 points, in what order did they come in the game and with how many points?

	NAME	POINTS
1ST		
2ND		
3RD		

REASONING

TWO DEFINITIONS 1

Two definitions for the same word are given. Fill in the correct word that matches both definitions.

1. To fight with your fists

   A container

   ANSWER _____

2. Area with no sun

   A tint of colour

   ANSWER _____

3. Part of a tree

   A large suitcase

   ANSWER _____

4. Smart

   Sunny

   ANSWER _____

5. A measurement

   Part of the body

   ANSWER _____

6. A stone

   To sway back and forth

   ANSWER _____

7. To hit with a fist

   A fruit drink

   ANSWER _____

8. To say clearly

   Temperament

   ANSWER _____

LANGUAGE

MATCHING CLUES 1

Match two of the word-parts to make a word that fits the clue. Each word-part is used only once.

je   jo   re   int

bel   jo   wel   ban

1. _____ a stringed musical instrument

_____ to rise in opposition

_____ a precious stone

_____ where two parts fit together

aj   ck   jo   ar

ke   ke   ba   ba

2. _____ a punch line

_____ slightly open

_____ to cook with dry heat

_____ toward the rear

LANGUAGE

SEQUENCING ITEMS 1

Discover a logical way to sequence these items, and explain the *reason* why you put them in that order. No alphabetical order allowed. There may be more than one correct answer.

1. Flea, Bumblebee, Ladybug, Butterfly

    1st _____ 2nd _____ 3rd _____ 4th _____

    Reason _____

2. Semester/term, Month, Centennial, Fiscal year

    1st _____ 2nd _____ 3rd _____ 4th _____

    Reason _____

3. Paint, Chop, Carve, Sand

    1st _____ 2nd _____ 3rd _____ 4th _____

    Reason _____

4. Millimetre, Kilometre, Metre, Centimetre

    1st _____ 2nd _____ 3rd _____ 4th _____

    Reason _____

5. Mortgage, Escrow, Credit check pre-approval, Offer

    1st _____ 2nd _____ 3rd _____ 4th _____

    Reason _____

6. Check mirrors, Press gas pedal, Put into drive, Fasten seat belt

    1st _____ 2nd _____ 3rd _____ 4th _____

    Reason _____

7. Bake, Gather ingredients, Mix, Pour into pan

    1st _____ 2nd _____ 3rd _____ 4th _____

    Reason _____

EXECUTIVE FUNCTIONING

8. Hill, Pebble, Mountain, Boulder

1st _____ 2nd _____ 3rd _____ 4th _____

Reason _____

9. Large intestine, Small intestine, Mouth, Stomach

1st _____ 2nd _____ 3rd _____ 4th _____

Reason _____

10. Cocoon, Butterfly, Caterpillar, Egg

1st _____ 2nd _____ 3rd _____ 4th _____

Reason _____

11. Night, Dawn, High noon, Dusk

1st _____ 2nd _____ 3rd _____ 4th _____

Reason _____

12. Nose, Blood, Body tissue, Lungs

1st _____ 2nd _____ 3rd _____ 4th _____

Reason _____

13. Bacteria, Cow, Yogurt, Milk

1st _____ 2nd _____ 3rd _____ 4th _____

Reason _____

14. Application, Attendance, Acceptance, Interview

1st _____ 2nd _____ 3rd _____ 4th _____

Reason _____

15. Hypothesis, Results, Experiment, Analysis

1st _____ 2nd _____ 3rd _____ 4th _____

Reason _____

FAMILY TREE GAME 1

Based on this family tree, answer the questions below with a specific name.

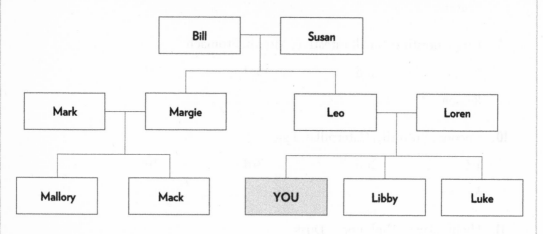

1. Who is your father's father's son?

   _____

2. Who is your mother's husband's mother?

   _____

3. Who is your uncle's daughter?

   _____

4. Who are your cousins?

   _____

5. Who is your aunt's husband?

   _____

6. Who is your grandfather's daughter-in-law?

   _____

REASONING

BOXED LETTERS – CARDS

Print the letters in the correct box to spell a type of card game reading across.

1. Print the letter O in box B2
    Print the letter H in box D6
    Print the letter I in box A4
    Print the letter F in box C3
    Print the letter S in box B5
    Print the letter G in box C1   ANSWER _____

	1	2	3	4	5	6
A						
B						
C						
D						

2. Print the letter K in box C3
    Print the letter R in box D5
    Print the letter E in box A4
    Print the letter P in box B1
    Print the letter O in Box A2   ANSWER _____

	1	2	3	4	5	6	7	8	9
A									
B									
C									
D									

VISUAL-SPATIAL

3. Print the letter A in A3
Print the letter S in C6
Print the letter E in D2
Print the letter T in B5
Print the letter H in B1
Print the letter R in C4   ANSWER _____

	1	2	3	4	5	6
A						
B						
C						
D						

4. Print the letter M in B6
Print the letter N in C3
Print the letter U in A5
Print the letter I in D2
Print the letter Y in C8
Print the letter G in B1
Print the letter M in A7
Print the letter R in D4   ANSWER _____

	1	2	3	4	5	6	7	8
A								
B								
C								
D								

VISUAL-SPATIAL

5. Print the letter A in B3
Print the letter S in C6
Print the letter P in C2
Print the letter E in D5
Print the letter S in B1
Print the letter D in A4   ANSWER _____

	1	2	3	4	5	6
A						
B						
C						
D						

6. Print the letter A in box B7
Print the letter A in box C3
Print the letter K in box D5
Print the letter K in box A9
Print the letter L in box C2
Print the letter C in box A8
Print the letter B in box D1
Print the letter J in Box B6
Print the letter C in Box C4   ANSWER _____

	1	2	3	4	5	6	7	8	9
A									
B									
C									
D									

TWO-LETTER PLACEMENT 1

Choose which two-letter combo will make a word when added to the letters below. There may be more than one possible answer.

er   ar   or   to   se   re   ra

1. __ __ d e r

2. a d h __ __ e

3. b __ __ w

4. f __ __ m

5. d r e __ __ y

6. a v __ __ a g e

7. c a __ __

8. h __ __ d

9. c o t __ __ n

10. p l u __ __ l

11. s h __ __ t

12. c a r e __ __

13. s p __ __ y

14. o r c h __ __ d

15. s e c __ __ t

16. s __ __ r e

17. p a __ __ n t

18. __ __ g u e

19. g __ __ e d

20. e __ __ l y

21. c o __ __ c e

22. m __ __ g i n a l

23. __ __ i g i n

24. g u __ __ d

25. i n __ __ r t

26. a v __ __ s i o n

27. c l o __ __ t

28. s c __ __ n

29. l a p __ __ p

30. t h __ __ a d

31. c __ __ a m i c

32. __ __ a s t

33. e r a __ __

34. c __ __ k

DECIPHER THE LETTER CODE 1

Complete the phrase by determining the number that is assigned to the used letters.

Begin by filling in the letters that you are given, then figure out which letters make sense to make words in the phrase. You don't have to figure out all the letters, just the ones you need.

For example, if the word is ___ H ___ , the word is likely THE, so 8 = T,
         8   13

therefore you can add in all 8s as Ts.

A	B	C	D	E	F	G	H	I	J	K	L	M
10		3		7		1	24					

N	O	P	Q	R	S	T	U	V	W	X	Y	Z
25						2			5		15	

MESSAGE:

___ ___ ___ ___   ___ ___ ___ ___ ___ ___ ___ ___ ___ ___   ___ ___
 5 24   7 25   7 19   7   9 15   2 24 18 25   1   18 23

___ ___ ___ ___ ___ ___   ___ ___ ___ ___   ___ ___ ___ ,
 3 12 14 18 25   1   15 12   8   9   5 10 15

___ ___ ___   ___ ___ ___   ___ ___   ___ ___ ___
15 12   8   10   9   7   18 25   2 24   7

___ ___ ___ ___ ___   ___ ___ ___ ___ .
 5   9 12 25   1   22 10 25   7

WHAT'S THAT PHRASE? 1

Fill in the letters to complete the familiar phrase. There is a clue to help.

1. A D____ ____ ____   A D____ ____ ____ ____

   When something is extremely common

2. A P____ ____ ____ ____   O____   C____ ____ ____

   A task that is simple to complete

3. A____ A____ ____ A____ ____ A L____ ____ ____

   When something is extremely expensive, it costs . . .

4. I____'____   A____ ____   G____ ____ ____ ____ ____   T____   M____

   When something is incomprehensible

5. B____ ____ ____   T____ T____ ____   D____ ____ W____ ____ ____ ____

   B____ ____ ____ D

   To start over again after a failed attempt is to go . . .

6. B____ ____ T A____ ____ ____ ____   D T____ ____   B____ ____ ____

   When someone avoids the main point or fails to get to the bottom line

7. B____ ____ W____ ____ ____   A R____ ____ K A____ ____   A

   H____ ____ D P____ ____ ____ E

   When someone is faced with two difficult decisions; a dilemma

8. B____ ____ ____ ____ K T____ ____   I____ ____

   To end the social awkwardness

9. B____ ____ ____ T Y____ ____ R B____ ____ ____ B____ ____ ____

   To ruin someone's happy mood

MEMORY

10. C___ ___ ___ E B___ ___ N___ C___ ___ ___ ___

To almost reach a successful outcome only to fall short at the end

11. C___ ___ T___ T___ ___ C___ ___ ___ E

To get to the point

12. D___ ___ N F___ ___ ___ T___ ___ C___ ___ ___ ___T

To look defeated or beaten

13. D___ ___ ___ T___ T___ ___ W___ ___ ___

When an outcome is determined in the last few seconds

14. D___ ___ P___ ___ ___ ___ L___ ___ ___ F___ ___ ___ S

To fall down in large numbers

15. E___ ___ ___ A___ P___ ___ ___

Something that is simple

16. E___ ___ ___ ___ ___ ___ T I___ T___ ___ R___ ___ ___

The large obvious problem that is being ignored

MEMORY

COUNT THE Us

As quickly as you can, count how many Us are in this paragraph. Scan each line from left to right.

a u l k d j f i s o d j h u i n d t u t y o e y k f s l y l k j l d f u i n f k s l l

w o q p o w r y r j k u l y s k d n f k s l u k s d n f u k j f k s d n f u n s k

d f n d l u k s d n f s k d u n k l p u n s d l f y a d f u l j u p i u w e r u p

o u w e r u l s u e r u l s i u s l d i u z m c v u z n u d n f u e r y u s d l k

f u u n l s u p i u r q w e u l s d f u l k j u l k u k l f s d i f u s d f u x c v

m n d f u s w e r u r y u x g u a d f g u l k j u o i u w e r u s d f u t w e r

u q w e u u u p o i u q w u a d f u z c v u m b n u k l j h s d f x c v i o s e

r k j a s d y s d f o l u n k e r j u s d f u w e r t w e m x g p q w i u y s d f

j n k u y t w e r l k d f u q w e r u x c b h s d f g b z v x c y t w e r u u s

e b f s u y g e w u a o d p e y x o s d i u d s w x p o t h d k b s k o e r t n

v u e r b n l d k f y u l s k d u s h s e t u t u s k d o u d t h k s d u

TOTAL Us _____

ATTENTION

AGING WORDS 1

The answer to each clue contains the letters "AGE."

1. A metal enclosure for confining animals

   ANSWER _____

2. A system of words to express thoughts

   ANSWER _____

3. A connective protein found in skin

   ANSWER _____

4. A restaurant fee for serving wine brought in from elsewhere

   ANSWER _____

5. A physical obstruction

   ANSWER _____

6. A small rural house situated in the countryside

   ANSWER _____

7. Discarded waste

   ANSWER _____

8. Something that passes from one generation to the next

   ANSWER _____

LANGUAGE

DOMINO ORDER 1

Starting with the domino marked "1st," find an order in which you can line up all these dominoes end to end. Wherever two dominoes touch, the numbered ends must match. You may rotate the dominoes, and there is more than one correct order.

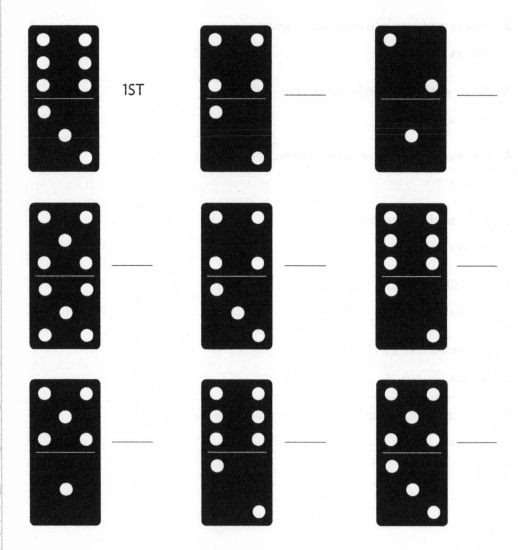

1ST

EXECUTIVE FUNCTIONING

VENN DIAGRAM – LANGUAGES

Answer the questions using the information displayed in the Venn diagram.

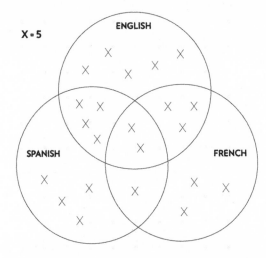

1. How many people speak only English and Spanish?

   ANSWER _____

2. Is it more common for people to speak all three languages or just Spanish and French?

   ANSWER _____

3. How many people speak only Spanish and French?

   ANSWER _____

4. How many people speak English?

   ANSWER _____

5. How many people speak only English?

   ANSWER _____

6. How many people do not speak French?

   ANSWER _____

VISUAL–SPATIAL

DOT COPY 1

Copy these patterns onto the blank graphs.

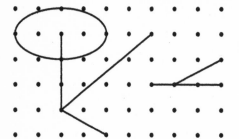

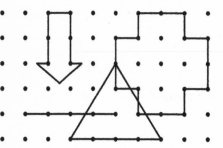

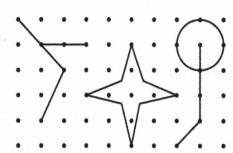

SHAPE MATCH 1

Circle the two matching shapes.

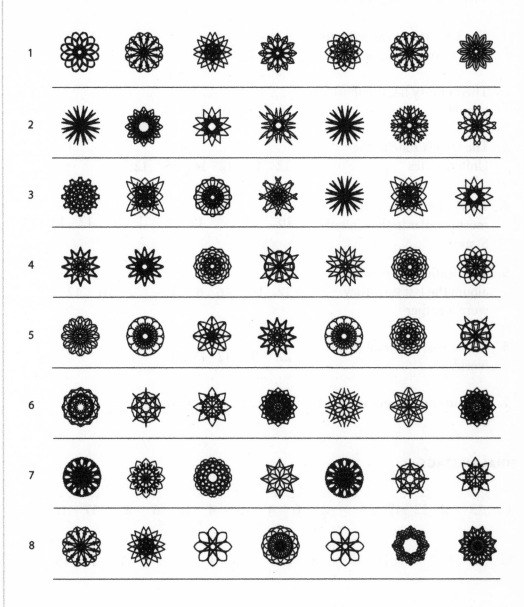

LETTER TRANSFER 1

Fill in the word to answer the clue, then transfer those numbered letters to the lines below for the final message.

1. The instrument Miles Davis, the jazz musician, played

   ___ ___ ___ ___ ___ ___ ___
   1   2   3   4   5   6   1

2. This country has the most people

   ___ ___ ___ ___ ___
   8   9   10 11 12

3. The largest state in the United States

   ___ ___ ___ ___ ___ ___
   12 13 12 14 15 12

4. This indoor sport is the most popular in the United States

   ___ ___ ___ ___ ___ ___ ___ ___ ___ ___
   16 12 14 15 6   1   16 12 13 13

5. The Beatles recorded this album the last time they were together

   ___ ___ ___ ___ ___ ___ ___ ___ ___
   12 16 16 6   17   2   18 12 19

6. The largest mammal in the world

   ___ ___ ___ ___ ___
   22 9   12 13 6

7. A young delinquent is called this

   ___ ___ ___ ___ ___ ___ ___ ___
   23 3   24 6   11 10 13 6

FINAL MESSAGE:

___ ___ ___ ___ ___ ___ ___ ___ ___ ___ ___ ___ ___ ___ ___ ___ ___
12 13 22 12 17 14   2   6   4   6   4   16 6   2   17 18 3

___ ___ ___ ___ ___ ___ _q_ ___ ___ , ___ ___ ___ ___ ___ ___ ___ ___
12 2   6   3   11 10   3   6   23 3   14 1   13 10 15 6

___ ___ ___ ___ ___ ___ ___ ___ ___ ___ ___ ___ .
6   24 6   2   17 16 18 19 17   6   13 14 6

MEMORY

Use the key code below to decode the words. Each space is one letter. Challenge yourself to go as quickly as you can. All of these words are in the category: **FAMILY**.

1. ___ ___ ___ ___ ___ ___

2. ___ ___ ___ ___ ___

3. ___ ___ ___ ___ ___ ___ ___

4. ___ ___ ___ ___ ___

5. ___ ___ ___ ___ ___ ___ ___ ___

KEY CODE

A	B	C	D	E	F	G	H	I	J	K	L	M

N	O	P	Q	R	S	T	U	V	W	X	Y	Z

MATCHING CLUES 2

Match two of the word-parts to make a word that fits the clue. Each word-part is used only once.

ot   ree   deg   ru

sir   tar   de   en

1. _____ a fortune-teller's cards

   _____ a temperature unit

   _____ a warning horn

   _____ unmannerly

st   la   ra   ep

re   rp   te   ta

2. _____ not common

   _____ a stair

   _____ a canvas cover

   _____ tardy

LANGUAGE

FIRST AND LAST LETTERS 1

Fill in the correct letters to make a word that matches the definition.

1. ___ rat ___   a wooden box

2. ___ estor ___   to renovate

3. ___ res ___   a printing machine

4. ___ ton ___   to make amends

5. ___ ddres ___   a house location

6. ___ ee ___   a fruit rind

7. ___ nti ___   to loosen laces

8. ___ ot ___   a musical tone

9. ___ em ___   an example model

10. ___ hee ___   steep, abrupt

11. ___ va ___   egg-shaped

12. ___ ria ___   a courtroom event

WORD MAZE – A LAZY SUNDAY

Find your way through the maze by connecting letters to spell out words.
Write the words on the next page. You may move right, left, up, or down, but no letters may be connected more than once.

START

A	P	T	R	W	Q	N	L	M	E	R	C
D	M	C	B	F	V	E	Y	K	P	D	O
G	N	O	L	S	E	W	S	P	A	H	F
W	H	K	J	R	H	X	T	H	L	E	F
A	L	K	Y	E	B	L	Y	O	D	E	Y
H	R	B	P	P	C	H	M	N	K	D	R
L	W	I	I	L	S	S	T	U	W	H	V
Q	Q	G	M	E	Q	L	K	A	C	B	Q
J	R	C	P	A	L	F	P	M	U	Y	P
O	L	N	B	V	F	A	C	B	S	O	T
M	A	S	D	B	A	M	U	P	V	B	N
B	K	P	B	I	M	B	C	K	N	F	B
G	J	C	Y	L	U	V	V	V	K	L	V

END

VISUAL–SPATIAL

WORDS

1. _____

2. _____

3. _____

4. _____

5. _____

6. _____

7. _____

8. _____

9. _____

LOGIC WORD PROBLEMS 1

These word problems require you to use the process of elimination to find the answer. It helps to use the grid provided to keep track of items eliminated.

X = No, not the correct answer; O = Yes, the correct answer

Using the clues, fill in the grid with Xs and Os. When there is only one choice left in a row or column, put an O there. Because it is the only option left, it is the correct answer. If a clue tells you the correct choice, you can put an O in that box and put Xs in the rest of the column and row because the other options cannot be correct too. Work through all of the clues this way.

1. You take your 4 grandchildren to the pet store to pick out one pet each. Can you determine which grandchild picked out which pet?

	CAT	DOG	FISH	GERBIL
BILLY				
SALLY				
CATHY				
JOHN				

CLUES
a. John chose the pet that lives in the water.
b. Cathy did not choose the pet that starts with the same letter as her name.
c. Billy is allergic to cats but not to dogs
d. Cathy wants a pet that will live in a cage.

2. At a picnic each of your friends picked a different piece of fruit for dessert. Can you determine which friend picked which fruit?

	APPLE	ORANGE	BANANA	GRAPES
IRMA				
BETTY				
RALPH				
JIM				

CLUES
a. Betty grabbed a handful of her fruit and some fell and bounced around on the ground.
b. Ralph makes a joke about slipping on Irma's peel.
c. As he ate his fruit Jim said: "Eat one of these a day to keep the doctor away."

REASONING

MIDDLE LETTERS 1

Fill in the correct letters to make a word that matches the definition.

1. a ___ ___ m   a minute particle

2. o ___ ___ ___ r   external

3. a ___ ___ ___ e   to concur

4. a ___ ___ ___ a   a sports location

5. d ___ ___ t   a small arrow

6. a ___ ___ ___ e   unaccompanied

7. s ___ ___ ___ p   to use a broom

8. a ___ ___ ___ a   fragrance

9. s ___ ___ ___ t   slumbered

10. o ___ ___ n   plow-pulling animals

11. v ___ ___ ___ e   worth

12. s ___ ___ ___ e   a fixed gaze

BAGS OF WORDS

The answer to each clue contains the letters "BAG."

1. A ring-shaped bread roll

   ANSWER _____

2. A vehicle safety device

   ANSWER _____

3. A long thin loaf of French bread

   ANSWER _____

4. Another word for a purse

   ANSWER _____

5. A talkative person who has little of interest or value to say

   ANSWER _____

6. A large cushion used as a seat

   ANSWER _____

7. A vegetable with a leafy head

   ANSWER _____

8. A pouch attached to a horse or motorcycle

   ANSWER _____

LANGUAGE

ALLITERATION – PEOPLE

Alliteration is when all the words start with the same sound. Complete these sentences with words that begin with the same letter. You can add articles (such as *a, an, the*) or prepositions (such as *with, on, as*) to help the sentence make sense.

For example: <u>Many moms making milkshakes.</u>

1. Lawyers lurch_____.

2. Busy burglars_____.

3. _____ pilots play.

4. _____ seamstresses sewing.

5. Merry maids _____.

6. Vertical ventriloquists _____.

7. Parents purchasing _____.

8. Fickle females _____.

9. Pleasant professors _____.

10. Senseless stewardesses _____.

11. Matchmakers make _____.

12. _____ rise rapidly.

13. Architects' adversaries are _____.

14. Engineers' education _____.

15. _____ nurses nurturing.

TRUE OR FALSE FACTS 1

Determine if each statement is True or False. Challenge yourself to answer as quickly as you can.

1. An elephant is larger than a tiger.   True   False

2. Grape juice is darker than red wine.   True   False

3. Healthy has more letters than particular.   True   False

4. Several means more than a couple.   True   False

5. Fifteen-year-olds can get a driver's license.   True   False

6. Gold is heavier than aluminium.   True   False

7. A car is more expensive than a plane.   True   False

8. Sirens are louder than bells.   True   False

9. Walnut shells are softer than egg shells.   True   False

10. All mushrooms are edible.   True   False

11. Knives can cut through cloth.   True   False

12. Aluminium foil can go in the microwave.   True   False

13. Bears have less fur than birds.   True   False

14. Both marbles and dice roll evenly.   True   False

15. Eagles are faster than jets.   True   False

16. Feathers are not lighter than air   True   False

17. Pillows are softer than hay.   True   False

18. Windshields shatter easier than plastic.   True   False

19. The word "screen" has more than one definition.   True   False

20. Rubber bands stretch easier than paper clips.   True   False

21. Orchestras never have a conductor.   True   False

22. Porcupines are larger than splinters.   True   False

23. Bulls are the same size as goats.   True   False

24. "Racecar" is the same when spelled backwards.   True   False

PROCESSING SPEED

SYMBOL CODING 1

Write the symbol that corresponds to each number in the empty boxes below. Challenge yourself to do this as quickly as you can, while maintaining accuracy. Do not do all of one symbol at a time. Complete each box in a row moving from left to right, and then continue to the next line.

KEY CODE

1	2	3	4	5	6	7	8	9
+	□	⬆	—	△	✕	◯	⅃	◇

2	5	4	7	6	3	8	5	9	1
3	6	7	8	3	4	9	1	2	5
5	9	1	4	2	7	5	9	8	6
6	2	3	6	9	8	1	3	4	5
7	9	3	1	4	2	7	8	5	6
4	1	6	8	2	9	3	5	4	2
1	5	7	4	3	6	2	1	9	3
6	3	1	7	2	5	9	8	2	1

PROCESSING SPEED

LETTERS-TO-WORD MATCH 1

There are 10 six-letter words that have been broken into chunks of three letters. These chunks have been mixed up, no chunk is used twice, and all chunks are used.

Can you determine what the 10 words are?

den	mag	det	est
ier	har	cal	use
ent	ach	fin	dam
blo	acq	net	uit
mer	bus	par	sel

1. _____

2. _____

3. _____

4. _____

5. _____

6. _____

7. _____

8. _____

9. _____

10. _____

THREE-LETTER PLACEMENT 1

Choose which three-letter combination will make a word when added to the letters below. There may be more than one correct answer.

bic   sal   gan   tin   ren   fan   dar

1. r a ___ ___ ___

2. s l o ___ ___ ___

3. a e r o ___ ___ ___

4. f r o s ___ ___ ___ g

5. a p p a ___ ___ ___ t

6. ___ ___ ___ a t i c

7. i n s ___ ___ ___ c t

8. ___ ___ ___ y c l e

9. ___ ___ ___ k e n

10. ___ ___ ___ e s

11. r e v e ___ ___ ___ t

12. i n ___ ___ ___ t

13. a c c u ___ ___ ___

14. m a ___ ___ ___ e e

15. b o u n ___ ___ ___ y

16. e l e ___ ___ ___ t

LANGUAGE

17. ___ ___ ___ a d

18. a r r o ___ ___ ___ t

19. r e ___ ___ ___ a

20. ___ ___ ___ k e r

21. o r ___ ___ ___ i s e

22. ___ ___ ___ v a g e

23. ___ ___ ___ g l e

24. p r o ___ ___ ___ e

25. s t ___ ___ ___ g t h

26. ___ ___ ___ l i n g

27. c u ___ ___ ___ l e

28. o r ___ ___ ___

29. ___ ___ ___ c y

30. o u ___ ___ ___ g

31. ___ ___ ___ e p s

32. w ___ ___ ___ c h

33. ___ ___ ___ u t e

ONLY THREE CLUES

Use these clues to answer each question.

1. You store things here.

   It is in the bottom part of a house.

   Mice like to live here.

   What is the place? _____

2. Kids like to play here.

   It is outside.

   There are paths to walk on here.

   What is the place? _____

3. It is made of soft fabric.

   It comes in many colours and designs.

   You use it in the bathroom or at a swimming pool.

   What is the item? _____

4. It cleans your house.

   It has a motor.

   Most dogs are afraid of it.

   What is the item?_____

5. It can be made of glass or plastic.

   It holds liquid.

   Its shape is a long cylinder.

   What is the item? _____

WHAT'S THE CATEGORY? 1

Put these words into the most correct category.

cabinet handles	poison ivy	calculator	duct tape
ladder	printer	floor wax	slide
hikers	concrete mix	landmark	stamps
wall mounts	paper weight	to-do list	fire pit
strollers	books		

1. Things found in a hardware store

   _____   _____

   _____   _____

   _____   _____

2. Things found in a park

   _____   _____

   _____   _____

   _____   _____

3. Things found in an office

   _____   _____

   _____   _____

   _____   _____

UNITS OF TIME 1

Determine the correct answer to each question. Try to do the math in your head first, then use scratch paper if needed. Do not use a calculator.

1. How many minutes are in 4 hours? _____

2. How many seconds are in 2 ½ hours? _____

3. How many hours do 120 minutes and 10,800 seconds equal?

   _____

4. In 8 hours, it will be 5:00 a.m. What time is it now? _____

5. In 14 hours, it will be 8:00 p.m. What time is it now? _____

6. In 4 ½ hours, you will be 30 minutes late for your 2:00 p.m. appointment.

   What time is it now? _____

7. You started doing garden work at 8:00 a.m. You spent 1 ½ hours weeding, 45 minutes planting seeds, 20 minutes watering, and then 15 minutes cleaning up.

   What time is it now? _____

8. You need to do all your errands before you meet friends for lunch at 12:30 p.m. First you need to go to the bank (20 minutes), pick up dry cleaning across town (35 minutes), buy household items at the store (45 minutes), return library books (15 minutes), and then pick up repaired jewelry (25 minutes).

   How long will it take you to do these errands? _____

9. What time do you need to leave the house to get all of these errands completed? _____

CALCULATION

10. You are flying from Denver to Seattle to visit you family for the summer. The morning of your flight, you hear that your plane is delayed 3 hours. You had a 1-hour layover midway, where you were supposed to change planes with the connection flight leaving at 11:00 a.m. You now have to change that connection flight.

If you are now flying out of Denver at 9:30 a.m., which connection flight to Seattle can you catch?   a. 1:00 p.m. flight   b. 7:50 p.m. flight

11. Your walk around the neighbourhood each day takes you 47 minutes. But today you stop to talk with Emma for 12 minutes, then you help Bruce pick up his trash can that fell overnight, and talk to him, for 7 minutes, then you help Lou look for his lost dog for 26 minutes, then Lynn calls you inside to taste her banana bread for 11 minutes, and then on the way home you stop and tell Emma all that happened for 4 minutes.

How much total time were you out in the neighbourhood today?

_____

If you left at 10:35 a.m., what time did you arrive back home?

_____

12. You are cooking dinner for your family who arrives at 6:00 p.m. The meat needs to simmer for 40 minutes on the stove, the scalloped potatoes bake for 105 minutes in the oven, and the green beans will take 35 minutes on the stove. You will need 30 minutes of preparation time to get started.

How much total time do you need to cook dinner? _____

What time do you need to start cooking to serve dinner at 6:30 p.m.?

_____

13. You live on the east coast of the US and your daughter lives on the west coast. You want to call her after she gets off work at 5:00 p.m. but before she eats dinner at 7:00 p.m. You are 3 hours ahead of her time. What is the time frame you have to call her in your eastern standard time? _____

CALCULATION

"B" WORDS

Using two clues, fill in the correct word that begins with "B."

1. A bee does this

   Excited talk

   ANSWER _____

2. The wind does this

   To project air

   ANSWER _____

3. To participate in this rough sport

   A cardboard carrier

   ANSWER _____

4. A horse does this

   A dollar

   ANSWER _____

5. To wax your car

   A muscular man is this

   ANSWER _____

6. Not the front

   Pain in your lower . . .

   ANSWER _____

7. A tied ribbon

   After a performance

   ANSWER _____

8. A short-legged omnivorous animal

   To pester someone

   ANSWER _____

9. To come together

   A group of instruments

   ANSWER _____

10. A wooden stick

    A winged animal

    ANSWER _____

11. A curve in the road

    To bow forward

    ANSWER _____

12. A colour

    A feeling

    ANSWER _____

13. To load a boat

    A flat piece of wood

    ANSWER _____

14. A type of wine

    To show embarrassment

    ANSWER _____

LANGUAGE

15. To schedule a flight

Bound written sheets of paper

ANSWER _____

16. Hard but breakable

Frail

ANSWER _____

17. To have no money

To snap into two pieces (past tense)

ANSWER _____

18. A lure

To deliberately taunt

ANSWER _____

WHAT IS THIS CALLED?

Use the clue to determine what is being described.

1. A wooden object used to hold up wet clothes to dry on a clothesline
    _____

2. A plush toy that children love to hug _____

3. Cheerleaders carry these in parades _____

4. This is made by stitching together squares of fabric and padding
    _____

5. A two-wheeled means of transportation _____

6. A petrified artifact found deep in the ground _____

7. These insects make a rhythmical chirping sound _____

8. This leisurely sport requires a line and pole _____

9. You win a game of chess with this final move _____

10. A plastic payment option _____

11. Skiing over flat, open terrain _____

12. Text of dialogue on a TV screen _____

DOMINO ORDER 2

Starting with the domino marked "1st," find an order in which you can line up all these dominoes end to end. Wherever two dominoes touch, the numbered ends must match. You may rotate the dominoes, and there is more than one correct order.

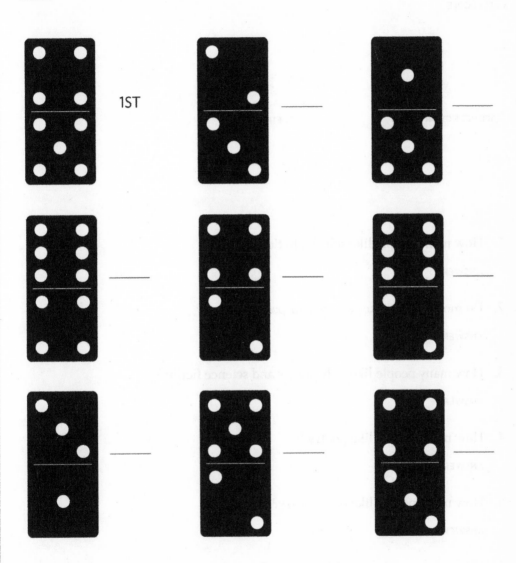

1ST

VENN DIAGRAM – BOOKS

Answer the questions using the information displayed in the Venn diagram.

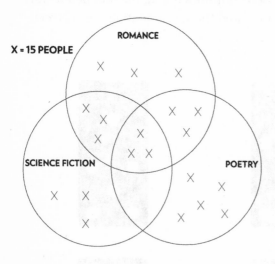

1. How many people like science fiction?

   ANSWER _____

2. Do more people like romance or poetry?

   ANSWER _____

3. How many people like only poetry and science fiction?

   ANSWER _____

4. How many people like poetry?

   ANSWER _____

5. How many people like only poetry?

   ANSWER _____

6. How many people do not like poetry?

   ANSWER _____

VISUAL–SPATIAL

DECIPHER THE LETTER CODE 2

Complete the phrase by determining the number that is assigned to the used letters.

Begin by filling in the letters that you are given, then figure out which letters make sense to make words in the phrase. You don't have to figure out all the letters, just the ones you need.

For example, if the word is ___ <u>H</u> ___ , the word is likely THE, so 8 = T,
                            8   13

therefore you can add in all 8s as Ts.

A	B	C	D	E	F	G	H	I	J	K	L	M
14	6						16				5	

N	O	P	Q	R	S	T	U	V	W	X	Y	Z
	15	4						17	9			

MESSAGE:

16 14 5 11   15 11   8 16 23   4 23 15 4 5 23

24 22   8 16 23   9 15 25 5 2   14 25 23

6 23 5 15 9   14 17 23 25 14 7 23 .

AGING WORDS 2

The answer to each clue contains the letters "AGE."

1. A loan agreement between borrower and lender

   ANSWER _____

2. To save something damaged for further use

   ANSWER _____

3. A quality of being brave

   ANSWER _____

4. The leaves of a plant or tree

   ANSWER _____

5. A legally recognised relationship

   ANSWER _____

6. An absence of something that is needed

   ANSWER _____

7. An organiser of a business

   ANSWER _____

8. Deliberate destruction

   ANSWER _____

LANGUAGE

COUNT THE Ts AND Ps

As quickly as you can, separately count how many Ts and Ps are in this paragraph. Scan each line from left to right. Keep a running tally of Ts in your mind while keeping a running tally of Ps separately. Do not do one letter at a time, try to do both at the same time.

a u l p d j f i s o d j h u i n d t u t y o e y k f s l y l k j l d p u i n f k s l l

w o q p o w r y t j k u l y s k d n f k t l u k s d n f u k p t k s d n f u n s p

d f n t l u k s d n f t k d u n k l p u n s d l f y a d f u l t u p i u w e r u p k

o u w e r u l s u e r u l s i u s l d i p z m c v u z n u d t f u e r y u s d l k

f u u n l s u p i u r q w e u l s d f u l p j u l k u t l f s d i f u s d t u x c v

m n d f t s w e r u r y u x g u a d t g u l k j p o i u w e r u s d f u t w e r

u q w e u u u p o i u q w u a d f u z c v u m b n u k l t h s d f x c v i o s e

r p j a s d y s d t o l u n k e r j u s d f u w e r t w e m x g p q w i u y s d f

j n k u y t w e r l k d f u q w e r u x c b h s d f g p z v x c y t w e r u u s

e b f s u y p e w u a o d p e y x o s d i u t s w x p o t h d k b s k o e r t n

TOTAL Ts _____

TOTAL Ps _____

MISMATCH 1

Pick out the one item that does not fit the category, and explain the *reason* why it does not fit.

1. Shoe, Grocery, Hardware, Tooth

   Mismatch item_____

   *Reason*_____

2. Goat, Horse, Eagle, Sheep

   Mismatch item_____

   *Reason*_____

3. Apple, Cauliflower, Carrot, Broccoli

   Mismatch item_____

   *Reason*_____

4. Elephant, Shark, Gorilla, Tiger

   Mismatch Item_____

   *Reason*_____

5. Turtle, Lizard, Parrot, Frog

   Mismatch item_____

   *Reason*_____

6. Colouring book, Lego, Building blocks, Model railway

   Mismatch item_____

   *Reason*_____

7. Pencil, Eraser, Marker, Pen

   Mismatch item_____

   *Reason*_____

8. Soccer, Lacrosse, Volleyball, Golf

   Mismatch item_____

   *Reason*_____

EXECUTIVE FUNCTIONING

9. Initiate, Dissolve, Originate, Create

Mismatch item_____

*Reason*_____

10. Entrance, Admission, Window, Door

Mismatch item_____

*Reason*_____

11. Being, Individual, Creature, Separate

Mismatch item_____

*Reason*_____

12. Various, Single, Only, Individual

Mismatch item_____

*Reason*_____

13. Pint, Cup, Ounce, Inch

Mismatch item_____

*Reason*_____

14. Vegetables, Rice, Pasta, Beans

Mismatch item_____

*Reason*_____

15. Skis, Boots, Snow, Resort

Mismatch item_____

*Reason*_____

16. Helicopters, Stars, Black holes, Planets

Mismatch item_____

*Reason*_____

EXECUTIVE FUNCTIONING

SIMILAR PROPERTIES

What do these two things have in common?

1. A Fish and a Lizard _____

2. Water and Steam _____

3. A Tornado and an Earthquake _____

4. A Coconut and a Safe _____

5. A Paper clip and Tape _____

6. A Coupon and a Credit card _____

7. A Budget and a Path _____

8. Fall and Spring _____

9. A Goal and a Target _____

10. A Wreath and an Ornament _____

11. A Mushroom and a Mountain _____

12. Sunflowers and Celery _____

BOXED LETTERS – GAMES

Print the letters in the correct box to spell a type of board game reading across.

1. Print the letter O in B4
   Print the letter O in C6
   Print the letter O in A2
   Print the letter N in D3
   Print the letter P in B5
   Print the letter L in A7
   Print the letter M in C1
   Print the letter Y in B8   ANSWER _____

	1	2	3	4	5	6	7	8
A								
B								
C								
D								

2. Print the letter I in box B9
   Print the letter E in box C6
   Print the letter A in box D2
   Print the letter H in box A8
   Print the letter T in box C3
   Print the letter S in box A7
   Print the letter L in box B5
   Print the letter T in box D4
   Print the letter P in Box A10
   Print the letter B in Box B1   ANSWER _____

	1	2	3	4	5	6	7	8	9	10
A										
B										
C										
D										

VISUAL-SPATIAL

3. Print the letter B in box B6
Print the letter A in box C4
Print the letter C in box A2
Print the letter L in box A7
Print the letter R in box C3
Print the letter E in box D8
Print the letter B in box B5
Print the letter S in box D1   ANSWER _____

	1	2	3	4	5	6	7	8
A								
B								
C								
D								

4. Print the letter S in box B5
Print the letter S in box C4
Print the letter E in box C3
Print the letter H in box D2
Print the letter C in box A1   ANSWER _____

	1	2	3	4	5	6	7	8
A								
B								
C								
D								

5. Print the letter A in box B5
Print the letter A in box C3
Print the letter S in box A8
Print the letter H in box A2
Print the letter E in box C7
Print the letter R in box D4
Print the letter D in box B6
Print the letter C in box B1   ANSWER_____

	1	2	3	4	5	6	7	8
A								
B								
C								
D								

6. Print the letter R in box B9
Print the letter I in box C2
Print the letter T in box D4
Print the letter N in box A7
Print the letter O in box C6
Print the letter I in box B5
Print the letter C in box B3
Print the letter Y in box C10
Print the letter P in Box C1
Print the letter A in Box B8   ANSWER_____

	1	2	3	4	5	6	7	8	9	10
A										
B										
C										
D										

VISUAL-SPATIAL

Fill in the word(s) to answer the clue, then transfer those numbered letters to the lines on the next page for the final message.

1. You get this colour if you mix red and yellow

   __ __ __ __ __ __
   1 2 3 4 5 6

2. This document contains this sentence: "We hold these truths to be self-evident, that all men are created equal."

   __ __ __ __ __ __ __ __ __ __ __   __ __
   7 6 8 9 3 2 3 10 11 1 4   1 12

   __ __ __ __ __ __ __ __ __ __ __ __
   11 4 7 6 13 6 4 7 6 4 8 6

3. Philadelphia is the capital of this US state

   __ __ __ __ __ __ __ __ __ __ __ __
   13 6 4 4 14 15 9 16 3 4 11 3

4. This American city is known as the home of jazz

   __ __ __   __ __ __ __ __ __ __
   4 6 17   1 2 9 6 3 4 14

5. This mountain range is home to the highest peak on earth

   __ __ __ __ __ __ __ __ __
   18 11 19 3 9 3 15 3 14

6. This scientist discovered the theory of relativity

   __ __ __ __ __ __ __ __
   6 11 4 14 10 6 11 4

MEMORY

FINAL MESSAGE:

17	18	6	4		11	10		8	1	19	6	14		10	1

u

| 10 | 18 | 1 | 5 | 18 | 10 | , | 14 | 1 | 19 | 6 | | 13 | 6 | 1 | 13 | 9 | 6 |

| 14 | 10 | 1 | 13 | | 3 | 10 | | 4 | 1 | 10 | 18 | 11 | 4 | 5 | .

PROFESSIONAL CHARACTERISTICS

Match the three top characteristics needed for each profession. You may only use each characteristics once.

creativity	ability to delegate	courage	inspired
articulate	logical	loyal	endurance
spontaneous	empathetic	thorough	confident

1. A CEO: _____ _____

   _____

2. An artist: _____ _____

   _____

3. A physician: _____ _____

   _____

4. A soldier: _____ _____

   _____

5. List any six characteristics you think are important for a person in the clergy.

   _____ _____

   _____ _____

   _____ _____

CALCULATION WORD PROBLEMS 1

Determine the correct answer to each question. Try to do the math in your head first, then use scratch paper if needed. Do not use a calculator.

1. You are having 6 friends over for a dinner party. You and your spouse want to make individual desserts for everyone but you have only 5 individual baking cups. How many more do you need to buy?
   _____ baking cups

2. Your 4 grandchildren are at your house playing. You have a pack of 30 stickers for them to use in colouring books. How many stickers does each child get if you divide them up evenly? How many stickers are left over?
   _____ stickers each   _____ are left over

3. Your book club meets once per month and the next book is 580 pages. How many pages do you have to read each day to have it completed by your next meeting if this month has 30 days? _____ pages

4. Your large family of 18 people is coming to your house for the Christmas holiday. There are 7 kids and 11 adults. You all decide that you will spend only £20 on each kid, and half that amount on each adult for presents. How much total money will you spend on gifts this year for your family, not including your spouse? _____ pounds

5. You are sitting in your back garden watching the birds in the tree. You watch 6 birds fly away, and then 4 more land. Now you count 14 birds total. How many birds were there in the beginning? _____ birds

6. While doing some garden work, you realise you need a really long rope. You have one piece of rope that is 8 feet 3 inches, and another piece of rope that is 12 feet 9 inches. If you use both, what is the total length of rope you have to use? _____ feet _____ inches

CALCULATION

CALENDAR QUIZ 1

Use the calendar clues to determine the correct date.

SUNDAY	MONDAY	TUESDAY	WEDNESDAY	THURSDAY	FRIDAY	SATURDAY
		1	2	3	4	5
6	7	8	9	10	11	12
13	14	15	16	17	18	19
20	21	22	23	24	25	26
27	28	29	30			

1. This date is on the middle day of the week.

    It is not in the first or last week of the month.

    It is a single digit date.

    What is the date? _____

2. This date is on a weekend.

    It falls in the middle week of the month.

    It is not the 19th.

    What is the date? _____

3. This date is between the 16th and the 23rd.

   It is on a day that begins with a "T."

   On this date there are only 8 more days of the month left.

   What is the date?_____

4. This date is a double digit.

   It is not in the last half of a week.

   Its digits add up to 4.

   It is not on a Sunday.

   What is the date? _____

A BIT OF WORDS

The answer to each clue contains the letters "BIT."

1. The curved path of a celestial object

   ANSWER _____

2. A burrowing, plant-eating animal with long ears

   ANSWER _____

3. A regular tendency or practice

   ANSWER _____

4. An amount of money removed from an account

   ANSWER _____

5. To formally forbid a person from doing something

   ANSWER _____

6. A public display in an art gallery

   ANSWER _____

7. Based on random choice or whim, rather than reason

   ANSWER _____

8. To live in or occupy

   ANSWER _____

REASONING

WHAT COMES NEXT?

Determine what comes next in this sequence and then explain the reason why.

1. Red, Orange, Yellow, Green, _____

   *Reason*_____

2. Do, Re, Mi, Fa, _____

   *Reason*_____

3. Baron, Earl, Duke, Prince, _____

   *Reason*_____

4. Day, Week, Month, Year, _____

   *Reason*_____

5. City, County, State, Country, _____

   *Reason*_____

6. Whisper, Talk, Yell, _____

   *Reason*_____

7. Two pair, Three of a kind, Straight, Flush, _____

   *Reason*_____

8. Finger, Knuckle, Wrist, Elbow, _____

   *Reason*_____

9. Pawn, Knight, Bishop, Rook, _____

   *Reason*_____

REASONING

PLACEMENT OF LETTERS 1

Use the letters on the left to turn the word-parts on the right into complete words. You can use each word-part only once.

1. ffu   ec _____ gy

      shi   am _____ fy

      ctf   in _____ cy

      pli   fa _____ on

      olo   be _____ it

      fic   ta _____ ul

      nef   di _____ se

      fan   of _____ er

2. cto   pe _____ rm

      fol   cl _____ fy

      ari   te _____ fy

      ffl   fa _____ ry

      sti   un _____ ds

      rfo   go _____ ng

      sti   wa _____ es

      lfi   ju _____ fy

3. ref   re _____ al

    oug   en _____ ge

    nan   ca _____ ul

    lar   fo _____ ge

    fus   en _____ ce

    for   br _____ ht

    aff   fi _____ ce

    ota   tr _____ ic

4. shf   se _____ sh

    rti   de _____ ce

    rba   wi _____ ul

    fen   fa _____ sy

    lfi   di _____ am

    lpf   ce _____ fy

    agr   ga _____ ge

    nta   he _____ ul

LANGUAGE

ABBREVIATIONS AND ACRONYMS

What do these abbreviations and acronyms stand for?

1. Capt. _____

2. UN _____

3. assoc _____

4. est. _____

5. AWOL _____

6. inc. _____

7. BA _____

8. cm _____

9. kg _____

10. lb _____

11. etc _____

12. cc _____

13. ltd _____

14. mph _____

15. Col. _____

16. NATO _____

17. oz _____

18. St. _____

MEMORY

LETTERS-TO-WORD MATCH 2

There are 10 six-letter words that have been broken into chunks of three letters. These chunks have been mixed up, no chunk is used twice, and all chunks are used.

Can you determine what the 10 words are?

can	hew	ble	ics
bou	act	fac	act
tor	pic	ach	kle
ual	nce	mas	ive
cot	opy	cas	eth

1. _____

2. _____

3. _____

4. _____

5. _____

6. _____

7. _____

8. _____

9. _____

10. _____

A BAN IN WORDS

The answer to each clue contains the letters "BAN."

1. A robber or outlaw belonging to a gang

   ANSWER _____

2. A kerchief tied around the head or neck

   ANSWER _____

3. To break up a group

   ANSWER _____

4. An elaborate and formal meal for many people

   ANSWER _____

5. To give up completely; cease to support

   ANSWER _____

6. An upright structure at the side of a staircase

   ANSWER _____

7. Residential; or dull and ordinary

   ANSWER _____

8. A stringed musical instrument with a long neck and rounded body

   ANSWER _____

9. Lacking in originality

   ANSWER _____

10. To send someone away from a place as an official punishment

    ANSWER _____

SYMBOL CODING 2

Write the number that corresponds to each symbol in the empty boxes below. Challenge yourself to do this as quickly as you can, while maintaining accuracy. Do not do all of one symbol at a time, complete each box in a row moving from left to right, and then continue to the next line.

KEY CODE

₪	φ	‡	◉	ʒ	§	¥	ɣ	ə
2	6	4	7	3	1	5	9	8

ʒ	₪	§	‡	φ	ə	◉	ɣ	‡	¥
◉	φ	ə	¥	§	‡	φ	ʒ	ə	ɣ
§	ʒ	‡	φ	◉	₪	¥	§	₪	φ
‡	ɣ	¥	ə	‡	§	ʒ	φ	‡	◉
₪	ə	◉	₪	ʒ	φ	¥	§	ɣ	ʒ
φ	ʒ	₪	§	‡	◉	ɣ	ə	¥	₪
◉	‡	¥	ʒ	ə	φ	₪	ə	‡	§

UNITS OF TIME 2

Determine the correct answer to each question. Try to do the math in your head first, then use scratch paper if needed. Do not use a calculator.

1. How many minutes are in 14 hours? _____

2. How many seconds are in 5 hours and 15 minutes? _____

3. How many hours equal 45 minutes and 8,100 seconds? _____

4. In 30 hours, it will be 8:00 a.m. What time is it now? _____

5. In 15 hours, it will be 10:00 p.m. What time is it now? _____

6. In 4 hours, you will be 15 minutes late for your 11:00 a.m. appointment.

   What time is it now? _____

7. You started cooking at 3:20 p.m. for your 6:00 p.m. dinner party. You spent 58 minutes on the appetiser soup, 14 minutes chopping vegetables, 44 minutes stir-frying, 6 minutes setting the table, and then 12 minutes cleaning up.

   What time is it now? _____

   How much time do you have to spare before the dinner party?

   _____

8. Your son lives on the west coast of the US and you live on the east coast. Both of you want to schedule a phone call when the grandchildren will be there. He gives you some available times: Saturday from 10:00 a.m. to 2:00 p.m. or after dinner between 8:00 and 9:00 p.m. You are 3 hours ahead of his time and you go to bed at 10:00 p.m your time.

   What is the time frame you have to call your son's family in your eastern standard time? _____

CALCULATION

DECIPHER THE LETTER CODE 3

Complete the phrase by determining the number that is assigned to the used letters.

Begin by filling in the letters that you are given, then figure out which letters make sense to make words in the phrase. You don't have to figure out all the letters, just the ones you need.

For example, if the word is ___ <u>H</u> ___ , the word is likely THE, so 8 = T,
                     8   13

therefore you can add in all 8s as Ts.

A	B	C	D	E	F	G	H	I	J	K	L	M
9						13	21				23	8

N	O	P	Q	R	S	T	U	V	W	X	Y	Z
	2				22				24		16	

MESSAGE:

| 8 | 6 | 11 | 11 | 23 | 19 | | 9 | 13 | 19 | | 6 | 22 | | 24 | 21 | 19 | 18 |

| 16 | 2 | 14 | 12 | | 9 | 13 | 19 | | 22 | 5 | 9 | 12 | 5 | 22 |

| 5 | 2 | | 22 | 21 | 2 | 24 | | 9 | 12 | 2 | 14 | 18 | 11 |

| 16 | 2 | 14 | 12 | | 8 | 6 | 11 | 11 | 23 | 19 | .

COUNT THE Ys AND Is

As quickly as you can, count how many Ys and Is are in this paragraph. Scan each line from left to right. Keep a running tally of both letters together. Don't do one letter at a time.

a u l k d j f i s o d j h u i n d t u t y o e y k f s l y l k j l d f u i n f k s l l

w o q p o w r y r j k u l y s k d n f k s l u k s d n f u k j f k s d n f u n s k

d f n d l u k s d n f s k d u n k l p u n s d l f y a d f u l j u p i u w e r u p

o u w e r u l s u e r u l s i u s l d i u z m c v u z n u d n f u e r y u s d l k

f u u n l s u p i u r q w e u l s d f u l k j u l k u k l f s d i f u s d f u x c v

m n d f u s w e r u r y u x g u a d f g u l k j y o i u w e r u s d f u t w e r

u q w e u u u p o i u q w u a d f u z c v u m b n u y l j h s d f x c v i o s

r k j a s d y s d f o l u n k e r j u s d f u w e r t w e m x g p q w i u y s d

j n k u y t w e r l k d f u q w e r u x c b h s d f g b z v x c y t w e r u u s

e b f s u y g e w u a o d p e y x o s d i u d s w x p o t h d k b s k o e i t n

v u e r b n l d k f y u l s k d u s h s e t u t u s k y i u d t h k s d u l o h g

TOTAL Ys AND Is _____

ATTENTION

AGING WORDS 3

The answer to each clue contains the letters "AGE."

1. To be enthusiastic and excited about doing something

   ANSWER _____

2. A long journey by sea or through space

   ANSWER _____

3. The remains after destruction

   ANSWER _____

4. Payment for work

   ANSWER _____

5. A settlement larger than a hamlet but smaller than a town

   ANSWER _____

6. To involve someone in an activity

   ANSWER _____

7. A communication in speech, writing, or signals

   ANSWER _____

8. Used for carrying personal items during a trip

   ANSWER _____

LANGUAGE

DOMINO ORDER 3

Starting with the domino marked "1st," find an order in which you can line up all these dominoes end to end. Wherever two dominoes touch, the numbered ends must match. You may rotate the dominoes, and there is more than one correct order.

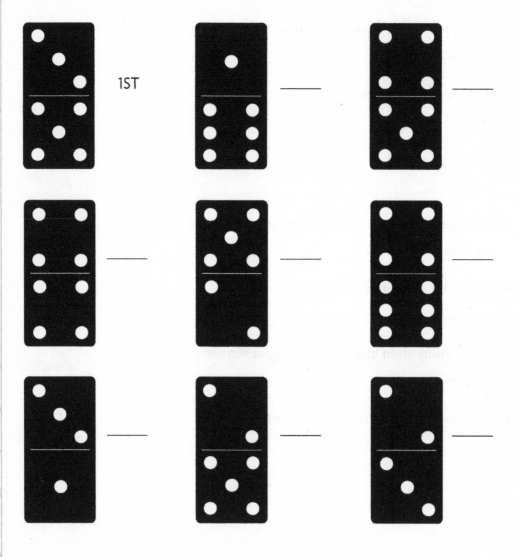

1ST

VENN DIAGRAM – MUSIC

Answer the questions using the information displayed in the Venn diagram.

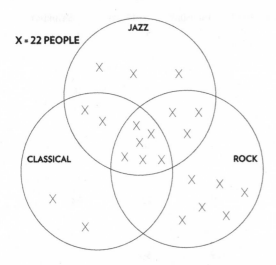

1. How many people like Jazz?

   ANSWER _____

2. How many people like only Jazz?

   ANSWER _____

3. How many people like both Classical and Rock?

   ANSWER _____

4. Which type of music do the most people like?

   ANSWER _____

5. How many people like all three types of music?

   ANSWER _____

6. How many people do not like Rock?

   ANSWER _____

VISUAL–SPATIAL

CALENDAR QUIZ 2

Use the calendar clues to determine the correct date.

SUNDAY	MONDAY	TUESDAY	WEDNESDAY	THURSDAY	FRIDAY	SATURDAY
				1	2	3
4	5	6	7	8	9	10
11	12	13	14	15	16	17
18	19	20	21	22	23	24
25	26	27	28	29	30	

1. This date is on a day that begins with "T."

   It is in the last half of the week.

   It is a single-digit date but not 1.

   What is the date? _____

2. This date is not on a weekend.

   Its digits add up to 9.

   It is not Friday the 9th.

   What is the date? _____

3. This date is between the 12th and the 21st.

It does not fall on a Monday or Friday.

It is on a Thursday.

What is the date? _____

4. This date is not a double digit.

It is in the middle of the week.

What is the date? _____

EXECUTIVE FUNCTIONING

DISCOVER THE PATTERN 1

Determine the number sequence pattern and complete the succeeding numbers. You may use a calculator for this excercise

1. 1, 4, 5, 9, 14, 23, _____, _____, _____, _____.

2. 5, 8, 12, 17, 23, _____, _____, _____, _____.

3. 60, 58, 54, 48, 40, _____, _____, _____.

4. 8, 10, 20, 32, 54, _____, _____, _____, _____.

5. 14, 56, 224, 896, _____, _____, _____.

6. 5, 15, 30, 90, 180 _____, _____, _____, _____.

7. 12, 14, 10, 12, 8, _____, _____, _____, _____, _____.

8. 40, 38, 35, 31, _____, _____, _____, _____.

9. 10, 16, 22, 28, _____, _____, _____, _____, _____.

10. 2, 7, 35, 40, 200, _____, _____, _____, _____.

SEQUENCING

CLOCK QUIZ 1

Use the clues to determine the correct time and then draw it in the clock.

1. This time is in the p.m.

   It is 50 minutes past 2:10.

   What is the time? _____

   Draw the clock and the time

2. This time is after noon.

   It is 200 minutes before midnight.

   What is the time? _____

   Draw the clock and the time

3. This time is in the morning.

   It is 915 minutes past noon.

   What is the time? _____

   Draw the clock and the time

4. This time is between 9:30 p.m. and 2:30 a.m.

   It is 345 minutes before 5:00.

   What is the time?_____

   Draw the clock and the time

TWO COMMON LETTERS 1

Scan each line to find the two letters each word has in common. The letters are next to each other. Challenge yourself to go as quickly as you can.

Example: bounce and balance both have "ce"

COMMON LETTERS

1. jigsaw   jicama   fajita   jinxed   jiggling   _____

2. abrupt   baptise   capture   disrupt   eruption   _____

3. academia   empty   condemn   memoir   ceremony   _____

4. eighteen   mightier   tougher   upright   weighted   _____

5. repulse   octopus   punched   tempura   sputter   _____

6. cashew   farewell   firework   renewal   withdrew   _____

7. absolve   involve   twelve   velvet   revolving   _____

8. abiding   edible   hardily   ordinal   dialog   _____

9. corkage   skaters   polka   kashmir   alkaline   _____

10. arranged   barrier   corridor   erratic   marriage   _____

PROCESSING SPEED

HOW MANY WORDS? 1

How many words can you make out of the letters in the two words below? You can rearrange the letters in any order you want and you do not have to use every letter in each new word.

1. Idiosyncratic

_____

_____

_____

_____

_____

_____

_____

_____

_____

_____

2. Scramble

_____

_____

_____

_____

_____

_____

_____

_____

_____

_____

ALLITERATION – CELEBRITIES

Alliteration is when all the words start with the same sound. Complete these sentences with words that begin with the same letter. You can add articles (such as *a, an, the*) or prepositions (such as *with, on, as*) to help the sentence make sense.

For example: <u>Mickey Mouse makes me melt.</u>

1. Ronald Reagan _____.

2. Christopher Columbus _____.

3. _____ muse with Marilyn Monroe.

4. _____ down with Daniel Defoe.

5. Lois Lane _____.

6. _____ suggests Secret Service.

7. Ford Focus _____.

8. Tiny Tim _____.

9. _____ beg Boris Becker.

10. Simon says _____.

11. _____ chose Charlie Chaplin.

12. Doris Day _____.

13. Sylvester Stallone _____.

14. Tina Turner _____.

15. _____ hugged Harry Houdini.

TWO DEFINITIONS 2

Two definitions for the same word are given. Fill in the correct word that matches both definitions.

1. Not common

   Undercooked

   ANSWER _____

2. A kind of dot

   A Polish dance

   ANSWER _____

3. Visible or reachable distance

   Mountains in a line

   ANSWER _____

4. Finished

   On the other side

   ANSWER _____

5. To propel a boat

   Objects arranged in a straight line

   ANSWER _____

6. A tool used to cut wood

   To see in the past tense

   ANSWER _____

7. The land edge of the ocean

   To glide along

   ANSWER _____

8. To move through the air

   Insect

   ANSWER _____

A BID ON WORDS

The answer to each clue contains the letters "BID."

1. To accept or act in accordance with a rule

   ANSWER _____

2. Relating to disturbing and unpleasant subjects

   ANSWER _____

3. To refuse to allow

   ANSWER _____

4. The sexual drive of a human

   ANSWER _____

5. Having an extreme or fanatical support for or belief in something

   ANSWER _____

6. A bid made in response to a previous bid by another person

   ANSWER _____

LANGUAGE

First, spend two minutes studying the images. Then turn the page for a quiz.

IMAGES MEMORY 1

(DON'T LOOK AT THIS PAGE UNTIL YOU'VE STUDIED PREVIOUS PAGE.)

Now look at the list of words below and circle the words that were images on the previous page.

SHELL

WINDOW

JACKET

TOWEL

UMBRELLA

RAIN

OCEAN

STARFISH

SHARK

SHOVEL

BOOTS

FLIP-FLOPS

FRISBEE

MEMORY

WHAT IS THIS LOCATION?

Determine the location based on the clues.

1. The Florida Air Force base where shuttles are launched

   _____

2. The highest mountain peak on earth _____

3. The home of the white cliffs _____

4. The location of the "Great Wall" _____

5. The home of Mardi Gras _____

6. The southernmost continent on earth _____

7. The Angkor Wat temple is located in this country _____

8. The location of the Colosseum _____

9. The highest peak in Great Britain _____

10. The world's largest ocean _____

11. Alcatraz prison sits on an island here _____

12. The USS *Arizona* Memorial is located here in Hawaii

    _____

13. The Hoover Dam is in this US state _____

14. The home of the tallest building in the world _____

15. St. Basil's Cathedral is located in this city _____

MEMORY

COMPLETE THE WORD SEARCH 1

First fill in the answers to the clues, then find those words in the word search grid on the next page. The first letter and number of letters in the word are given.

1. The main ingredient to an omelet   E ____ ____

2. Another word for satire   I ____ ____ ____ ____

3. When something is absolutely necessary
   E ____ ____ ____ ____ ____ ____ ____ ____

4. A bar bill is called a   T ____ ____

5. The home of the Leaning Tower   P ____ ____ ____

6. When someone is being very open in conversation
   C ____ ____ ____ ____ ____

7. Another word for fast   S ____ ____ ____ ____

8. Little girls tie their hair up in a   P ____ ____ ____ ____ ____ ____ ____

9. Part of a suit   V ____ ____ ____

10. You catch butterflies with this   N ____ ____

COMPLETE THE WORD SEARCH 1

Words can be in any direction.

```
A   W   L   B   Q   R   M   D   J   E   P   R   A   L
D   F   Y   O   V   B   I   C   E   P   M   D   D   Y
G   S   S   K   E   D   N   E   A   I   N   H   G   S
W   K   L   P   N   J   I   S   D   S   R   E   W   L
A   R   M   A   O   E   U   S   N   A   W   R   A   M
H   P   C   I   C   N   L   E   H   O   P   I   H   K
R   V   T   C   I   R   Y   N   Y   C   O   H   F   T
Q   E   A   L   Q   E   G   T   P  [E   G   G]  Q   T
J   S   N   E   T   R   O   I   A   H   K   F   J   N
O   T   C   O   F   L   B   A   A   I   R   O   N   Y
M   B   U   N   A   O   P   L   M   T   L   B   M   U
B   I   C   B   M   C   K   P   B   A   K   F   B   C
G   L   V   V   U   A   V   C   V   B   J   L   G   V
```

Using the code key, determine what words the numbers are spelling.

CODE KEY

A = 16	E = 33	I = 74	M = 67	P = 80	U = 22
C = 24	G = 64	K = 27	N = 42	S = 51	R = 6
D = 44	H = 58	L = 46	O = 92	T = 38	Y = 7

1. 46 16 42 44 67 16 6 27   WORD: _____

2. 24 16 67 16 6 16 44 33 6 74 33   WORD: _____

3. 67 16 6 74 92 42 33 38 38 33   WORD: _____

4. 92 22 38 51 67 16 6 38   WORD: _____

5. 67 16 6 16 38 58 92 42   WORD: _____

6. 44 33 67 16 6 24 16 38 33   WORD: _____

7. 24 22 51 38 92 67 16 6 7   WORD: _____

8. 67 16 6 64 74 42 16 46   WORD: _____

9. 64 6 16 67 67 16 6   WORD: _____

10. 80 6 33 67 16 6 74 38 16 46   WORD: _____

MISSPELLED WORDS 1

Pick out the words that are misspelled words, and correct their spelling.

wiegh	_____	adress	_____
calandar	_____	hierarchy	_____
amateur	_____	noticable	_____
libary	_____	balanse	_____
colunm	_____	precede	_____
inoculate	_____	untill	_____
concheince	_____	wheather	_____
cemetery	_____	arguement	_____
excede	_____	beleive	_____
foriegn	_____	indispensable	_____
dicsipline	_____	kernel	_____
miniature	_____	determine	_____
inteligance	_____	leopard	_____

LOGIC WORD PROBLEMS 2

These word problems require you to use the process of elimination to find the answer. It helps to use the grid below.

X = No, not the correct answer; O = Yes, the correct answer

Using the clues, fill in the grid with Xs and Os. When there is only one choice left in a row or column, put an O there. Because it is the only option left, it is the correct answer. If a clue tells you the correct choice, you can put an O in that box and put Xs in the rest of the column and row because the other options cannot be correct too. Work through all of the clues this way.

1. At a local street party, there are 5 different kinds of pies. Each friend takes a slice of a different kind of pie. Can you determine which friend chose which pie?

	APPLE	CUSTARD	COCONUT	CHOCOLATE	RASPBERRY
HELEN					
FRANK					
EDDY					
JOYCE					
EMMA					

CLUES
a. Frank is the only one not allergic to coconut.
b. Helen says that chocolate is her therapist.
c. Eddy doesn't like fruit pies.
d. Emma doesn't like getting seeds in her teeth.

2. Some friends are meeting at the park. Each person is taking a different kind of transportation in different colours. Can you determine which person took which type of transportation and in which colour?

	CAR	BUS	BIKE	RED	YELLOW	SILVER
LOU						
CONNIE						
STUART						

CLUES
a. Connie loves yellow, but she hates taking public transportation
b. Stuart did not take the red vehicle.
c. Lou had to wear a helmet.

WHAT'S THE CATEGORY? 2

Put these words into the most correct category.

baseball	wrench	wire cable	book light
boots	fishing net	a jack	sweatshirts
brake light	cricket helmet	seat cover	adapters
grease	headphones	power cord	umbrella
overalls	camera		

1. Things found in the sporting goods section of store

   _____   _____

   _____   _____

   _____   _____

2. Things found in a mechanics repair shop

   _____   _____

   _____   _____

   _____   _____

3. Things found in an electronics store

   _____   _____

   _____   _____

   _____   _____

REASONING

FIRST AND LAST LETTERS 2

Fill in the correct letters to make a word that matches the definition.

1. ___ isl ___   a church walkway

2. ___ is ___   to stand up

3. ___ as ___   to struggle for breath

4. ___ or ___   additional

5. ___ lad ___   a part of a knife

6. ___ asco ___   a team's symbol

7. ___ es ___   to try it out

8. ___ an ___   a lion's hair

9. ___ di ___   to revise and make changes

10. ___ ti ___   to mix

11. ___ ea ___   letter greeting

12. ___ de ___   you brainstorm this

LANGUAGE

ORDERED LETTERS 1

Pick the one statement that is WRONG.

1. ASZCV

A) Z is in the middle.
B) C is after Z.
C) V is at the end.
D) S is between Z and C.

2. BNDFG

A) N is second.
B) F is between D and G.
C) F is last.
D) D is in the middle.

3. HJMOK

A) J is to the left of H.
B) M is third.
C) O is between M and K.
D) J is to the right of H.

4. LPTUI

A) U is between P and I.
B) P is second.
C) L is before P.
D) T is fourth.

5. QREWY

A) E is right of R.
B) W is left of Y.
C) Q is right of R.
D) Y is last.

6. UWYVX

A) Y is between W and X.
B) X is not last.
C) V is between Y and X.
D) W is second.

7. FACNL

A) N is after C.
B) C is left of N.
C) C is right of A.
D) N is between F and C.

8. JTICD

A) T is before I.
B) C is between T and D.
C) T is left of J.
D) I is in the middle.

SHARED FOOD LETTERS

Write in a letter that completes each word so that a food reads down using your letters.

1. cha___e
   c___ast
   bl___e
   ___ast

2. a___le
   ___at
   l___ft
   ___all

3. ___ome
   b___ke
   kic___
   m___nu

4. ___oap
   b___il
   ___oud
   st___rt
   ___ate

5. ___egun
   t___ail
   s___ed
   r___lly
   bri___e

6. b___aid
   n___ture
   dr___p
   ___ave
   pa___d
   ___ice

7. di___e
   c___at
   d___se
   ___ite
   k___d
   ___asy

8. a___he
   fa___m
   dar___
   se___l
   swi___

9. ___air
   t___de
   ver___e
   ___air

10. na___
    t___le
    v___st

LANGUAGE

SHAPE ADDITION

Which shape was added to the first image to create the second image?

1.

   a. b. c. d.

2.

   a. b. c. d.

3.

   a. b. c. d.

4.

   a. b. c. d.

5.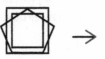

   a. b. c. d.

6.

   a. b. c. d.

7.

   a. b. c. d.

8.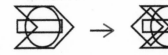

   a. b. c. d.

VISUAL-SPATIAL

PURCHASING PROBLEMS

Determine which items you can buy with the amount you have to spend. Always try to make maximum use of the money available.

1. You have £22.35 to spend on your grandson's birthday present. You want to buy him the most present(s) you can. Choosing the most items possible, which items can you afford to purchase?

BATMAN FIGURE	COLOURING BOOK	FOOTBALL	REMOTE CONTROL CAR
£14.79	£3.15	£7.95	£19.05

ANSWER _____

2. You have £70 to spend on new cookware. Choosing the most items possible, which items can you afford to purchase?

SKILLET	CASSEROLE PAN	BOILING POT	SERVING DISH
£30.29	£55.78	£24.35	£14.69

ANSWER _____

3. You have £30 to spend on snacks for the party. Choosing the most items possible, which items can you afford to purchase?

3 OZ. OF CHEESE	4 LBS OF NUTS	2 LBS OF DELI MEAT	12 OZ. OF CRACKERS
AT £5.90 PER OUNCE	AT £3.20 PER POUND	AT £1.25 PER POUND	AT £0.79 PER OUNCE

ANSWER _____

4. You have £7 to spend on office supplies. Choosing the most items possible, which items can you afford to purchase?

10 PENCILS	3 NOTEPADS	CALCULATOR	2 BOXES OF FOLDERS
AT £0.12 EACH	AT £1.15 EACH	£5.65	AT £3.85 EACH

ANSWER _____

CALCULATION

5. You have £25.25 to spend on dinner for four people. Choosing the most items possible, which items can you afford to purchase?

6 LBS OF POTATO	3 LBS OF BEEF	4 LBS OF BROCCOLI	20 OZ. OF RICE
AT £1.32 PER POUND	AT £5.20 PER POUND	AT £0.79 PER POUND	AT £0.32 PER OUNCE

ANSWER _____

6. You have £670 to spend on new furniture. Choosing the most items possible, which items can you afford to purchase?

COUCH	END TABLE	LAMP	ARMCHAIR
£375	£79	£127	£215

ANSWER _____

DECIPHER THE LETTER CODE 4

Complete the phrase by determining the number that is assigned to the used letters.

Begin by filling in the letters that you are given, then figure out which letters make sense to make words in the phrase. You don't have to figure out all the letters, just the ones you need.

For example, if the word is ___ H ___ , the word is likely THE, so 8 = T,
$\qquad\qquad\qquad\quad$ 8 $\quad$ 13

therefore you can add in all 8s as Ts.

A	B	C	D	E	F	G	H	I	J	K	L	M
8		18										15

N	O	P	Q	R	S	T	U	V	W	X	Y	Z
20	14			26	5				22			

MESSAGE:

— — — — — — —   — — — — — —
4   8   1   22 8   2   5   22 8   20 24 6   21

— —   — —   — — — — — — — — ,
24 14   13 6   5   14 15 6   13 14 21 2

— — —   — — — —   — — — — — — —
13 11 24   20 14 22 4   26 6   8   1   4   10 6

—   — — — — — —   — — — —   — — — —
4   5   16 14 11 1   21   16 8   3   6   13 6   6   20

— — — —   — — — — — — — — .
15 14 26 6   5   7   6   18 4   25 4   18

COUNT THE VOWELS

As quickly as you can, count all of the vowels (a, e, i, o, u) in this paragraph. Scan each line from left to right. Keep a running tally of all letters, don't do one letter at a time.

m n d f u s w e r u r y u x g u a d f g u l k j u o i u w e r u s d f u t w e r

j n k u y t w e r l k d f u q w e r u x c b h s d f g b z v x c y t w e r u u s

d f n d l u k s d n f s k d u n k l p u n s d l f y a d f u l j u p i u w e r u p

a u l k d j f i s o d j h u i n d t u t y o e y k f s l y l k j l d f u i n f k s l l

o u w e r u l s u e r u l s i u s l d i u z m c v u z n u d n f u e r y u s d l k

r k j a s d y s d f o l u n k e r j u s d f u w e r t w e m x g p q w i u y s d f

e b f s u y g e w u a o d p e y x o s d i u d s w x p o t h d k b s k o e r t n

f u u n l s u p i u r q w e u l s d f u l k j u l k u k l f s d i f u s d f u x c v

w o q p o w r y r j k u l y s k d n f k s l u k s d n f u k j f k s d n f u n s k

u q w e u u u p o i u q w u a d f u z c v u m b n u k l j h s d f x c v i o s e

TOTAL VOWELS _____

AGING WORDS 4

The answer to each clue contains the letters "AGE."

1. A large-scale stage production representing historical events

    ANSWER _____

2. To search through things

    ANSWER _____

3. To bet on an outcome

    ANSWER _____

4. A list of things to do in a specific order

    ANSWER _____

5. An actual or mental picture

    ANSWER _____

6. A place to keep your car

    ANSWER _____

7. A professional representing another person in business

    ANSWER _____

8. These fill a book

    ANSWER _____

LANGUAGE

DOMINO ORDER 4

Starting with the domino marked "1st," find an order in which you can line up all these domines end to end. Wherever two dominoes touch, the numbered ends must match. You may rotate teh dominoes, and there is more than one correct order.

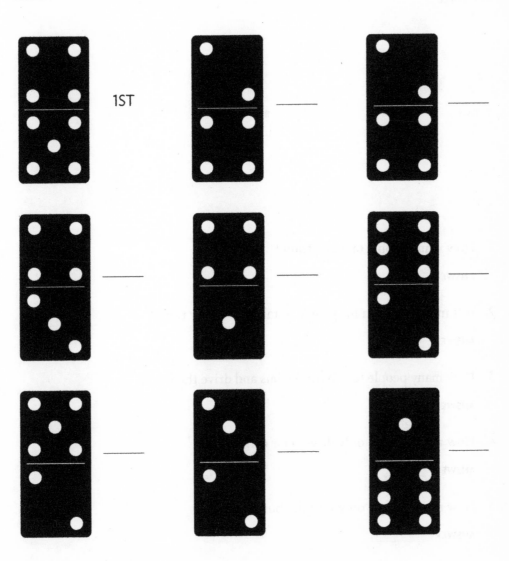

VENN DIAGRAM – TRANSPORTATION

Answer the questions using the information displayed in the Venn diagram.

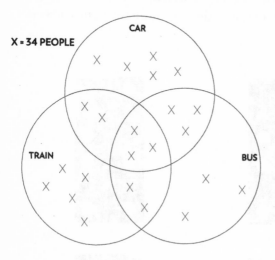

1. How many people take the train?

   ANSWER _____

2. Is it more common for people to take the bus or train?

   ANSWER _____

3. How many people take both the bus and drive their car?

   ANSWER _____

4. How many people only drive their car?

   ANSWER _____

5. How many people only take the bus?

   ANSWER _____

6. How many people take all three types of transportation?

   ANSWER _____

VISUAL–SPATIAL

NAME SOMETHING 1

1. Name five professions that start with "P."

   _____

   _____

   _____

   _____

   _____

2. Name five professions that start with "S."

   _____

   _____

   _____

   _____

   _____

3. Name five book or movie titles that begin with "M."

   _____

   _____

   _____

   _____

   _____

LETTERS-TO-WORD MATCH 3

There are 10 six-letter words that have been broken into chunks of three letters. These chunks have been mixed up, no chunk is used twice, and all chunks are used.

Can you determine what the 10 words are?

abs	any	inj	net
dle	hor	bot	lon
mob	joc	kin	urd
ure	don	key	gra
vel	ger	ile	par

1. _____

2. _____

3. _____

4. _____

5. _____

6. _____

7. _____

8. _____

9. _____

10. _____

LANGUAGE

WHAT'S NEXT? 1

Determine which shape comes next in the pattern.

1. à ÿ ý à ÿ ÿ ý à ÿ
   a. ý   b. à   c. ÿ

2. € £ © © ∞ € £ © © ∞
   a. £   b. €   c. ©

3. ± ± ± ≤ μ μ ± ±
   a. ±   b. ≤   c. μ

4. ¥ ß α ¥ ¥ ß α ¥ ¥
   a. α   b. ß   c. ¥

5. π ɰ δ ɤ π ɰ δ ɤ
   a. π   b. ɰ   c. δ

6. ϑ ϑ ß ώ ï ϑ ϑ ϑ ß ώ ï ϑ
   a. ß   b. ώ   c. ϑ

7. Ϛ ς ɧ ӽ Ϛ ς ɧ ӽ Ϛ
   a. Ϛ   b. ς   c. ɧ

CALCULATION WORD PROBLEMS 2

1. While gardening, you have a group of friends come by for a visit. There are 3 women and 2 men. You want to give a bouquet of 6 flowers from your garden to each woman, and a basket of 8 apples from your apple tree to each man. How many total items will you be picking from your garden?

   _____

2. Each time one of your grandchildren visits, you measure their height. Last time Sally was 3 feet 10 inches and Billy was 4 feet 5 inches. Today Sally is 4 feet even, and Billy is 4 feet 8 inches. How many total inches did they both grow together?

   _____ inches

3. You are going to bring pies to a local street party. There are going to be 28 people attending. If each pie yields 6 slices, how many pies should you bring so that everyone can get at least one piece?

   _____ pies

4. Your family drinks one gallon of milk every 4 days. At the grocery store, you want to buy enough milk to last for at least 2 weeks. How many gallons of milk should you buy?

   _____ gallons

5. You need to buy a large floor carpet for your living room. It needs to be twice as long in length as the width. The width should be 8 feet. How long should the length of the carpet be?

   _____ feet

6. You want to walk 2 ½ miles each day. The distance around your block is ¼ of a mile. How many times would you have to walk around your block in one day to accomplish your goal?

   _____

CALCULATION

ACCOMPLISH THIS TASK 1

Determine two different ways you could accomplish each task. There is not one right answer, so be as creative as you like.

Keep papers together   1. _____

2. _____

Join two pieces of wood   1. _____

2. _____

Make a blanket   1. _____

2. _____

Climb a hill   1. _____

2. _____

Travel across the country   1. _____

2. _____

Clean the car   1. _____

2. _____

Cook an egg breakfast   1. _____

2. _____

Catch up on current events   1. _____

2. _____

REASONING

BAD WORDS

The answer to each clue contains the letters "BAD."

1. A small distinctive piece of metal to show rank

    ANSWER _____

2. To order someone not to do something; not allow (past tense)

    ANSWER _____

3. A game with nets and rackets

    ANSWER _____

4. A burrowing mammal related to the weasel

    ANSWER _____

5. To criticise or make disparaging remarks about somebody

    ANSWER _____

6. A medieval poet or singer of lyric verses about love, who performs while strolling

    ANSWER _____

MATCH THE PARTS 1

Match a word-part on the left with a word-part on the right to form a word and write it on the line. You can only use each word-part once.

1. dan   any   _____

    acc   mal   _____

    lea   ade   _____

    for   cer   _____

    bot   son   _____

    par   use   _____

    can   der   _____

    rea   ary   _____

2. enl   ges   _____

    cav   ium   _____

    ima   ear   _____

    inv   ive   _____

    lin   ist   _____

    sod   ity   _____

    act   lic   _____

    fro   ent   _____

LANGUAGE

TWO COMMON LETTERS 2

Scan each line to find the two letters each word has in common. The letters are next to each other. Challenge yourself to go as quickly as you can.

Example: bounce and balance both have "ce"

COMMON LETTERS

1. faith   infant   loofah   safari   unfair   _____

2. amoeba   nebula   debtor   rebate   zebra   _____

3. brain   afraid   cobra   brandy   corals   _____

4. amount   county   fungus   hunter   ounce   _____

5. eject   deduct   action   victim   sector   _____

6. compass   impair   keypad   parent   unpaid   _____

7. muscle   escrow   rescue   scents   rascal   _____

8. thirdly   stirrup   upstairs   twirled   wiring   _____

9. barley   eyelids   survey   hockey   obeying   _____

10. hourly   pearl   burlap   uncurl   worldly   _____

PROCESSING SPEED

DISCOVER THE PATTERN 2

Determine the number sequence pattern and complete the succeeding numbers. You may use a calculator for this excercise.

1. 2, 6, 10, ———, ———, ———, ———.

2. 5, 10, 20, 40, ———, ———, ———, ———.

3. 3, 5, 4, 6, ———, ———, ———, ———, ———.

4. 8, 12, 10, 14, 12, ———, ———, ———, ———, ———.

5. 8, 32, 16, 64, ———, ———, ———, ———, ———.

6. 3, 9, 6, 18, 15, ———, ———, ———, ———, ———.

7. 5, 10, 10, 15, 15, ———, ———, ———, ———, ———.

8. 12, 14, 13, 16, 15, 19, ———, ———, ———, ———, ———.

9. 4, 8, 4, 12, 4, 16, ———, ———, ———, ———, ———, ———.

10. 6, 6, 12, 36, ———, ———, ———, ———.

COMPOUND WORDS 1

Make as many compound words as you can with these beginnings.

1. be _____

    be _____

    be _____

    be _____

    be _____

    be _____

    be _____

    be _____

2. in _____

    in _____

    in _____

    in _____

    in _____

    in _____

    in _____

    in _____

3. out _____

    out _____

    out _____

    out _____

    out _____

    out _____

    out _____

    out _____

    out _____

    out _____

    out _____

    out _____

    out _____

    out _____

MEMORY

SYMBOL CODING 3

Write the symbol that corresponds to each number in the empty boxes below. Challenge yourself to do this as quickly as you can, while maintaining accuracy. Do not do all of one number at a time, complete each box in a row moving from left to right, and then continue to the next line.

KEY CODE

1	2	3	4	5	6	7	8	9
□	✕	⌐	◇	△	↑	—	○	+

7	9	3	1	4	2	7	8	5	6
4	1	6	8	2	9	3	5	4	2
5	9	1	4	2	7	5	9	8	6
3	6	7	8	3	4	9	1	2	5
7	9	3	1	4	2	7	8	5	6
6	3	1	7	2	5	9	8	2	1
2	9	8	5	1	4	7	3	6	8
1	5	7	4	3	6	2	1	9	3

SEQUENCING ITEMS 2

Discover a logical way to sequence these items, and explain the *reason* why you put them in that order. No alphabetical order allowed.

1. Rough draft, Outline, Final copy, Editing

    1st _____ 2nd _____ 3rd _____ 4th _____

    Reason _____

2. Precipitation, Condensation, Evaporation, Accumulation

    1st _____ 2nd _____ 3rd _____ 4th _____

    Reason _____

3. Bird, Plankton, Fish, Cat

    1st _____ 2nd _____ 3rd _____ 4th _____

    Reason _____

4. Novel, Flyer, Pamphlet, Paragraph

    1st _____ 2nd _____ 3rd _____ 4th _____

    Reason _____

5. Basement, Roof, Attic, Foundation

    1st _____ 2nd _____ 3rd _____ 4th _____

    Reason _____

6. Ford, Kennedy, Bush, Reagan

    1st _____ 2nd _____ 3rd _____ 4th _____

    Reason _____

7. Bulgaria, Portugal, Hungary, Italy

    1st _____ 2nd _____ 3rd _____ 4th _____

    Reason _____

8. Election, Ballot counting, Campaign, Voting

1st _____ 2nd _____ 3rd _____ 4th _____

Reason _____

9. Ankle, Forehead, Waist, Thigh

1st _____ 2nd _____ 3rd _____ 4th _____

Reason _____

10. Take home, Customer, Store, Purchase

1st _____ 2nd _____ 3rd _____ 4th _____

Reason _____

11. Blueberry, Avocado, Cantaloupe, Mushroom

1st _____ 2nd _____ 3rd _____ 4th _____

Reason _____

12. Rosa Parks, *Apollo 11*, Nixon resigns, The Beatles go to America

1st _____ 2nd _____ 3rd _____ 4th _____

Reason _____

13. Appeal, Hearing, Sentencing, Trial

1st _____ 2nd _____ 3rd _____ 4th _____

Reason _____

14. Atom, Element, Electron, Molecule

1st _____ 2nd _____ 3rd _____ 4th _____

Reason _____

WORDS THAT CAN

The answer to each clue contains the letters "CAN."

1. Empty; having no furniture or inhabitants

   ANSWER _____

2. An action or event regarded as morally or legally wrong and causing general public outrage

   ANSWER _____

3. A narrow boat with pointed ends, propelled by paddles

   ANSWER _____

4. Truthful; straightforward; frank

   ANSWER _____

5. A brown nut with an edible kernel

   ANSWER _____

6. A cylinder block of wax with a wick

   ANSWER _____

7. To decide or announce that an event will not take place

   ANSWER _____

8. A strong coarse cloth used for sails, tents, or paintings

   ANSWER _____

LANGUAGE

FAMILY TREE GAME 2

Based on this family tree, answer the questions below with a specific name.

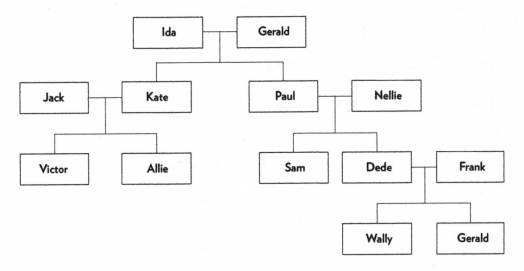

1. Who is Dede's grandmother? _____

2. Who is Kate's sister-in-law? _____

3. Who is the youngest Gerald named after? _____

4. Who are Ida's grandsons? _____

5. Who is Paul's sister's daughter? _____

6. Who is Wally's grandfather? _____

MATCHING CLUES 3

Match two of the word-parts to make a word that fits the clue. Each word-part is used only once.

loc   ck   ak   nap

kin   mo   ket   pe

1. _____ a small ornamental case

   _____ to tease

   _____ a square piece of cloth

   _____ greatest; maximun

ken   ket   ta   nk

pac   sil   pra   sk

2. _____ a container

   _____ duty

   _____ a mischievous joke

   _____ soft and lustrous

WHAT'S THE CATEGORY? 3

Put these words into the most correct category.

zippers	tubes	cheques	tellers
slides	hangers	vault	mothballs
hooks	change	photo albums	goggles
eyewash kit	loans	element chart	funnels
hat box	interest		

1. Things found in a closet

   _____   _____

   _____   _____

   _____   _____

2. Things found in a science lab

   _____   _____

   _____   _____

   _____   _____

3. Things found in a bank

   _____   _____

   _____   _____

   _____   _____

ORDERED LETTERS 2

Pick the one statement that is CORRECT.

1. ASZCV

A) C is fifth.
B) C is between A and Z.
C) S is between A and Z.
D) V is not last.

2. BNDFG

A) D is right of F.
B) F is left of G.
C) F is last.
D) D is first.

3. HJMOK

A) O is between H and M.
B) M is not in the middle.
C) K is left of O.
D) J is right of H.

4. LPTUI

A) U is between T and L.
B) P is left of L.
C) L is left of P.
D) T is fourth.

5. QREWY

A) W is left of Y.
B) R is left of Q.
C) E is left of Q.
D) E is fourth.

6. UWYVX

A) V is right of X.
B) W is right of V.
C) V is between U and Y.
D) Y is right of W.

7. FACNL

A) C is after N.
B) A is left of C.
C) C is left of A.
D) N is between F and C.

8. JTICD

A) J is right of C.
B) I is between J and C.
C) T is left of J.
D) D is left of C.

EXECUTIVE FUNCTIONING

WHAT'S THE ITEM? 2

Determine what item these clues are describing and write it on the line.

1. This stuff lies all around our houses.

   We don't like to see it around, so we wipe it up.

   Scientists say it is mostly made of dead skin cells.

   What is this item? _____

2. Today kids like to use these for crafts.

   Their original purpose was to dry clothes.

   You use them on a line outside.

   What are these items? _____

3. You can use this to drink.

   It usually comes in a glass.

   Some people like to chew on them.

   What is this item? _____

4. These are small and round.

   They are made to fit through holes.

   They can keep your shirt on.

   What are these items? _____

5. These are made of porous material.

   They are used to clean up liquid.

   They can be squeezed out.

   What are these items? _____

CLOCK QUIZ 2

Use the clues to determine the correct time and then draw it in the clock.

1. This time is not in the a.m.

   It is 98 minutes past 2:00.

   What is the time? _____

   Draw the clock and the time

2. This time is before lunch.

   It falls between 6:00 and 8:00.

   It is 390 minutes past midnight.

   What is the time? _____

   Draw the clock and the time

3. This time is at night.

   It 560 minutes past noon.

   What is the time? _____

   Draw the clock and the time

4. This time is between 2:30 a.m. and 2:30 p.m.

   It is 45 minutes before 6:15.

   What is the time? _____

   Draw the clock and the time

EXECUTIVE FUNCTIONING

DECIPHER THE LETTER CODE 5

Complete the phrase by determining the number that is assigned to the used letters.

Begin by filling in the letters that you are given, then figure out which letters make sense to make words in the phrase. You don't have to figure out all the letters, just the ones you need.

For example, if the word is ___ H ___ , the word is likely THE, so 8 = T,
                                    8   13

therefore you can add in all 8s as Ts.

A	B	C	D	E	F	G	H	I	J	K	L	M
	13	17		3						6		16

N	O	P	Q	R	S	T	U	V	W	X	Y	Z
	23	4			10					11		

MESSAGE:

___ ___ ___ ___ ___ ___ ___ ___ ___   ___ ___ ___ ___
5   17 23 16   4   2 25   3 24   23 14 17   3

___ ___ ___ ___   ___ ___   ___ ___   ___ ___ ___ ___ ___ ,
13   3   5 25   16   3   5 25   17   1   3 10 10

___ ___ ___   ___ ___   ___ ___ ___   ___ ___
13   2 25   20 25   21   5 10   14 23

___ ___ ___ ___ ___   ___ ___ ___   ___ ___   ___ ___
16   5 25 17   1   9 23 24   16   3   5 25

___ ___ ___ ___ ___ ___ ___ ___ ___ ___ .
6   20 17   6 13 23 11 20 14 19

COUNT THE CONSONANTS

As quickly as you can, count all of the consonants (any letter that is not a vowel) in this paragraph. Scan each line from left to right. Keep a running tally of all letters, don't do one letter at a time.

a e i f u s w e r u r y u x g u a d f a e o k j u o i u w e r u s d f u t w e r

j a k u y t w e r l a e o u q w e r u x c b a e l f g a z v x c a t w e r u u s

d f a e l u k s d n f s k d u a e l p u n s a l f y a d f u l j u p i u w e r u p

a u l k a j f i s o a a h u i n d t u t y o e y a f s a y l k a l a f u i n f k s a l

o u w e r u a s u e r u a s i u e o d i u z m c v u z n u d n f u e r y u s d l

r k j a s d y s e d f o l u n k e r j u s e f u w e r t w e m x g p q w i u y s

e b o s u y g e w u a o d p e y x o s d i u d s w x p o t h e k a s k o e r t n

f u u n l s u p i u r q w e u l s d f u l k j u l k u k l f s d i f u s d f u x c v

w o q e o w r y r j k u l y s k d n f a s l u k s d n f u a j e k s d n e u n s k

u q w e u a u p o i u q w u a d f u z c v u m e i u k l j h s d f x c v i o s e

TOTAL CONSONANTS _____

WORDS FULL OF AWE

The answer to each clue contains the letters "AWE."

1. You do this to a domesticated house pet to prevent damage to your furniture

   ANSWER _____

2. To be filled with overwhelming emotion; enthralled, captivated

   ANSWER _____

3. A storage compartment in a piece of furniture

   ANSWER _____

4. Having imperfections

   ANSWER _____

5. To chew at something persistently (past tense)

   ANSWER _____

6. To make illegal (past tense)

   ANSWER _____

7. Plants that grow in the ocean

   ANSWER _____

8. To melt something (past tense)

   ANSWER _____

DOT COPY 2

Copy these patterns onto the blank graphs.

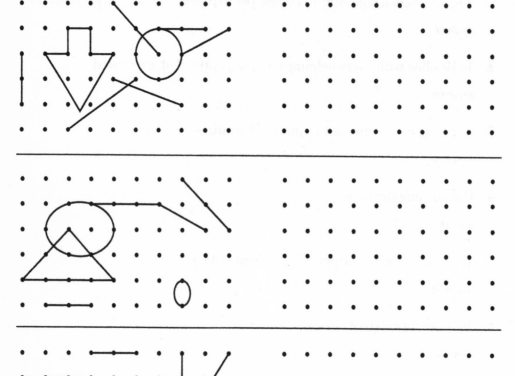

NAME SOMETHING 2

1. Name five countries that start with "C."

   _____

   _____

   _____

   _____

   _____

2. Name five drinks that start with "G."

   _____

   _____

   _____

   _____

   _____

3. Name five things that begin with "Y."

   _____

   _____

   _____

   _____

   _____

LOGIC WORD PROBLEMS 3

These word problems require you to use the process of elimination to find the answer. It helps to use the grid below.

X = No, not the correct answer; O = Yes, the correct answer

Using the clues, fill in the grid with Xs and Os. When there is only one choice left in a row or column, put an O there. Because it is the only option left, it is the correct answer. If a clue tells you the correct choice, you can put an O in that box and put Xs in the rest of the column and row because the other options cannot be correct too. Work through all of the clues this way.

1. Five people are waiting in line at the grocery store. What is the order of the line?

	FIRST	SECOND	THIRD	FOURTH	FIFTH
SARAH					
WALTER					
ABBY					
NEAL					
MALLORY					

CLUES
a. Abby is not first or last.
b. Abby is directly in front of Mallory.
c. Walter is in the middle.
d. Sarah is after Neal.

REASONING

2. Lori, Amy, Hank, and Randy went out dancing together. Each danced a different type of dance with a partner not in their group. Can you determine who danced which type of dance and with whom?

	LEO	JANE	BRIAN	NATALIE	JITTERBUG	SALSA	SWING	LINDY HOP
LORI								
AMY								
HANK								
RANDY								

CLUES

a. Each person danced with a partner of the opposite sex.

b. Hank did not do the jitterbug nor dance with Natalie.

c. Lori danced with a man who has the same letter as her name to a dance with the same letter as her name.

d. Randy loves to salsa dance.

TWO DEFINITIONS 3

Two definitions for the same word are given. Fill in the correct word that matches both definitions.

1. He goes out of a place; he . . .

   They grow on trees

   ANSWER _____

2. Remaining

   Not right

   ANSWER _____

3. A hammer hits it

   It grows on your finger

   ANSWER _____

4. To not eat for a determined time

   Quick

   ANSWER _____

5. To put in alphabetical order

   It smooths out an edge

   ANSWER _____

6. A formal dance

   A round object

   ANSWER _____

7. A measure of weight

   A home for lost dogs

   ANSWER _____

8. To be unkind

   Average

   ANSWER _____

EDIT THE WORD 1

In the first column, change one letter in the original word to make a new word. In the second column, take out one letter from the original word and keep the rest of the letters in the same order to form a new word.

For example:

	CHANGE ONE LETTER	TAKE OUT ONE LETTER
Spank	Spark	Sank

	CHANGE ONE LETTER	TAKE OUT ONE LETTER
1. Table	_____	_____
2. Hurt	_____	_____
3. Race	_____	_____
4. Tail	_____	_____
5. Fuse	_____	_____
6. Scan	_____	_____
7. Bark	_____	_____
8. Tank	_____	_____

ACCOMPLISH THIS TASK 2

Determine two things you would need to accomplish each task. There is not one right answer, so be as creative as you like.

For example: To fill a prescription, you would need

1. A physician's signature, and 2. patience for the line at the pharmacy.

Dial a phone   1. _____

2. _____

Make coffee   1. _____

2. _____

Grocery shop   1. _____

2. _____

Wrap a gift   1. _____

2. _____

Go on a date   1. _____

2. _____

Take a photo   1. _____

2. _____

Play a game   1. _____

2. _____

Feed your pet   1. _____

2. _____

Take a nap   1. _____

2. _____

Play an instrument   1. _____

2. _____

REASONING

Use a flashlight 1. _____

2. _____

Write a cheque 1. _____

2. _____

Wash your hair 1. _____

2. _____

Keep a secret 1. _____

2. _____

Ride a bike 1. _____

2. _____

Hem a dress 1. _____

2. _____

Go swimming 1. _____

2. _____

Bake a cake 1. _____

2. _____

Put out a fire 1. _____

2. _____

Replace a lightbulb 1. _____

2. _____

Make ice 1. _____

2. _____

Walk around the block 1. _____

2. _____

Tell a joke 1. _____

2. _____

REASONING

LETTER TRANSFER 3

Fill in the word to answer the clue, then transfer those numbered letters to the lines on the next page for the final message.

1. This is the capital city of the Italian region of Tuscany

   ___   ___   ___   ___   ___   ___   ___   ___

   1   6   18   4   2   7   16   2

2. The seafaring armed forces of a nation

   ___   ___   ___   ___

   7   5   8   9

3. This bodily organ has four chambers

   ___   ___   ___   ___   ___

   12   2   5   4   13

4. US Presidents Kennedy and Johnson both died in this state

   ___   ___   ___   ___   ___

   13   2   14   5   15

5. This scientist wrote *The Origin of Species*

   ___   ___   ___   ___   ___   ___

   3   5   4   19   17   7

MEMORY

6. The past tense of the word "swing"

—— —— —— —— ——
15 19 20 7   21

FINAL MESSAGE:

—— —— —— —— —— —— —— —— —— —— —— —— —— —— —— ——
13 12 2   4 18 5   3   13 18   15 20 16 16 2   15 15
—— —— —— —— —— —— —— —— —— —— —— —— ——
17 15   5   6 19 5   9   15   20 7   3   2   4
—— —— —— —— —— —— —— —— —— —— —— —— .
16 18 7   15 13 4   20 16 13 17 18 7

A CUP OF WORDS

The answer to each clue contains the letters "CUP."

1. A job or profession

   ANSWER _____

2. To recover from illness or exertion

   ANSWER _____

3. A cabinet with shelves for storage

   ANSWER _____

4. A classical mythological character known as the son of the goddess of love

   ANSWER _____

5. An involuntary spasm of the diaphragm making a sudden sound

   ANSWER _____

6. To reside in a location

   ANSWER _____

7. A large rodent with defensive quills on its body

   ANSWER _____

LANGUAGE

CODING – OCCUPATIONS

Use the key code below to decode the words. Each space is one letter. Challenge yourself to go as quickly as you can. All of these words are in the category: **OCCUPATIONS**.

1. P H Y S I C I A N

2. T E A C H E R

3. A C C O U N T A N T

4. E L E C T R I C I A N

5. P I L O T

KEY CODE

A	B	C	D	E	F	G	H	I	J	K	L	M

N	O	P	Q	R	S	T	U	V	W	X	Y	Z

LOGIC WORD PROBLEMS 4

These word problems require you to use the process of elimination to find the answer. It helps to use the grid below.

X = No, not the correct answer; O = Yes, the correct answer

Using the clues, fill in the grid with Xs and Os. When there is only one choice left in a row or column, put an O there. Because it is the only option left, it is the correct answer. If a clue tells you the correct choice, you can put an O in that box and put Xs in the rest of the column and row because the other options cannot be correct too. Work through all of the clues this way.

1. Sally, Rick, Jay, and Beverly were playing a card game. They had to figure out which person had the ace of spades, jack of hearts, queen of clubs, and king of diamonds. Can you determine which person had which card?

	ACE/SPADES	JACK/HEARTS	QUEEN/CLUBS	KING/DIAMONDS
SALLY				
RICK				
JAY				
BEVERLY				

CLUES
a. Jay did not have a heart or club.
b. Rick was the only person to have a spade.
c. Sally wished she had a queen because they were always her lucky cards.

REASONING

2. Five friends were shopping for home goods together. Which person bought which item at the store?

	LAWN CHAIR	HAMMER	SCISSORS	DOOR HINGE	WRENCH
HARRY					
EMMA					
JOANNE					
LEO					
DIANE					

CLUES

a. Joanne had already replaced all her old creaky door hinges last month and didn't need any now, but she had some good advice for Leo.
b. Emma was in the middle of a sewing project when she realised she needed a supply.
c. Harry did not need any tools, but Joanne did.
d. Diane needed a different size wrench for her project.

ORDERED NUMBERS 1

Pick the one statement that is WRONG.

1.   **53691**

A) 3 is second.
B) 9 is between 6 and 1.
C) 5 is not first.
D) 6 is in the middle.

2.   **74182**

A) 4 is after 1.
B) 1 is in the middle.
C) 8 is between 4 and 2.
D) 8 is fourth.

3.   **64823**

A) 8 is right of 4.
B) 2 is left of 3.
C) 4 is between 6 and 3.
D) 3 is fourth.

4.   **91734**

A) 3 is between 4 and 7.
B) 7 is fourth.
C) 9 is before 1.
D) 3 is right of 7.

5.   **67928**

A) 2 is right of 6.
B) 6 is left of 2.
C) 9 is in the middle.
D) 8 is not last.

6.   **35421**

A) 2 is between 1 and 4.
B) 4 is left of 2.
C) 1 is right of 2.
D) 2 is fifth.

7.   **65283**

A) 2 is after 8.
B) 5 is left of 2.
C) 8 is right of 5.
D) 8 is fourth.

8.   **57139**

A) 7 is between 3 and 5.
B) 3 is right of 1.
C) 1 is right of 9.
D) 1 is in the middle.

EXECUTIVE FUNCTIONING

MATCHING CLUES 4

Match two of the word-parts to make a word that fits the clue. Each word-part is used only once.

rk   shi   thi   spa

ver   tch   ske   nk

1. _____ a rough drawing

_____ to shake slightly

_____ a small fiery particle

_____ to ponder

yo   ck   ke   sli

nk   wic   ya   ker

2. _____ smooth and glossy

_____ to pull with a jerk

_____ woven twigs

_____ a wooden crosspiece

START HERE – END THERE

Find at least three ways to get from the first number to the second number. You may use any combination of operations: addition (+), subtraction (-), multiplication (x), or division (/) to reach your goal. Remember the order of operations when working out an equation: First do any multiplication and division (working left to right), then do any addition and subtraction (working left to right).

For example: 8   = 27

$$8 + 20 - 1 = 27 \qquad 8 \times 3 + 3 = 27 \qquad 8 / 2 + 23 = 27$$

This column must include:

	ADDITION & SUBTRACTION	MULTIPLICATION	DIVISION
1. 2 = 15	_____	_____	_____
2. 3 = 17	_____	_____	_____
3. 4 = 22	_____	_____	_____
4. 5 = 48	_____	_____	_____
5. 6 = 74	_____	_____	_____
6. 7 = 88	_____	_____	_____
7. 8 = 30	_____	_____	_____
8. 9 = 25	_____	_____	_____
9. 10 = 48	_____	_____	_____

CALCULATION

Now you can use any combination of operations you choose:

10. 12 = 62 _____ _____ _____

11. 15 = 86 _____ _____ _____

12. 24 = 92 _____ _____ _____

WORDS THAT FIT

The answer to each clue contains the letters "FIT."

1. To receive an advantage; gain

   ANSWER _____

2. A person whose behavior or attitude sets them apart from others in an uncomfortably conspicuous way

   ANSWER _____

3. A set of clothing worn together for a particular occasion

   ANSWER _____

4. A financial gain or advantage

   ANSWER _____

5. To add a component to a product that did not have it when manufactured

   ANSWER _____

6. A writing or drawing sprayed illicitly on a wall in a public place

   ANSWER _____

7. To be appropriate for

   ANSWER _____

8. The condition of being physically healthy

   ANSWER _____

LETTERS-TO-WORD MATCH 4

There are 10 six-letter words that have been broken into chunks of three letters. These chunks have been mixed up, no chunk is used twice and all chunks are used.

Can you determine what the 10 words are?

cha	orc	cac	ace
tus	att	sec	anc
sce	hid	rge	tic
ach	hor	pal	lau
kle	nch	ret	nic

1. _____

2. _____

3. _____

4. _____

5. _____

6. _____

7. _____

8. _____

9. _____

LANGUAGE

SYMBOL CODING 4

Write the number that corresponds to each symbol in the empty boxes below. Challenge yourself to do this as quickly as you can, while maintaining accuracy. Do not do all of one symbol at a time, complete each box in a row moving from left to write, and then continue to the next line.

KEY CODE

ꝰ	ℛ	Ϙ	ℭ	Ξ	Δ	Ⱶ	Ɥ	Ӿ
5	9	3	2	4	7	1	8	6

Δ	ℭ	Ξ	ꝰ	Ɥ	ℛ	Ⱶ	Ӿ	Ϙ	ꝰ
Ξ	Ɥ	Ⱶ	ℛ	Δ	Ϙ	Ӿ	ꝰ	Ɥ	ℭ
Ⱶ	ꝰ	Ϙ	Ӿ	ℭ	Ξ	Δ	Ɥ	ℛ	Ⱶ
ℛ	Δ	Ɥ	Ⱶ	Ӿ	Δ	ꝰ	ℭ	Ϙ	Ξ
ꝰ	Ⱶ	Ӿ	Ⱶ	Ξ	Ɥ	ℛ	Ӿ	Δ	Ⱶ
ℭ	Ɥ	ℛ	ꝰ	Δ	Ⱶ	Ӿ	Ϙ	Ξ	ℛ
Ⱶ	Ӿ	Δ	Ⱶ	Ɥ	Ӿ	Ϙ	ꝰ	Ⱶ	Δ

PROCESSING SPEED

SUNNY WORDS

The answer to each clue contains the letters "SUN."

1. An ice cream dessert with toppings

    ANSWER _____

2. Submerged beneath the surface of the water

    ANSWER _____

3. To lie outside to get a tan

    ANSWER _____

4. Not praised or honored, such as an _____ hero

    ANSWER _____

5. A piece of women's clothing worn in hot weather

    ANSWER _____

6. Protects skin from damaging UV rays

    ANSWER _____

7. A large destructive ocean wave

    ANSWER _____

8. An instrument that shows time by using shadows

    ANSWER _____

CALENDAR QUIZ 3

Use the calendar clues to determine the correct date.

SUNDAY	MONDAY	TUESDAY	WEDNESDAY	THURSDAY	FRIDAY	SATURDAY
	1	2	3	4	5	6
7	8	9	10	11	12	13
14	15	16	17	18	19	20
21	22	23	24	25	26	27
28	29	30	31			

1. This date is on a day that begins with "S."

   It is in the middle week of the month.

   It is not the 20th.

   What is the date? _____

2. This date is not on a weekday.

   It is a single digit.

   It is not on a Sunday.

   What is the date? _____

EXECUTIVE FUNCTIONING

3. This date is between the 21st and the 31st.

   It is on a Wednesday.

   It is not the last day of the month.

   What is the date? _____

4. This date is in the first half of the month.

   It is in the middle of the week.

   It is not the 3rd.

   What is the date? _____

TWO COMMON LETTERS 3

Scan each line to find the two letters each word has in common. The letters are next to each other. Challenge yourself to go as quickly as you can.

Example: bounce and balance both have "ce"

COMMON LETTERS

1. allegory   egotist   illegal   neglect   vinegar   _____

2. allocate   bachelor   cloister   employee   lockable   _____

3. caffeine   divinity   finalist   linger   ceiling   _____

4. crumple   entrust   grueling   protrude   ruminate   _____

5. leftovers   aircraft   grifters   shoplift   softness   _____

6. disrobe   newsroom   misread   pressrun   misrule   _____

7. billiard   ambrosia   cardiac   enviable   partial   _____

8. ensemble   amenable   dribble   humble   blue   _____

9. betrayer   doctrine   atrocity   geometry   mistrust   _____

10. bicycle   diabolical   efficacy   evicted   justice   _____

PROCESSING SPEED

CLOCK QUIZ 3

Use the clues to determine the correct time and then draw it in the clock.

1. This time is in the p.m.

   It is 80 minutes past 8:25.

   What is the time? _____

   Draw the clock and the time

2. This time is in the morning.

   It is 145 minutes after 1:35.

   What is the time? _____

   Draw the clock and the time

3. This time is not in the afternoon.

   It is 425 minutes past midnight.

   What is the time? _____

   Draw the clock and the time

4. This time is between 1:00 a.m. and 1:00 p.m.

   It is 130 minutes before 3:00.

   What is the time? _____

   Draw the clock and the time

HOW MANY WORDS? 2

How many words can you make out of the letters in the two words below? You can rearrange the letters in any order you want and you do not have to use every letter in each new word.

1. Accoutrement

_____

_____

_____

_____

_____

_____

_____

_____

_____

_____

2. Gardening

_____

_____

_____

_____

_____

_____

_____

_____

_____

_____

LANGUAGE

FURRY WORDS

The answer to each clue contains the letters "FUR."

1. A yellow combustible chemical element that smells bad

   ANSWER _____

2. To make or become spread out from a rolled or folded state

   ANSWER _____

3. An appliance fired by gas, oil, or wood in which air or water is heated

   ANSWER _____

4. Extremely angry

   ANSWER _____

5. To renovate and redecorate a building

   ANSWER _____

6. Large movable objects to make a space suitable for living or working

   ANSWER _____

7. A narrow trench, or a wrinkle in the brow

   ANSWER _____

MIDDLE LETTERS 2

Fill in the correct letters to make a word that matches the definition.

1. s ___ ___ ___ e   to look happy

2. h ___ n   the source of an egg

3. e ___ ___ o   when a sound reverberates

4. u ___ ___ ___ ___ ___ l a fork, spoon, or knife

5. d ___ ___ i   a sandwich store

6. e ___ ___ ___ ___ ___ n a feeling

7. a ___ ___ ___ s   pains

8. s ___ ___ ___ ___ ___ s spring, summer, fall, winter

9. p ___ ___ h   a garden walkway

10. s ___ ___ ___ ___ e   a gesture to show respect in the military

11. c ___ ___ t   an informal talk

12. s ___ ___ ___ d   swiftness

LANGUAGE

MEMORY CROSSWORD 1

First, spend two minutes studying the words in this crossword. Then turn the page for a quiz.

```
                        R
  B  A  T  T  L  E
     M              P
     U        C  A  S  I  N  O
     S              I
  S  E  N  D  E  R
        E
        A
        R
```

MEMORY CROSSWORD 1

(DON'T LOOK AT THIS PAGE UNTIL YOU'VE STUDIED PREVIOUS PAGE.)

Now look at the list of words below and circle the words that were in the crossword on the previous page.

GLORY

POKER

NEAR

AMUSE

ENTERTAIN

BATTLE

RECEIVE

REPAIR

POSTAGE

SENDER

CASINO

GALLOP

REWARD

MEMORY

IMAGES MEMORY 2

First, spend two minutes studying the images. Then turn the page for a quiz.

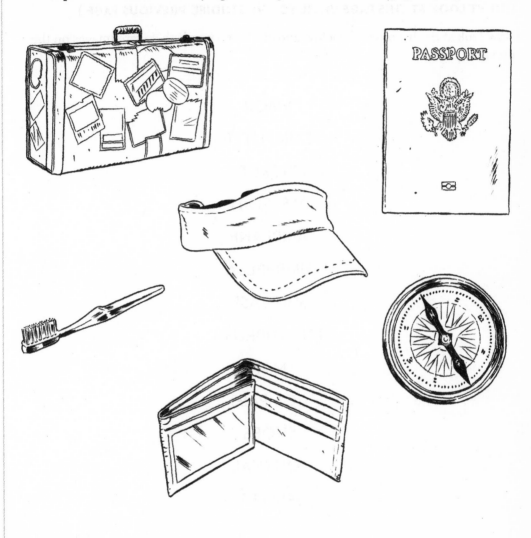

IMAGES MEMORY 2

(DON'T LOOK AT THIS PAGE UNTIL YOU'VE STUDIED PREVIOUS PAGE.)

Now look at the list of words below and circle the words that were images on the previous page.

VISOR

COMPUTER

TICKET

PASSPORT

AIRPLANE

UMBRELLA

SUITCASE

TOOTHBRUSH

MAP

COMPASS

SHOES

JOURNAL

WALLET

DOT COPY 3

Copy these patterns onto the blank graphs.

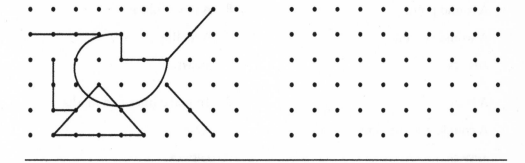

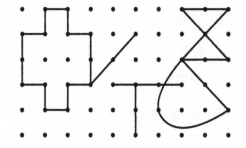

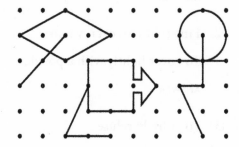

"D" WORDS

Using two clues, fill in the correct word that begins with "D."

1. A round point
   A woman's name

   ANSWER _____

2. A fruit
   A couple goes on one

   ANSWER _____

3. An individual feature
   A small detachment of troops

   ANSWER _____

4. To call on a phone
   The face of a clock or watch

   ANSWER _____

5. To aim in a direction
   To speak clearly

   ANSWER _____

6. To become incorporated into a liquid
   To close down

   ANSWER _____

7. A product not made abroad
   An indoor pet

   ANSWER _____

8. A lower place
   A feeling

   ANSWER _____

9. To make lines and marks
   A tie

   ANSWER _____

10. To let fall
    A small portion of liquid

    ANSWER _____

11. To operate a car
    To urge to attain a goal

    ANSWER _____

12. Fine particles everywhere
    To cover lightly with a powder

    ANSWER _____

13. To politely refuse
    To become less

    ANSWER _____

14. To push into low position
    To make someone feel bad

    ANSWER _____

15. Lacking excitement

Not bright

ANSWER _____

16. To plunge steeply

To go headfirst

ANSWER _____

17. A quantity of medicine

A portion

ANSWER _____

18. A structure extending across a ship

To decorate festively

ANSWER _____

WORD MAZE – PATRIOTIC

Find your way through the maze by connecting letters to spell out words. Write the words on the next page. You may move forward, backward, up, or down, but no letters may be connected more than once.

START

R	F	P	R	W	Q	C	L	M	E	R	C
E	M	I	B	F	V	I	Y	K	P	D	O
E	D	H	L	S	E	T	E	N	A	T	I
W	O	S	N	E	Z	I	C	H	W	E	O
A	M	I	N	D	E	P	N	O	D	D	N
F	E	C	P	P	C	E	E	N	K	E	R
L	W	I	I	L	S	N	D	C	O	M	V
A	Q	T	S	E	Q	L	K	R	C	B	Q
G	V	E	U	J	C	I	T	A	U	Y	P
O	L	T	B	V	H	A	C	B	S	O	T
M	A	E	D	B	A	M	U	P	V	B	N
B	K	R	B	I	M	B	C	K	N	F	B
G	J	A	N	L	U	V	V	V	K	L	V

END

VISUAL–SPATIAL

WORDS

1. _____

2. _____

3. _____

4. _____

5. _____

6. _____

7. _____

8. _____

BETTING WORDS

The answer to each clue contains the letters "BET."

1. More pleasing or acceptable than something else

   ANSWER _____

2. Disloyal; to act in a way that is contrary to a promise made

   ANSWER _____

3. A frozen dessert made with fruit syrup and ice

   ANSWER _____

4. To and from; from one place to another

   ANSWER _____

5. Act of becoming engaged to marry someone

   ANSWER _____

6. All the letters used to represent a language

   ANSWER _____

7. A medical disorder producing excessive urine

   ANSWER _____

LANGUAGE

SHAPE MATCH 2

Circle the two matching shapes.

1

2

3

4

5

6

7

8

TRUE OR FALSE FACTS 2

Determine if each statement is True or False. Challenge yourself to answer as quickly as you can.

1. A customer serves the waitress.   True   False

2. Rinse with mouthwash to prevent bad breath.   True   False

3. Mould can be used in making cheese.   True   False

4. Roses smell worse than cat litter.   True   False

5. Dehydration can cause delirium.   True   False

6. Golf requires less walking than Ping-Pong.   True   False

7. Dogs are never man's best friend.   True   False

8. Calculus is not as hard as basic math.   True   False

9. Jury trials are held in a courtroom.   True   False

10. Auctioneers rarely learn to talk fast.   True   False

11. A cotton shirt is not as warm as a wool jacket.   True   False

12. A plate will hold anything a bowl can hold.   True   False

13. Herbivores eat meat.   True   False

14. Botanists always study plants.   True   False

15. Toothpaste is sweeter than fudge.   True   False

16. Elbows are the largest joints in the body.   True   False

17. Hard-boiled eggs take more than 2 minutes to make.   True   False

PROCESSING SPEED

18. In math, multiplying two negatives equals a positive.   True   False

19. Every part of a true sentence must be true.   True   False

20. September is after March.   True   False

21. Cats love to take baths.   True   False

22. Thunder always comes before rain.   True   False

23. If yesterday was Wednesday, then tomorrow is Friday.   True   False

24. ½ never equals 50 percent.   True   False

MISMATCH 2

Pick out the one item that does not fit the category, and explain the *reason* why it does not fit.

1. Car, Jet Ski, Truck, Golf cart

   Mismatch item_____

   *Reason*_____

2. Shred, Cube, Mix, Slice

   Mismatch item_____

   *Reason*_____

3. Tenderloin, Ham, Rump, Sirloin

   Mismatch item_____

   *Reason*_____

4. Fountain, Steam, Ice, Droplets

   Mismatch item_____

   *Reason*_____

5. Lagoon, Waves, Lake, Swamp

   Mismatch item_____

   *Reason*_____

6. Aisle, Road, Stream, Sidewalk

   Mismatch item_____

   *Reason*_____

7. A pup, A joey, A sheep, A fawn

   Mismatch item_____

   *Reason*_____

8. Facts, Truth, Proof, Report

Mismatch item_____

*Reason*_____

9. Invention, Story, Reality, Fiction

Mismatch item_____

*Reason*_____

10. Manuscript, Pamphlet, Brochure, Flyer

Mismatch item_____

*Reason*_____

11. Emotion, Reaction, Answer, Sentiment

Mismatch item_____

*Reason*_____

12. Kinship, Branch, Relative, Tribe

Mismatch item_____

*Reason*_____

13. Ocean, Beach towel, Sunglasses, Sunblock

Mismatch item_____

*Reason*_____

14. Striker, Bowler, Winger, Full-back

Mismatch item_____

*Reason*_____

15. Pistol, Knife, Armour, Dart

Mismatch item_____

*Reason*_____

16. Rome, Paris, Sydney, Washington DC

Mismatch item_____

*Reason*_____

17. Small, Microscope, Tiny, Miniscule

Mismatch item_____

*Reason*_____

WORDS FULL OF FUN

The answer to each clue contains the letters "FUN."

1. An activity or purpose natural to a person or thing

   ANSWER _____

2. A sum of money saved or made available for a particular purpose

   ANSWER _____

3. Spore-producing organisms feeding on organic matter

   ANSWER _____

4. A tube that is wide at the top and narrow at the bottom

   ANSWER _____

5. To pay back

   ANSWER _____

6. A ceremony to honor a person who passed away

   ANSWER _____

7. To fail to function normally

   ANSWER _____

WHAT'S THE CATEGORY? 4

Put these words into the most correct category.

menu	shells	booths	sheets
cashier	needles	wreckage	utensils
bandages	coral	medication	elevator
sand	insurance	divers	oil
spices	tide		

Things found in an ocean:

_____   _____

_____   _____

_____   _____

8. Things found in a hospital

_____   _____

_____   _____

_____   _____

9. Things found in a restaurant

_____   _____

_____   _____

_____   _____

REASONING

WHAT'S NEXT? 2

Determine which shape comes next in the pattern.

1. [\ ]   [^]   ~   [^]   [\ ]   ~   [\ ]   [

   a. ^   b.]   c. \

2. «   «   ¤   »   »   »   «   «   ¤

   a. «   b. ¤   c. »

3. ʆ   ʅ   ƥ   ɷ   ʆ   ʅ   ƥ   ɷ   ʆ

   a. ʅ   b. ƥ   c. ɷ

4. ⌐   ǂ   ǂ   ¬   ±   ⌐   ǂ

   a. ¬   b. ǂ   c. ±

5. ð   ø   ö   Ö   Õ   ð   ø   ö

   a. Õ   b. ð   c. Ö

6. Ɣ   ƛ   ƛ   ƛ   ý   ý   Ɣ   Ɣ   ƛ   ƛ

   a. Ɣ   b. ƛ   c. ý

7. д   Д   Й   Њ   ħ   ɯ   д   Д   Й   Њ   ħ

   a. д   b. ħ   c. ɯ

CALCULATIONS

Calculate the correct answer for each question.

1. The sum total of all 10 of your grandchildrens' ages is 110. If they are all 2 years apart in age, what are their ages?

    ANSWER _____

2. While at Katy's ballet recital you see that the auditorium holds 240 people. Two-thirds of the seats are full. How many empty seats are open?

    ANSWER _____

3. You are putting away savings to go on a cruise. The cruise leaving 1st November costs £1,800. It is now February; how much do you have to save each month to afford the cruise?

    ANSWER _____

4. You have 24 yards of ribbon to wrap 8 presents. How much ribbon does each box get?

    ANSWER _____

5. You have to divide up your bowl of sweets among your 6 grandchildren. The 3 oldest grandkids get four more each than the younger ones. If there are 48 sweets, how many do the younger ones get?

    ANSWER _____

6. While building your porch steps, you determine that it takes 3 ¾ planks of wood to build one step. You want the staircase to be 8 steps. How many planks of wood do you need to buy?

    ANSWER _____

7. You are driving 57 miles per hour on the freeway. You want to get to Atlanta, which is 228 miles away. How long will it take you to get there?

    ANSWER _____

8. You are ordering dinner tables for a party of 70 people. The company you called said they have small tables that fit 5 people and large tables that fit 12 people. How many large and small tables should you order so that you have the exact amount of seating?

ANSWER _____

9. You are using your large coat closet to hold guests' coats during the party. When the party begins 4 coats are put in. Then 8 coats are put in and 2 taken out. Then 4 coats are put in before half of the coats in the closet are taken out. Finally, at the end of the night, 6 coats are taken out of the closet. How many coats are left inside the closet?

ANSWER _____

HOW MANY WORDS? 3

How many words can you make out of the letters in the two words below? You can rearrange the letters in any order you want and you do not have to use every letter in each new word.

1. Prestidigitation

_____

_____

_____

_____

_____

_____

_____

_____

_____

_____

2. Mellow

_____

_____

_____

_____

_____

_____

_____

_____

_____

_____

LANGUAGE

WORDS FULL OF INK

The answer to each clue contains the letters "INK."

1. To use your mind to actively form ideas

   ANSWER _____

2. A connection between two things

   ANSWER _____

3. To descend below the surface of a liquid

   ANSWER _____

4. To have a strong unpleasant odor

   ANSWER _____

5. A liquid to swallow

   ANSWER _____

6. To attempt to repair something in a casual way

   ANSWER _____

7. To make smaller in size

   ANSWER _____

8. A slight fold in something

   ANSWER _____

TWO-LETTER PLACEMENT 2

Choose which two-letter combo will make a word when added to the letters below.

al   ac   is   in   la   ca   si

1. c a n ___ ___ e

2. ___ ___ t u a l

3. d ___ ___ c o

4. ___ ___ l o w

5. i n ___ ___ n d

6. ___ ___ l m

7. f a ___ ___ t

8. f ___ ___ t o r

9. g o s ___ ___ p

10. f l o r ___ ___

11. ___ ___ b o u r

12. c r ___ ___ p y

13. i n ___ ___ d e

14. k ___ ___ d l e

15. f o s ___ ___ l

16. l o c ___ ___

17. ___ ___ g n

18. ___ ___ s u e

19. d i ___ ___ o g u e

20. b ___ ___ n k

21. d e ___ ___ r e

22. l e g ___ ___

23. l o ___ ___ l

24. e n ___ ___ t

25. c o u ___ ___ n

26. s ___ ___ i v a

27. s ___ ___ r f

28. r a ___ ___ e

29. p ___ ___ q u e

30. g r a ___ ___

31. l ___ ___ e a r

32. f i s c ___ ___

33. r e ___ ___ t

34. w ___ ___ e

ORDERED NUMBERS 2

Pick the one statement that is CORRECT.

1. 53691

A) 9 is right of 1.
B) 9 is between 3 and 1.
C) 5 is not first.
D) 6 is left of 3.

2. 74182

A) 1 is not in the middle.
B) 4 is right of 1.
C) 8 is between 1 and 2.
D) 4 is third.

3. 64823

A) 4 is right of 2.
B) 3 is left of 2.
C) 2 is between 6 and 8.
D) 8 is right of 6.

4. 91734

A) 3 is between 4 and 7.
B) 9 is not first.
C) 7 is not in the middle.
D) 4 is left of 3.

5. 67928

A) 2 is right of 8.
B) 6 is right of 9.
C) 8 is right of 7.
D) 8 is not last.

6. 35421

A) 2 is between 3 and 4.
B) 5 is left of 3.
C) 4 is not in the middle.
D) 2 is fourth.

7. 65283

A) 2 is after 8.
B) 5 is left of 6.
C) 8 is left of 5.
D) 5 is left of 2.

8. 57139

A) 7 is between 1 and 9.
B) 3 is right of 1.
C) 1 is left of 5.
D) 1 is first.

ORDERED SYMBOLS 1

Pick the one statement that is WRONG.

1. ☆ ○ □ △ ⇨

A) Circle is before Triangle.
B) Square is between Star and Arrow.
C) Triangle is right of Arrow.
D) Star is left of Circle.

2. ◇ + ☾ = ▯

A) Crescent is right of Plus.
B) Diamond is left of Plus.
C) Equals is before Cylinder.
D) Cylinder is third.

3. ☀ ◺ ♡ ○ ▭

A) Sun is left of Heart.
B) Rectangle is between Sun and Circle.
C) Triangle is left of Heart.
D) Circle is right of Triangle.

4. ⇨ △ ▯ ♡ ◇

A) Cylinder is between Heart and Arrow.
B) Heart is fourth.
C) Diamond is left of Heart.
D) Arrow is not last.

5. ▯ ☆ = + ◺

A) Star is between Equals and Plus.
B) Cylinder is left of Star.
C) Plus is right of Star.
D) Triangle is fifth.

6. ○ ☾ ☀ △ ▭

A) Crescent is left of Sun.
B) Triangle is between Sun and Circle.
C) Rectangle is right of Triangle.
D) Circle is left of Crescent.

7. □ △ ▭ ◇ ♡

A) Diamond is right of Triangle.
B) Triangle is between Square and Rectangle.
C) Heart is right of Diamond.
D) Rectangle is second.

8. = ☾ ⇨ ☆ +

A) Star is between Arrow and Plus.
B) Crescent is left of Arrow.
C) Star is right of Arrow.
D) Plus is left of Star.

THREE-LETTER PLACEMENT 2

Choose which three-letter combo will make a word when added to the letters below.

ous   ear   ran   tar   ker   nor   cue

1. e n d ___ ___ ___

2. t a r ___ ___ ___

3. s p ___ ___ ___ e

4. w a l ___ ___ ___

5. b ___ ___ ___ d

6. c l ___ ___ ___

7. h ___ ___ ___ e

8. a l ___ ___ ___

9. e ___ ___ ___ m o u s

10. b ___ ___ ___ i n g

11. e r ___ ___ ___ d

12. c a l l ___ ___ ___

13. s e e ___ ___ ___

14. s ___ ___ ___ t

15. ___ ___ ___ t h

16. o ___ ___ ___ g e

17. w _ _ _ y

18. f u r i _ _ _

19. _ _ _ n e l

20. h _ _ _ t

21. s _ _ _ e

22. _ _ _ d

23. g _ _ _ d

24. r e s _ _ _

25. s e r i _ _ _

26. _ _ _ t h

27. b a _ _ _ s

28. s _ _ _ c h

29. b a r b e _ _ _

30. r o c _ _ _

31. u n l _ _ _ n

32. l _ _ _ y

33. c _ _ _ k y

34. s _ _ _ s

LANGUAGE

ASKING WORDS

The answer to each clue contains the letters "ASK."

1. A face covering to hide identity

   ANSWER _____

2. A small flat container for alcohol

   ANSWER _____

3. A job assigned to somebody

   ANSWER _____

4. Off center or at an angle

   ANSWER _____

5. A woven container with a handle

   ANSWER _____

6. A rubber seal used to render a joint impermeable to gas or liquid

   ANSWER _____

LANGUAGE

MATCHING CLUES 5

Match two of the word-parts to make a word that fits the clue. Each word-part is used only once.

abr   cab   upt   lad

abs   bal   orb   le

1. _____ a thick rope of wire

   _____ to soak up

   _____ sudden; unexpected

   _____ a song narrating a story

bar   bad   bal   dou

let   ger   ble   ely

2. _____ to pester

   _____ a formal artistic dance

   _____ to almost not

   _____ twice as many

SHARED NATURE LETTERS

Write in a letter that completes each word so that a nature word reads down.

1. w a i ___
     c ___ a s h
     l ___ a d
     ___ a s y

2. f i ___ r e
     o b ___ y
     l ___ u g h
     ___ a l l
     c ___ a p e l

3. s ___ i n g
     n ___ g h t
     k i ___ g
     ___ a r t

4. s t a ___ e
     g ___ a r
     l e ___ p
     e ___ e n
     n ___ a r
     ___ o l d

5. s ___ u g
     ___ l l e y
     ___ i n d
     r ___ a d

6. c a ___ é
     s o u ___
     r ___ a d
     ___ a l k
     k e ___ p
     t ___ y

7. c a ___ e l
     c ___ l a
     ___ s e
     ___ a m e
     s p i ___
     ___ i r
     l ___ t r e
     c o i ___

8. ___ e l t
     ___ a i n
     h ___ a r t
     v ___ i n
     g a ___ e
     t r u ___

9. s u p e ___
     b e ___ r d
     h ___ d e
     l e ___ d

WORDS FULL OF AIR 1

The answer to each clue contains the letters "AIR."

1. A finger-shaped cream pastry

    ANSWER _____

2. A feeling of hopelessness

    ANSWER _____

3. Chief presiding officer of a company board

    ANSWER _____

4. A device to spray makeup or paint

    ANSWER _____

5. A treeless grass-covered US plain

    ANSWER _____

6. A card game for one

    ANSWER _____

7. To weaken something; to lessen the quality or strength

    ANSWER _____

8. A wealthy person whose net worth is more than a million dollars

    ANSWER _____

CALCULATION WORD PROBLEMS 3

1. You head out for a walk at 9:15 and walk for 75 minutes. What time do you arrive back home?

   _____

2. You are finished shopping at the grocery store and walk to the checkout registers. You have 2 boxes of granola bars, a gallon of milk, a canister of coffee, coffee filters, tea bags, a pound of sugar, and 3 boxes of cereal. Can you go in the express lane that says 15 items or fewer?

   _____

3. You take your grandchildren to a local park. There are 35 kids playing at the park today. If there are 16 more kids than adults, how many adults are there at the park today?

   _____

4. You count 14 red flowers and 18 yellow flowers in your garden. The next morning when you wake up and go outside, you see that 3 red flowers died and 2 yellow flowers died, but you see 6 more flowers that bloomed overnight. Now, how many total flowers do you have in your garden?

   _____

5. You are having family over and want to buy enough sodas for everyone to have one and then have some left over for yourself for one week. There will be 4 adults and 3 kids plus you and your spouse. You drink one soda each day. How many sodas will you have to buy?

   _____

6. You are making flyers for your 32 club members to advertise the fund-raiser. You want each person to take and hand out 20 flyers. How many copies of the flyer should you make?

   _____

CALCULATION

"G" WORDS

Using two clues, fill in the correct word that begins with "G."

1. Soccer's posts and net

   The object of your effort

   ANSWER _____

2. Happy

   Pleased

   ANSWER _____

3. A form of play or sport

   Wild bird hunted for food

   ANSWER _____

4. Simple elegance

   Unmerited favour

   ANSWER _____

5. A person invited to your home

   Company

   ANSWER _____

6. To prepare someone for a particular purpose

   To brush a horse

   ANSWER _____

7. A diagram

   To plot and measure variables

   ANSWER _____

8. A metal cooker used outside

   To question intensely

   ANSWER _____

9. To watch over

   Worn to prevent injury

   ANSWER _____

10. Disgusting

    Without tax

    ANSWER _____

MATCH THE PARTS 2

Match a word-part on the left with a word-part on the right to form a word and write it on the line. You can use each word-part only once.

1. beh   ive   _____

    got   our   _____

    loc   our   _____

    rum   ten   _____

    spa   ave   _____

    mot   rse   _____

    par   ody   _____

    col   ket   _____

2. the   nel   _____

    wor   ble   _____

    bun   ory   _____

    dev   dle   _____

    fun   nce   _____

    inj   ker   _____

    nua   our   _____

    hum   ure   _____

OUR WORDS

The answer to each clue contains the letters "OUR."

1. The business of providing information to people visiting places of interest

   ANSWER _____

2. An attractive quality that makes certain people seem appealing or special

   ANSWER _____

3. A place, person, or thing from which something comes or can be obtained

   ANSWER _____

4. Act of traveling from one place to another

   ANSWER _____

5. Presided over by a judge

   ANSWER _____

6. Taste and enjoy it completely

   ANSWER _____

7. Postpone a meeting

   ANSWER _____

8. A messenger who transports goods or documents

   ANSWER _____

9. A connoisseur of good food with a discerning palate

   ANSWER _____

LANGUAGE

PLACEMENT OF LETTERS 2

Choose a word-part from the left and fit it into letters on the right to make a word.
You can use each word-part only once.

1. gn   ch ____ ____ ge

    ng   ag ____ ____ cy

    an   re ____ ____ on

    en   to ____ ____ ue

    gi   fi ____ ____ er

    ng   ma ____ ____ et

    ld   vo ____ ____ ge

    ya   go ____ ____ en

2. no   di ____ ____ ogue

    go   hi ____ ____ er

    ng   si ____ ____ al

    si   ig ____ ____ re

    gh   vi ____ ____ ur

    al   as ____ ____ gn

    go   wa ____ ____ ns

    gn   mi ____ ____ le

LANGUAGE

3. og   ga ____ ____ op

    ri   be ____ ____ ng

    ge   or ____ ____ ge

    ow   cr ____ ____ ch

    ll   du ____ ____ ng

    lo   sl ____ ____ an

    un   gr ____ ____ th

    an   le ____ ____ nd

4. rb   en ____ ____ ne

    ig   ti ____ ____ ng

    ci   ge ____ ____ le

    gi   ha ____ ____ our

    vi   br ____ ____ ht

    ig   or ____ ____ in

    nt   ra ____ ____ ng

    mi   lo ____ ____ ng

SOLUTIONS TO A PROBLEM

Describe two different ways to solve these problems. There is not one right answer, so be as creative as you like.

Feeling stressed out 1. _____
                      2. _____

Car won't start 1. _____
                 2. _____

Can't find keys 1. _____
                 2. _____

Have a headache 1. _____
                 2. _____

Electricity goes out 1. _____
                      2. _____

Burn your hand 1. _____
                2. _____

A fly in the kitchen 1. _____
                      2. _____

Neighbour's dog won't stop barking 1. _____
                                    2. _____

Double-booked appointments 1. _____
                            2. _____

Fallen out with an old friend 1. _____
                               2. _____

Shrunk a knit in the wash 1. _____
                           2. _____

REASONING

ORDERED SYMBOLS 2

Pick the one statement that is CORRECT.

1. ☆ ○ □ △ ⇨

   A) Circle is right of Triangle.
   B) Square is between Star and Circle.
   C) Triangle is right of Square.
   D) Star is right of Circle.

2. ◇ + ☾ = ⬭

   A) Crescent is left of Plus.
   B) Diamond is left of Equals.
   C) Equals is right of Cylinder.
   D) Cylinder is fourth.

3. ☼ △ ♡ ○ ▭

   A) Triangle is right of Rectangle.
   B) Circle is between Sun and Heart.
   C) Heart is not in the middle.
   D) Sun is left of Triangle.

4. ⇨ △ ⬭ ♡ ◇

   A) Cylinder is right of Arrow.
   B) Heart is third.
   C) Diamond is left of Heart.
   D) Arrow is not first.

5. ⬭ ☆ = + △

   A) Star is right of Plus.
   B) Cylinder is right of Star.
   C) Plus is right of Star.
   D) Equals is fourth.

6. ○ ☾ ☼ △ ▭

   A) Crescent is right of Rectangle.
   B) Triangle is between Sun and Circle.
   C) Sun is left of Crescent.
   D) Circle is left of Triangle.

7. □ △ ▭ ◇ ♡

   A) Diamond is not fourth.
   B) Triangle is right of Rectangle.
   C) Rectangle is left of Square.
   D) Heart is right of Diamond.

8. = ☾ ⇨ ☆ +

   A) Star is between Arrow and Equals.
   B) Crescent is left of Star.
   C) Plus is left of Arrow.
   D) Equals is right of Crescent.

WORDS THAT HAM IT UP 1

The answer to each clue contain the letters "HAM."

1. A lizard that changes colour

   ANSWER _____

2. The river that runs through London

   ANSWER _____

3. A pounding tool

   ANSWER _____

4. Something fake that is presented as genuine

   ANSWER _____

5. To make movement or progress difficult

   ANSWER _____

6. A hair-cleaning product

   ANSWER _____

7. A meeting place of legislature or court

   ANSWER _____

8. A hanging bed made of canvas or netting

   ANSWER _____

COMPOUND WORDS 2

Make at least three compound words with these beginnings.

1. Bed _____ _____ _____

2. News _____ _____ _____

3. Lady _____ _____ _____

4. Pig _____ _____ _____

5. Hand _____ _____ _____

6. Life _____ _____ _____

7. Sand _____ _____ _____

8. Fire _____ _____ _____

9. Eye _____ _____ _____

10. Back _____ _____ _____

11. Rain _____ _____ _____

12. Moon _____ _____ _____

13. Butter _____ _____ _____

14. Book _____ _____ _____

15. Door _____ _____ _____

16. Head _____ _____ _____

SEQUENCING ITEMS 3

Discover a logical way to sequence these items, and explain the reason why you put them in that order. No alphabetical order allowed.

1. Algebra, Calculus, Geometry, Trigonometry

   1st _____ 2nd _____ 3rd _____ 4th _____

   Reason _____

2. *Chariots of Fire, Ben-Hur, Casablanca, The Sound of Music*

   1st _____ 2nd _____ 3rd _____ 4th _____

   Reason _____

3. Moon landing, Amelia Earhart, Berlin Wall torn down, United Nations founded

   1st _____ 2nd _____ 3rd _____ 4th _____

   Reason _____

4. Orange, Black, Yellow, Blue

   1st _____ 2nd _____ 3rd _____ 4th _____

   Reason _____

5. Reading a brochure, Running a marathon, Dialing a phone number, Writing a novel

   1st _____ 2nd _____ 3rd _____ 4th _____

   Reason _____

6. Put in mailbox, Stamp, Write letter, Address envelope

   1st _____ 2nd _____ 3rd _____ 4th _____

   Reason _____

7. Light match, Stack firewood, Dig hole, Gather kindling

   1st _____ 2nd _____ 3rd _____ 4th _____

   Reason _____

8. Belt, Shoes, Trousers, Socks

1st _____ 2nd _____ 3rd _____ 4th _____

Reason _____

9. Water, Dig hole, Cover with dirt, Place seed

1st _____ 2nd _____ 3rd _____ 4th _____

Reason _____

10. Constructing, Planning, Buying supplies, Designing

1st _____ 2nd _____ 3rd _____ 4th _____

Reason _____

11. Running, Jogging, Walking, Sprinting

1st _____ 2nd _____ 3rd _____ 4th _____

Reason _____

12. Anniversary, Courting, Vows, Reception

1st _____ 2nd _____ 3rd _____ 4th _____

Reason _____

13. Spain, Slovenia, Serbia, Switzerland

1st _____ 2nd _____ 3rd _____ 4th _____

Reason _____

14. Christmas Day, Halloween, Valentine's Day, Easter

1st _____ 2nd _____ 3rd _____ 4th _____

Reason _____

15. Change, Receipt, Pay, Choose

1st _____ 2nd _____ 3rd _____ 4th _____

Reason _____

MISSPELLED WORDS 2

Pick out the words that are misspelled words, and correct their spelling.

acceptible	_____	acomodate	_____
liason	_____	occasionally	_____
exhilarat	_____	personnel	_____
manoeuvre	_____	pastime	_____
receit	_____	guarranttee	_____
harass	_____	sargent	_____
greatful	_____	accidentally	_____
independent	_____	threshole	_____
miniscule	_____	humerous	_____
consensus	_____	ignorence	_____
lisenc	_____	milinium	_____
restaurant	_____	existence	_____
jewlry	_____	fiery	_____
rymth	_____	priority	_____

LANGUAGE

TWO COMMON LETTERS 4

Scan each line to find the two letters each word has in common. The letters are next to each other. Challenge yourself to go as quickly as you can.

Example: bounce and balance both have "ce"

1. although   fight   higher   ghost   laugh   _____

2. calmer   ailment   filmed   mailman   almond   _____

3. basket   bearskin   outskirt   sketch   masking   _____

4. afraid   carefree   frowning   unfreeze   suffrage   _____

5. billable   backstab   reasonable abstract   laborer   _____

6. butcher   fabulous   abundant   tabulate   debutant   _____

7. artistic   bruising   discern   baptism   finished   _____

8. assembly   amenable   dribble   humble   crucible   _____

9. banished   cheapen   coherent   heavenly   mustache   _____

10. conjured   justice   reinjured   adjunct   perjury   _____

BLANK CROSSWORD

Fill in the crossword with your own words. There is no one right answer.

LANGUAGE

MATCHING CLUES 6

Match two of the word-parts to make a word that fits the clue. Each word-part is used only once.

edi	bel	ble	ore
ong	bef	ble	hum

1. _____ preceding

   _____ to be in the rightful place

   _____ fit to eat

   _____ modest

bon	our	lab	ain
obt	mar	rib	ble

2. _____ to work hard

   _____ a ball of coloured glass

   _____ to acquire

   _____ narrow strips of fabric

WORDS WITH OUT

The answer to each clue contains the letters "OUT."

1. A sequence of actions regularly followed

   ANSWER _____

2. To put forth shoots of a plant

   ANSWER _____

3. To utter a loud call or cry

   ANSWER _____

4. A way directed along a specified course

   ANSWER _____

5. The projecting nose and mouth of an animal

   ANSWER _____

6. The period between childhood and adult age

   ANSWER _____

7. Money given as compensation or a dividend

   ANSWER _____

8. A person sent out ahead of a main force to gather information

   ANSWER _____

9. A small store selling fashionable clothes or accessories

   ANSWER _____

PARTS OF A WHAT? 1

Put these words into the most correct category.

lens	window	rudder	cord
deck	ignition	shutter	receiver
speaker	flash	hood	aperture
keypad	wheel	masthead	tiller

1. Parts of a camera

   _____   _____

   _____   _____

2. Parts of a phone

   _____   _____

   _____   _____

3. Parts of a car

   _____   _____

   _____   _____

4. Parts of a boat

   _____   _____

   _____   _____

REASONING

WHAT'S THAT PHRASE? 2

Fill in the letters to complete the familiar phrase. There is a clue to help.

1. E __ __ __ __ Y C __ __ __ D H __ __ __
   S __ __ __ __ R L __ __ __ __ G
   To be optimistic even in difficult times

2. F __ __ H O __ __ O __ W __ __ __ R
   Someone in a situation they are unfamiliar with or unsuited for

3. G __ F __ __ B __ __ __ E
   To risk it all

4. G __ O __ __ O __ A L __ __ __ __
   To put yourself in a risky situation to help someone

5. G __ __ __ Y T __ __ - S __ __ __ __ __
   A smugly virtuous person

6. H __ __ __ __ __ A __ A C __ __ __ __
   A state of being delighted

7. H __ __ D P __ __ L T __ S __ __ __ __ __ W
   Something that is difficult to accept

8. H __ __ __ O __ __ __ H __ __ __ __
   Fall deeply in love

9. I __ __ __ P __ __ __ __ __ __
   To be in a difficult situation

MEMORY

10. J __ __ __ - __ __ - A __ __ - T __ __ __ __ __ S

To have skill in multiple trades

11. J __ __ __ T __ __ G __ __

When something happens too early; starting too soon

12. K __ __ P O __ T __ __ __ __ __ __ N'

To press forward, not stop

13. K __ __ __ __ Y __ __ S __ __ __ __ O __ __

To be taken by surprise

14. A M __ __ __ __ __ __ __ O __ __ O __ __

M __ __ __ __ __ __ __

To escalate a small thing and turn it into a big problem

15. M __ C __ __ O __ T __ __

Something you find delightful

16. O __ C __ __ __ __ N __ __ __

Strong feelings of happiness and satisfaction

17. R __ __ __ O __ Y __ __ __ P __ __ __ __ __

To spoil someone's fun

LETTER TRANSFER 4

Fill in the word(s) to answer the clue, then transfer those numbered letters to the lines on the next page for the final message.

1. Elephant tusks are made out of this material

   ___ ___ ___ ___ ___
   1   2   3   4   5

2. This is the hardest substance known

   ___ ___ ___ ___ ___ ___ ___
   6 1 7 8 3 9 6

3. The last name of the second man on the moon

   ___ ___ ___ ___ ___ ___
   7 10 6 4 1 9

4. The Grand Canyon is in this state

   ___ ___ ___ ___ ___ ___ ___
   7 4 1 11 3 9 7

5. The name of the cartoon starring Charlie Brown

   ___ ___ ___ ___ ___ ___ ___
   12 13 7 9 14 15 16

6. The country where reggae music originated

— — — — — — —
17 7 8 7 1 18 7

7. The sport in which you would use a "sand iron"

— — — —
19 3 10 20

FINAL MESSAGE:

— — — — — — q— — — — — — — — —
7 19 13   1 16   7   14 13 16 15 1 3 9   3 20

— — — — — — — — — — — — —:
8 1 9 6   3 2 13 4   8 7 15 15 13 4

— — — — — — — — — — —, — — — — —,
1 20 5   3 14 6 3 9   15   8 1 9 6

— — — — — — —, — — — — — — —.
7 19 13   6 3 9 15   8 7 15 15 13 4

COMPLETE THE WORD SEARCH 2

First fill in the answers to the clues, then find those words in the word search grid.

The first letter and number of letters in the word are given.

1. To secretly get married   E __ __ __ __

2. Dried grass   H __ __

3. To give to a charity   D __ __ __ __ __

4. A doorway is an   E __ __ __ __ __ __ __

5. You inherit these   G __ __ __ __

6. To not listen to someone speaking   I __ __ __ __ __

7. To calm and train a horse   T __ __ __

8. A penny   C __ __ __

9. A large spoon you use to serve soup   L __ __ __ __

10. Formal choirs wear these   R __ __ __ __

MEMORY

COMPLETE THE WORD SEARCH 2

Words can be in any direction.

```
A  W  L  B  Q  R  M  T  H  E  P  R  A  L
D  F  Y  O  G  B  K  L  A  D  L  E  Q  Y
T  S  S  K  E  L  N  O  J  E  N  H  G  S
W  A  L  F  N  L  I  S  D  S  R  E  W  L
A  R  M  T  E  R  O  B  E  S  E  R  A  M
H  P  K  E  S  P  L  P  H  O  N  D  H  K
L  L  T  C  S  T  U  E  E  C  T  H  L  T
Q  H  A  Y  N  E  T  G  P  E  R  B  E  A
J  A  N  E  L  A  O  C  T  R  A  R  J  N
O  V  C  T  N  T  B  N  A  S  N  O  O  C
M  B  U  O  A  N  P  S  M  N  C  B  M  U
B  I  D  B  M  I  G  N  O  R  E  F  B  C
G  L  V  V  U  C  E  I  Y  K  J  L  G  V
```

UPSIDE DOWN

Determine which image is the original image upside down.

1. ANSWER _____

a.   b.   c.   d.

2. ANSWER _____

a.   b.   c.   d.

3. ANSWER _____

a.   b.   c.   d.

4. ANSWER _____

a.   b.   c.   d.

VISUAL–SPATIAL

HOT WORDS

The answer to each clue contains the letters "HOT."

1. An image produced on light-sensitive film

   ANSWER _____

2. A place for overnight stays

   ANSWER _____

3. An injection of a medicine

   ANSWER _____

4. A direct telephone link to a service, often available 24-7

   ANSWER _____

5. A small Y-shaped weapon used to propel objects

   ANSWER _____

6. The science of medical devices such as braces

   ANSWER _____

7. A person who has lost contact with reality

   ANSWER _____

8. A division into two groups of contradictory things

   ANSWER _____

LETTER-NUMBER SUBSTITUTION CODE 2

Using the code key, determine what words the numbers are spelling.

CODE KEY

A = 4	D = 92	U = 34	R = 23	O = 52
B = 19	E = 71	P = 87	S = 38	N = 96
C = 55	I = 26	L = 63	T = 45	V = 12

1. 4 87 87 63 26 55 4 19 63 71

WORD: _____

2. 87 23 4 55 45 26 55 71

WORD: _____

3. 71 23 4 92 26 55 4 45 71

WORD: _____

4. 23 71 87 63 26 55 4 45 71

WORD: _____

5. 92 71 38 87 26 55 4 19 63 71

WORD: _____

6. 87 23 71 92 26 55 45 4 19 63 71

WORD: _____

7. 71 92 34 55 4 45 26 52 96

WORD: _____

8. 4 63 63 52 55 4 45 71

WORD: _____

9. 23 71 12 52 55 4 19 63 71

WORD: _____

10. 55 4 19 26 96 71 45

WORD: _____

TWO DEFINITIONS 4

Two definitions for the same word are given. Fill in the correct word that matches both definitions.

1. A boat's standing area

   A stack of cards

   ANSWER _____

2. Not heavy

   Shines bright

   ANSWER _____

3. To sway back and forth

   Larger than a pebble

   ANSWER _____

4. Employees

   A walking stick

   ANSWER _____

5. Students receive these

   Scuffs or stains on a surface

   ANSWER _____

6. A short letter

   A musical component

   ANSWER _____

7. The answer after subtracting one number from another

   The quality that makes one thing unlike another

   ANSWER _____

8. The task of cleaning a fish to eat

   A tool to measure weight

   ANSWER _____

FIRST AND LAST LETTERS 3

Fill in the correct letters to make a word that matches the definition.

1. ___ antru ___   a burst of bad temper

2. ___ ola ___   a type of eclipse

3. ___ tla ___   a book of maps

4. ___ ea ___   to show the way

5. ___ ear ___   listened to

6. ___ eig ___   a royal rule

7. ___ bov ___   over

8. ___ ati ___   a silky smooth fabric

9. ___ in ___   fishing string

10. ___ is ___   an aspiration

11. ___ tai ___   a laundry problem

12. ___ ro ___   to let fall

CALENDAR QUIZ 4

Use the calendar clues to determine the correct date.

SUNDAY	MONDAY	TUESDAY	WEDNESDAY	THURSDAY	FRIDAY	SATURDAY
	1	2	3	4	5	6
7	8	9	10	11	12	13
14	15	16	17	18	19	20
21	22	23	24	25	26	27
28	29	30	31			

1. This date is in the last week of the month.

   It is on a weekend.

   What is the date? _____

2. This date is on a weekday.

   It is not a single digit.

   It is on a Friday.

   It does not begin with a 1.

   What is the date? _____

EXECUTIVE FUNCTIONING

3. This date is between the 2nd and the 19th .

   It is on a weekend.

   It is not in the first weekend of the month.

   It is not the 14th.

   What is the date? _____

4. This date is not in the first half of the month.

   It is not in the middle of the week.

   It begins with a 3.

   What is the date? _____

RAPPING WORDS

The answer to each clue contains the letters "RAP."

1. A device designed to allow entry but not exit

   ANSWER _____

2. To cover in paper or material

   ANSWER _____

3. A strip of material with a buckle used to secure or carry something

   ANSWER _____

4. Happening in a short time or at a fast pace

   ANSWER _____

5. To arrange cloth loosely or casually around something

   ANSWER _____

6. To push or pull a hard, sharp implement across a surface to remove matter

   ANSWER _____

7. To deceive or trick

   ANSWER _____

8. Relating to visual art

   ANSWER _____

LANGUAGE

ONE COMMON LETTER 1

Scan each line to find the one letter each word has in common. Challenge yourself to go as quickly as you can.

Example: baker and milk both have "k"

COMMON LETTER

1. accept	baptise	chirp	group	hippo	_____
2. sedan	adult	bends	blonde	tuned	_____
3. grump	bluff	church	aunt	menu	_____
4. radium	sermon	amazed	compass	manure	_____
5. parlour	Velcro	zealot	wallet	uphold	_____
6. entice	gothic	jockey	launch	peace	_____
7. abysmal	boyish	clingy	gypsy	hymnal	_____
8. jacket	banker	drunk	knife	parked	_____
9. finish	mashed	north	phlegm	school	_____
10. before	effect	faithful	softer	toffee	_____

MIDDLE LETTERS 3

Fill in the correct letters to make a word that matches the definition.

1. p ___ ___ a   an earnest request

2. n ___ ___ e   kind

3. t ___ ___ t   a camp shelter

4. i ___ ___ ___ r   not outer

5. a ___ ___ ___ e   an orchard fruit

6. m ___ ___ ___ c   to imitate

7. n ___ ___ ___ ___ e to deny

8. l ___ ___ e   fishing bait

9. t ___ ___ ___ e   not those

10. c ___ ___ ___ l   infants do this

11. p ___ ___ ___ l   a bicycle part

12. t ___ ___ d   a warty amphibian

LANGUAGE

MEMORY CROSSWORD 2

First, spend two minutes studying the words in this crossword. Then turn the page for a quiz.

```
                      D
A   C   C   R   U   E
M                   T
O           M   A   R   K   E   R
E                   I
B   U   S   H   E   L
A           I
            N
            G
```

MEMORY CROSSWORD 2

(DON'T LOOK AT THIS PAGE UNTIL YOU'VE STUDIED PREVIOUS PAGE.)

Now look at the list of words below and circle the words that were in the crossword on the previous page.

MARKER

PALE

GATOR

ACCRUE

AMOEBA

PROTON

MERRY

OFFICE

DETAIL

GARDEN

BUSHEL

SING

PRIZE

MEMORY

IMAGES MEMORY 3

First, spend two minutes studying the images. Then turn the page for a quiz.

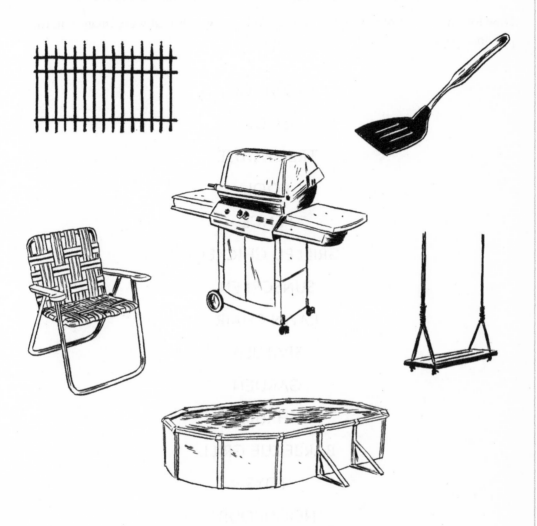

(DON'T LOOK AT THIS PAGE UNTIL YOU'VE STUDIED PREVIOUS PAGE.)

Now look at the list of words below and circle the words that were images on the previous page.

SWING

SLIDE

TREE HOUSE

POOL

FENCE

GRILLED CHICKEN

SUNSCREEN

LAWN CHAIR

SPATULA

GARDEN

SHRUBS

BARBECUE GRILL

TOYS

NEIGHBOUR

CALCULATION WORD PROBLEMS 4

1. A. You are painting bird houses to sell at a craft fair booth. You bought 15 bird houses that cost £6.98 each, and the paint costs £27. How much does each bird house cost to make?

   _____

   B. You want to make a profit on the birdhouses. If you sell them for £25 each, how much profit would you make on each birdhouse?

   _____

   C. If you sell all 15 birdhouses, how much total profit would you make?

   _____

2. A group of 4 friends go picking strawberries at a farm field. Each basket holds 8 strawberries and each friend brings back 3 baskets. How many total strawberries does the group have?

   _____

3. There were 562 people at the county fair when it started raining. Half of them went home and 24 waited in their cars to see if the rain would stop. How many people stayed outside to enjoy the county fair despite the rain?

   _____

4. A museum reports that 214 tickets were sold ahead of time for an art exhibit, but half of those people brought a friend with them to see the exhibit too and bought their tickets at the door. How many total people came to see the art exhibit?

   _____

5. Your grandson saved up 562 pennies to buy toys at the toy store. He wants to buy 6 army men that cost £0.85 each. Does he have enough money?

   _____

WORDS FULL OF AIR 2

The answer to each clue contains the letters "AIR."

1. A series of steps

   ANSWER _____

2. Strands growing on a head or body

   ANSWER _____

3. A small imaginary creature with magical powers

   ANSWER _____

4. Not equal or just

   ANSWER _____

5. A farm for milk production

   ANSWER _____

6. Two similar things used together

   ANSWER _____

7. An event or occurrence that is known about; a social event

   ANSWER _____

8. To fix or mend something

   ANSWER _____

LANGUAGE

MATCHING CLUES 7

Match two of the word-parts to make a word that fits the clue. Each word-part is used only once.

lev par pat en

ent tree el ade

1. _____ a formal procession

 _____ a type of leather

 _____ smooth

 _____ starter dish

ket ase no er

eal bas te id

2. _____ wicker carrier

 _____ rub out a mark

 _____ a quick letter

 _____ perfect

EDIT THE WORD 2

In the first column, change one letter in the original word to make a new word. In the second column, take out one letter from the original word and keep the rest of the letters in the same order to form a new word.

For example:

	CHANGE ONE LETTER	**TAKE OUT ONE LETTER**
Spank	Spark	Sank

		CHANGE ONE LETTER	**TAKE OUT ONE LETTER**
1.	Dusty	_____	_____
2.	Farm	_____	_____
3.	Rear	_____	_____
4.	Shut	_____	_____
5.	Fast	_____	_____
6.	What	_____	_____
7.	Here	_____	_____
8.	Pair	_____	_____

LANGUAGE

WHO IS THIS PERSON?

Determine the name of the person described by the clues.

1. This singer won an Oscar for *From Here to Eternity* in 1954 _____

2. This woman wrote *Silas Marner* and *The Mill on the Floss* _____

3. This political figure gave his "Iron Curtain" speech in 1946 _____

4. This author published his book *1984* in 1949 _____

5. This woman refused to give up her seat on a bus in 1955 _____

6. This film director released *Psycho* in 1960 _____

7. This president gave "The Man on the Moon" speech _____

8. This artist exhibited his piece *Campbell Soup Can* in 1962 _____

9. This pop singer was the frontman of The Shadows _____

10. This political figure gave a speech titled "I Have a Dream" _____

11. This woman became the first female Prime Minister of The United Kingdom _____

12. This American man was the first man on the moon _____

13. In 1974, this president was the first ever to resign _____

14. This TV mogul established BSkyB in 1990 _____

15. This actor starred in *Rebel Without a Cause* in 1955 _____

MEMORY

TWO COMMON LETTERS 5

Scan each line to find the two letters each word has in common. The letters are next to each other. Challenge yourself to go as quickly as you can.

Example: bounce and balance both have "ce"

COMMON LETTERS

1.	allows	floats	blooms	clowns	locker	_____
2.	alumni	solemn	hymnal	columns	gymnast	_____
3.	fabric	hubris	abroad	rubric	bruise	_____
4.	chewed	flower	glowed	skewer	towels	_____
5.	mildly	holder	seldom	yield	remold	_____
6.	gothic	behind	orchid	hinges	rhinos	_____
7.	whiskers	sketch	asking	frisky	risked	_____
8.	charge	margin	purged	target	argyle	_____
9.	protect	bootleg	brother	denote	idiotic	_____
10.	buckle	attack	clocks	pocket	unpack	_____

PROCESSING SPEED

SHAPE MATCH 3

Circle the two matching shapes.

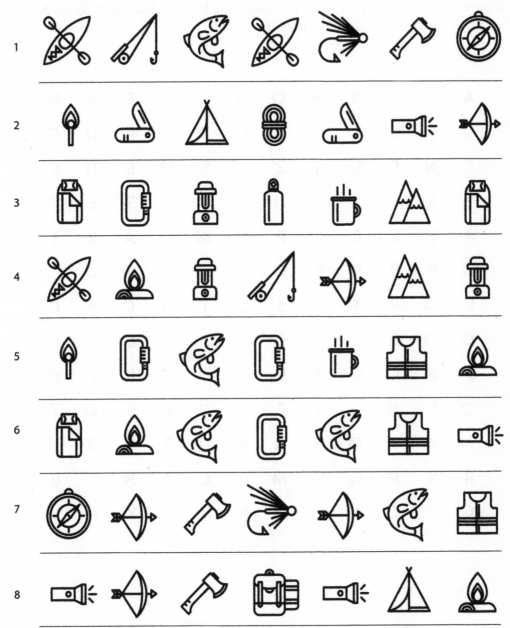

WORD MAZE – NEWS

Find your way through the maze by connecting letters to spell out words. Write the words on the next page. You may move forward, backward, up, or down, but no letters may be connected more than once.

START

END

VISUAL–SATIAL

WORDS

1. _____

2. _____

3. _____

4. _____

5. _____

6. _____

7. _____

8. _____

PARTS OF A WHAT? 2

Put these words into the most correct category.

path	attic	desks	wings
fertiliser	cockpit	notebooks	motor
pantry	rules	passengers	sunshine
staircase	rulers	fountain	foyer

1. Parts of a house

_____   _____

_____   _____

2. Parts of a classroom

_____   _____

_____   _____

3. Parts of an airplane

_____   _____

_____   _____

4. Parts of a garden

_____   _____

_____   _____

REASONING

WORDS THAT HAM IT UP 2

The answer to each clue contains the letters "HAM."

1. A small rodent with cheek pouches

   ANSWER _____

2. Negative emotion; state of disgrace

   ANSWER _____

3. A white sparkling wine for special occasions

   ANSWER _____

4. A patty of ground meat

   ANSWER _____

5. A dried flower head used to make an herbal tea

   ANSWER _____

6. Disorganised failure; a state of messy disorder

   ANSWER _____

7. Supreme victor in a contest

   ANSWER _____

8. Leg tendon

   ANSWER _____

LANGUAGE

CODING – LANGUAGES

Use the key code below to decode the words. Each space is one letter. Challenge yourself to go as quickly as you can. All of these words are in the category: **LANGUAGES**.

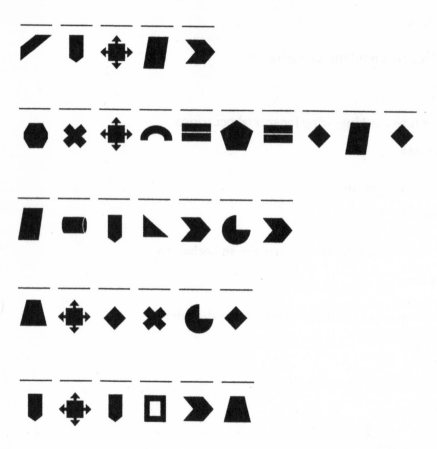

KEY CODE

A B C D E F G H I J K L M

N O P Q R S T U V W X Y Z

SYMBOL CODING 5

Write the number that corresponds to each symbol in the empty boxes below. Challenge yourself to do this as quickly as you can, while maintaining accuracy. Do not do all of one symbol at a time, complete each box in a row moving from left to right, and then continue to the next line.

KEY CODE

1	2	3	4	5	6	7	8	9
△	T	\	◯	◇	✚	⬈	▭	✕

2	9	8	5	1	4	7	3	6	8
6	3	1	7	2	5	9	8	2	1
2	4	6	9	5	3	4	7	1	8
1	5	2	4	7	9	3	6	8	3
3	6	7	8	3	4	9	1	2	5
5	9	1	4	2	7	5	9	8	6
4	1	6	8	2	9	3	5	4	2
7	9	3	1	4	2	7	8	5	6

LOGIC WORD PROBLEMS 5

These word problems require you to use the process of elimination to find the answer. It helps to use the grid below.

X = No, not the correct answer; O = Yes, the correct answer

Using the clues, fill in the grid with Xs and Os. When there is only one choice left in a row or column, put an O there. Because it is the only option left, it is the correct answer. If a clue tells you the correct choice, you can put an O in that box and put Xs in the rest of the column and row because the other options cannot be correct too. Work through all of the clues this way.

1. Jerry was landscaping his back garden and trying to bring in a lot of different colours. He wanted a fruit tree, a rosebush, a scrub with flowers, and a succulent plant with a bloom. Can you determine what colour each item was?

	RED	ORANGE	YELLOW	PINK
FRUIT TREE				
ROSEBUSH				
SCRUB				
SUCCULENT				

CLUES

a. Apples are Jerry's favourite fruit, so he definitely wanted those in his garden.
b. The succulent did not have a pink or yellow bloom.
c. Jerry could not find a scrub with pink blooms.

2. Each of Bonnie's grandchildren play a different sport. Can you determine who plays which sport?

	CRICKET	SOCCER	BASKETBALL	GOLF
BILLY				
KEVIN				
SANDRA				
KELLY				

CLUES

a. Kevin wants to be a cricketer player when he grows up.

b. Sandra has never wanted to play any team sport.

c. Kelly can't use her hands in her sport.

REASONING

MISMATCH 3

Pick out the one item that does not fit the category, and explain the *reason* why it does not fit.

1. Jazz, Opera, Classical, Guitar

   Mismatch item_____

   *Reason*_____

2. Sailboat, Jet ski, Kayak, Canoe

   Mismatch item_____

   *Reason*_____

3. Oboe, Flute, Piano, Clarinet

   Mismatch item_____

   *Reason*_____

4. Roses, Lilies, Daisies, Thistle

   Mismatch item_____

   *Reason*_____

5. Blue, Hues, Tints, Shades

   Mismatch item_____

   *Reason*_____

6. Echo, Movement, Hum, Buzz

   Mismatch item_____

   *Reason*_____

7. Volume, Sound, Clamor, Bright

   Mismatch item_____

   *Reason*_____

EXECUTIVE FUNCTIONING

8. Painter, Cartoonist, Sculptor, Illustrator

Mismatch item_____

*Reason*_____

9. Baubles, Jewellery, Lights, Tinsel

Mismatch item_____

*Reason*_____

10. Loop, Ring, Clang, Jingle

Mismatch item_____

*Reason*_____

11. Seeds, Juice, Nectar, Sap

Mismatch item_____

*Reason*_____

12. Store, House, Apartment, Studio

Mismatch item_____

*Reason*_____

13. Mandate, Inquire, Query, Probe

Mismatch item_____

*Reason*_____

14. Lift, Boost, Raise, Advance

Mismatch item_____

*Reason*_____

15. Spaniel, Fox, Hound, Retriever

Mismatch item_____

*Reason*_____

16. Pretzels, Nuts, Peppers, Crisps

Mismatch item_____

*Reason*_____

17. Headland, Island, Peninsula, Cape

Mismatch item_____

*Reason*_____

PARTS OF A WHAT? 3

Put these words into the most correct category.

lyrics	board	cards	a toast
cover	harmony	applause	rules
chapters	speech	players	characters
decorations	instruments	chorus	index

1. Parts of a book

   _____   _____

   _____   _____

2. Parts of a game

   _____   _____

   _____   _____

3. Parts of a ceremony

   _____   _____

   _____   _____

4. Parts of a song

   _____   _____

   _____   _____

REASONING

REARRANGE THESE

Rearrange the letters of these words to create a new word.

1. Friend _____
2. March _____
3. Talks _____
4. Eager _____
5. Meats _____
6. Ought _____
7. Peaks _____
8. Brief _____
9. Field _____
10. Verse _____
11. Melon _____
12. Ports _____
13. Shelf _____
14. Grate _____
15. Hooks _____
16. Needs _____
17. Votes _____
18. Hoses _____
19. Items _____
20. Night _____
21. Relay _____
22. Roses _____
23. Shout _____
24. Lapse _____
25. Ocean _____
26. Warts _____
27. Siren _____
28. Panel _____
29. Spray _____
30. Parks _____
31. Races _____
32. Saint _____
33. Shrub _____
34. Study _____
35. Vases _____
36. Causes _____

LANGUAGE

TWO DEFINITIONS 5

Two definitions for the same word are given. Fill in the correct word that matches both definitions.

1. A large furry animal

To carry a large load

ANSWER _____

2. A shepherd's stick

To provide workforce

ANSWER _____

3. Power

To state a possibility

ANSWER _____

4. The edge of a river

A place to store money

ANSWER _____

5. To have permission to do something

A month of the year

ANSWER _____

6. A place to wash your hands

To not float

ANSWER _____

7. To stumble

A vacation

ANSWER _____

8. The noise of a clock

A parasite

ANSWER _____

9. The stem of a plant

To follow

ANSWER _____

"L" WORDS

Using two clues, fill in the correct word that begins with "L."

1. To strike with a whip
   Eyelid
   ANSWER _____

2. A fine knitted fabric
   A part of a sneaker
   ANSWER _____

3. To be in charge
   To take someone by the hand
   ANSWER _____

4. To go back in a chair
   A sloping position
   ANSWER _____

5. Behind schedule
   Near the end of a time period
   ANSWER _____

6. Most recent in time
   Final
   ANSWER _____

7. Attached to a stem
   To turn pages quickly
   ANSWER _____

8. It will be returned
   To contribute to
   ANSWER _____

9. Unable to find your way
   Can't be recovered
   ANSWER _____

10. To overlap sheets of a substance
    A covering
    ANSWER _____

11. A narrow horizontal strip of paper attached to an object to describe it
    A company that produces music
    ANSWER _____

12. To go away from
    To allow to remain
    ANSWER _____

LANGUAGE

13. A traditional story
A famous person

ANSWER _____

14. Legitimate

Permitted by law

ANSWER _____

15. Probably

Might happen or be true

ANSWER _____

16. Makes things visible

Ignite

ANSWER _____

MATCHING CLUES 8

Match two of the word-parts to make a word that fits the clue. Each word-part is used only once.

key   bas   oke   nk

ket   bla   don   br

1. _____ carries things

_____ bare or plain

_____ out of money

_____ a hoofed mammal

eal   ely   ker   ke

hi   app   ep   lik

2. _____ climbs mountains

_____ an urgent request

_____ to retain possession

_____ probable

LANGUAGE

ONE COMMON LETTER 2

Scan each line to find the one letter each word has in common. Challenge yourself to go as quickly as you can.

Example: baker and milk both have "k"

						COMMON LETTER
1.	debtor	fabric	abroad	harbor	phobic	_____
2.	bestow	growth	fellow	newest	reward	_____
3.	eagle	forget	digest	jingle	malign	_____
4.	belief	citrus	avidly	filter	hobbit	_____
5.	funder	ground	extinct	inhale	lineage	_____
6.	Frisbee	gators	hinder	inward	longer	_____
7.	savour	cavity	evict	gravel	wolves	_____
8.	lumbar	insult	jurors	mumble	outrun	_____
9.	fajita	hijack	deject	adjoin	unjust	_____
10.	filter	adopt	busted	country	invite	_____

CREATE YOUR OWN FAMILY TREE

Fill in the names of your family in the appropriate positions. Add or take away more children or grandchildren as needed. If you have great-grandchildren, add them too.

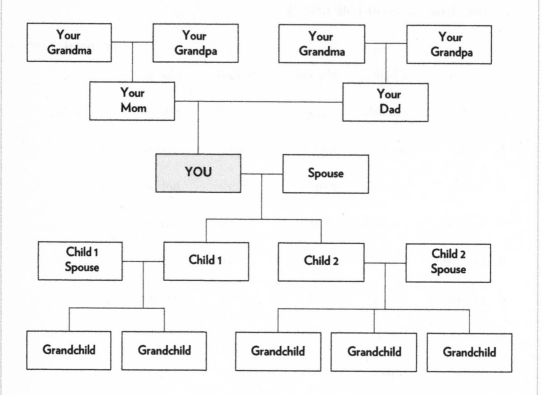

MEMORY

AN INVITATION— KEEP GOING!

SO **HOW DO** you feel after 201 exercises for your brain? Do you feel like you can think a little clearer, a little faster? Well then keep going! Your brain exercise regimen should not stop here. Research supports that brain stimulation must be regular and long-term in order for it to make a real difference. Just like physical exercise, we don't stop after a few months and expect the benefits to last. You must keep challenging your brain.

Find unique and novel activities in which to engage. From simple tasks like driving a different way home to more difficult tasks like learning a new instrument, do all you can to stimulate your brain. We can often live on autopilot, just going through the motions of habit. Break your habits! Try new things! If you have never done crafts before, try painting or making pottery. Every small action counts towards building up brain strength!

You really can keep your brain stronger for longer!

ANSWERS

GRANDCHILDREN COMPARISONS   pages 2–3

1. 1st Melanie, 2nd Patrick, 3rd Jimmy, 4th Cathy
2. 1st Lucy, 2nd Tom, 3rd Sally, 4th Amber
3. 1st Kate, 2nd Joe, 3rd Henry
4. 1st Marie, 2nd Neil, 3rd Yvonne, 4th Albert
5. 1st Robert, 2nd Olivia, 3rd Tamra, 4th Louie
6. 1st Vivian 44 pts, 2nd Eva 36 pts, 3rd William 32 pts

TWO DEFINITIONS 1   page 4

1. Box
2. Shade
3. Trunk
4. Bright
5. Foot
6. Rock
7. Punch
8. State

MATCHING CLUES 1   page 5

1. Banjo, rebel, jewel, joint
2. Joke, ajar, bake, back

SEQUENCING ITEMS 1   pages 6–7

The answers listed can go in either direction.

1. **Smallest to largest:** Flea, Ladybug, Bumblebee, Butterfly
2. **Shortest to longest duration:** Month, Semester/term, Fiscal year, Centennial
3. **Process of sculpting wood:** Chop, Carve, Sand, Paint
4. **Smallest to largest:** Millimetre, Centimetre, Metre, Kilometre
5. **Process of a buying house:** Credit check pre-approval, Offer, Escrow, Mortgage
6. **Process of starting a car:** Fasten seat belt, Check mirrors, Put into drive, Press gas pedal
7. **Process of baking:** Gather ingredients, Mix, Pour into pan, Bake
8. **Smallest to largest:** Pebble, Boulder, Hill, Mountain
9. **Process of digestion:** Mouth, Stomach, Small intestine, Large intestine
10. **Lifecycle of a butterfly:** Egg, Caterpillar, Cocoon, Butterfly
11. **Path of the sun:** Dawn, High noon, Dusk, Night
12. **Route of oxygen through the body:** Nose, Lungs, Blood, Body tissue
13. **Process of making yogurt:** Cow, Milk, Bacteria, Yogurt
14. **Process of getting accepted to university:** Application, Interview, Acceptance, Attendance
15. **Scientific method:** Hypothesis, Experiment, Analysis, Results

FAMILY TREE GAME 1   page 8

1. Leo
2. Susan
3. Mallory
4. Mallory and Mack
5. Mark
6. Loren

BOXED LETTERS – CARDS   pages 9–11

1. Go Fish
2. Poker
3. Hearts
4. Gin Rummy
5. Spades
6. Blackjack

TWO-LETTER PLACEMENT 1   page 12

1. order
2. adhere
3. brew
4. farm or form
5. dreary
6. average
7. case or care
8. hard or herd
9. cotton
10. plural
11. short
12. career
13. spray
14. orchard
15. secret
16. store
17. parent
18. argue
19. greed
20. early
21. coerce
22. marginal
23. origin
24. guard
25. insert
26. aversion
27. closet
28. scorn
29. laptop
30. thread
31. ceramic
32. toast
33. erase
34. cork

DECIPHER THE LETTER CODE 1   page 13

Message: When everything is coming your way, you are in the wrong lane.

WHAT'S THAT PHRASE? 1   pages 14–15

1. A dime a dozen
2. A piece of cake
3. An arm and a leg
4. It's all Greek to me

5. Back to the drawing board
6. Beat around the bush
7. Between a rock and a hard place
8. Break the ice
9. Burst your bubble
10. Close but no cigar
11. Cut to the chase
12. Down for the count
13. Down to the wire
14. Dropping like flies
15. Easy as pie
16. Elephant in the room

COUNT THE Us   page 16

There are 72 Us.

AGING WORDS 1   page 17

1. Cage
2. Language
3. Collagen
4. Corkage
5. Blockage
6. Cottage
7. Garbage
8. Heritage

DOMINO ORDER 1   page 18

Here is one possible order:

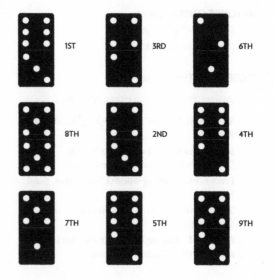

VENN DIAGRAM – LANGUAGES   page 19

1. 20 people
2. All three languages
3. 5 people
4. 70 people
5. 25 people
6. 65 people

DOT COPY 1   page 20

Go back and check yourself, or have a friend check your copied design.

SHAPE MATCH 1   page 21

1. 2nd and 6th shapes match
2. 1st and 5th shapes match
3. 2nd and 6th shapes match
4. 3rd and 6th shapes match
5. 2nd and 5th shapes match
6. 4th and 7th shapes match
7. 1st and 5th shapes match
8. 3rd and 5th shapes match

LETTER TRANSFER 1   page 22

1. Trumpet
2. China
3. Alaska
4. Basketball
5. Abbey Road
6. Golf
7. Whale
8. Juvenile

Final message: Always remember you are unique, just like everybody else.

CODING – FAMILY   page 23

1. Cousin
2. Niece
3. Grandma
4. In-Law
5. Relative

MATCHING CLUES 2   page 24

1. Tarot, Degree, Siren, Rude
2. Rare, Step, Tarp, Late

FIRST AND LAST LETTERS 1   page 25

1. Crate
2. Restore
3. Press
4. Atone
5. Address
6. Peel
7. Untie
8. Note
9. Demo
10. Sheer
11. Oval
12. Trial

WORD MAZE – A LAZY SUNDAY   pages 26–27

1. Newspaper
2. Coffee
3. Donuts
4. Slippers
5. Long
6. Walk
7. Big
8. Meal
9. Family

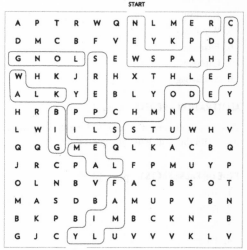

LOGIC WORD PROBLEMS 1   page 28

1. Billy – Dog
   Sally – Cat
   Cathy – Gerbil
   John – Fish
2. Irma – Banana
   Betty – Grapes
   Ralph – Orange
   Jim – Apple

MIDDLE LETTERS 1   page 29

1. Atom
2. Outer
3. Agree
4. Arena
5. Dart
6. Alone
7. Sweep
8. Aroma
9. Slept
10. Oxen
11. Value
12. Stare

BAGS OF WORDS   page 30

1. Bagel
2. Airbag
3. Baguette
4. Handbag
5. Windbag
6. Beanbag
7. Cabbage
8. Saddlebag

ALLITERATION – PEOPLE   page 31

There is no one correct answer. As long as every word starts with the same letter you got it right.

TRUE OR FALSE FACTS 1   pages 32–33

1. True
2. False
3. False
4. True
5. False
6. True
7. False
8. True
9. False
10. False
11. True
12. False
13. False
14. False
15. False
16. True
17. True
18. True
19. True
20. True
21. False
22. True
23. False
24. True

SYMBOL CODING 1   page 34

Go back and check yourself, or have a friend check your answers.

LETTERS-TO-WORD MATCH 1   page 35

Acquit, Blouse, Busier, Calmer, Damsel, Detach, Finest, Harden, Magnet, Parent

THREE-LETTER PLACEMENT 1   pages 36–37

1. radar
2. slogan
3. aerobic
4. frosting
5. apparent
6. fanatic
7. instinct
8. bicycle
9. darken
10. sales, dares, tines, or fanes
11. reverent
12. infant
13. accusal
14. matinee
15. boundary
16. elegant
17. salad
18. arrogant
19. retina
20. bicker, tinker, or darker
21. organise
22. salvage

23. tingle
24. profane
25. strength
26. darling
27. cubicle
28. organ
29. fancy
30. outing
31. biceps
32. wrench
33. salute

ONLY THREE CLUES   page 38
1. Basement
2. Park
3. Towel
4. Vacuum
5. Bottle

WHAT'S THE CATEGORY? 1   page 39
1. **Hardware store:** cabinet handles, ladder, wall mounts, concrete mix, floor wax, duct tape
2. **Park:** hikers, strollers, poison ivy, landmark, slide, fire pit
3. **Office:** printer, paper weight, books, calculator, to-do list, stamps

UNITS OF TIME 1   pages 40–41
1. 240 minutes
2. 9,000 seconds
3. 5 hours
4. 9:00 p.m.
5. 6:00 a.m.
6. 10:00 a.m.
7. 10:50 a.m.
8. 2 hours and 20 minutes, 10:10 a.m.
9. Since the flight time is 3 ½ hours you can't catch the 1:00 p.m., you'll have to take the 7:50 p.m. flight.
10. 1 hours and 47 minutes, 12:22 p.m.
11. 2 hours and 15 minutes, 4:15 p.m.
12. 8:00 – 10:00 p.m.

"B" WORDS   pages 42–43
1. Buzz
2. Blow
3. Box
4. Buck
5. Buff

6. Back
7. Bow
8. Badger
9. Band
10. Bat
11. Bend
12. Blue
13. Board
14. Blush
15. Book
16. Brittle
17. Broke
18. Bait

WHAT IS THIS CALLED?   page 44
1. Clothes peg
2. Teddy bear
3. Pom-poms
4. Quilt
5. Bicycle
6. Fossil
7. Cricket or grasshopper
8. Fishing
9. Checkmate
10. Credit card
11. Cross-country skiing
12. Subtitles

DOMINO ORDER 2   page 45
Here is one possible order:

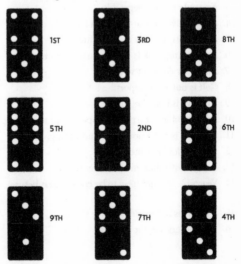

VENN DIAGRAM – BOOKS   page 46

1. 135 people
2. Romance
3. 0 people
4. 165 people
5. 75 people
6. 135 people

DECIPHER THE LETTER CODE 2   page 47

Message: Half of the people in the world are below average.

AGING WORDS 2   page 48

1. Mortgage
2. Salvage
3. Courage
4. Foliage
5. Marriage
6. Shortage
7. Manager
8. Sabotage

COUNT THE Ts AND Ps   page 49

There are 22 Ts and 19 Ps.

MISMATCH 1   pages 50–51

1. A tooth is not a type of store.
2. An eagle does not have four legs.
3. An apple is not a vegetable.
4. A shark lives in water, not on land.
5. A parrot is the only one that flies.
6. A colouring book is not a construction toy.
7. An eraser does not write.
8. Golf is not a team sport.
9. Dissolve is not a beginning.
10. Admission is not a physical opening to a building.
11. Separate is not a noun to name a thing.
12. Various does not mean one.
13. Inch is not a fluid measurement.
14. Vegetables do not have to be cooked first before eating.
15. A resort is not mandatory for skiing.
16. Helicopters are not in space

SIMILAR PROPERTIES   page 52

1. Have scales
2. Made of H_2O
3. Natural disasters
4. Can be cracked
5. Keep things together
6. Can be used to purchase items
7. Should be followed
8. Seasons
9. Must aim for them, or can hit them
10. Christmas decorations
11. Have caps
12. Grow on a stalk

BOXED LETTERS – GAMES   pages 53–55

1. Monopoly
2. Battleship
3. Scrabble
4. Chess
5. Charades
6. Pictionary

LETTER TRANSFER 2   pages 56–57

1. Orange
2. Declaration of Independence
3. Pennsylvania
4. New Orleans
5. Himalayas
6. Einstein

Final message: When it comes to thought, some people stop at nothing.

PROFESSIONAL CHARACTERISTICS   page 58

1. CEO: articulate, ability to delegate, confident
2. Artist: creativity, spontaneous, inspired
3. Physician: logical, empathetic, thorough
4. Soldier: courage, loyal, endurance
5. There are no right or wrong answers!

CALCULATION WORD PROBLEMS 1   page 59

1. 3 baking cups
2. 7 stickers each, 2 are left over
3. 19 pages for 20 days and 20 pages for 10 days
4. £250
5. 16 birds
6. 21 feet, 0 inches

CALENDAR QUIZ 1   pages 60–61

1. Wednesday the 9th
2. Sunday the 13th
3. Tuesday the 22nd
4. Tuesday the 22nd

A BIT OF WORDS   page 62

1. Orbit
2. Rabbit
3. Habit
4. Debit
5. Prohibit
6. Exhibit
7. Arbitrary
8. Inhabit

WHAT COMES NEXT?   page 63

1. Blue – ROYGBIV colour spectrum order
2. Sol – Musical tone order
3. King – Hierarchy of royalty
4. Decade – Lengths of times
5. Continent – Locations, small to large
6. Scream – Voice volumes
7. Full house – Rank of poker hands
8. Shoulder – Joints, working up the arm
9. Queen – Rank order of chess pieces

PLACEMENT OF LETTERS 1   pages 64–65

1. ecology
   amplify
   infancy
   fashion
   benefit
   tactful
   diffuse
   officer
2. perform
   clarify
   testify
   factory
   unfolds
   golfing
   waffles
   justify
3. refusal
   enlarge
   careful
   footage
   enforce
   brought
   finance
   traffic
4. selfish
   defence
   wishful
   fantasy
   diagram
   certify
   garbage
   helpful

ABBREVIATIONS AND ACRONYMS   page 66

1. Captain
2. United Nations
3. Association
4. Established
5. Absence without leave
6. Incorporated
7. Bachelor of Arts
8. Centimetre
9. Kilogram
10. Pound
11. Et cetera
12. Carbon copy, cubic centimeter, chief clerk, closed-captioned, common carrier, community college, and country club
13. Limited
14. Miles per hour
15. Colonel
16. North Atlantic Treaty Organisation
17. Ounce
18. Street or saint

LETTERS-TO-WORD MATCH 2   page 67

Active, Actual, Bounce, Bleach, Canopy, Cashew, Ethics, Factor, Mascot, Pickle

A BAN IN WORDS   page 68

1. Bandit
2. Bandana
3. Disband
4. Banquet
5. Abandon
6. Banister
7. Suburban
8. Banjo
9. Banal
10. Banish

SYMBOL CODING 2   page 69

Go back and check yourself, or have a friend check your answers.

UNITS OF TIME 2   page 70

1. 840 minutes
2. 18,900 seconds
3. 3 hours
4. 2:00 a.m.
5. 7:00 a.m.
6. 7:15 a.m.
7. 5:34 p.m., 26 minutes
8. 1:00 p.m. – 5:00 p.m. EST

DECIPHER THE LETTER CODE 3 page 71

Message: Middle age is when your age starts to show around your middle.

COUNT THE Ys AND Is page 72

There are 35 Ys and Is

AGING WORDS 3 page 73

1. Eager
2. Voyage
3. Wreckage or carnage
4. Wage
5. Village
6. Engage
7. Message
8. Luggage or baggage

DOMINO ORDER 3 page 74

Here is one possible order:

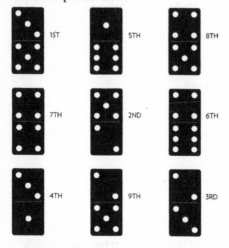

VENN DIAGRAM – MUSIC page 75

1. 308 people
2. 66 people
3. 132 people
4. Rock
5. 132 people
6. 154 people

CALENDAR QUIZ 2 pages 76–77

1. Thursday the 8th
2. Tuesday the 27th
3. Thursday the 15th
4. Wednesday the 7th

DISCOVER THE PATTERN 1 page 78

1. 37, 60, 97, 157; each number is the sum of the 2 preceding numbers
2. 30, 38, 47, 57; add 3, add 4, add 5, add 6
3. 30, 18, 4; subtract 2, subtract 4, subtract 6, subtract 8
4. 88, 144, 234, 380; add the 2 preceding numbers plus 2
5. 3,584, 14,336, 57,344; multiply by 4 each step
6. 540, 1,080, 3,240, 6,480; multiply by 3, multiply by 2, multiply by 3, multiply by 2
7. 10, 6, 8, 4, 6; add 2, subtract 4, add 2, subtract 4
8. 26, 20, 13, 5; subtract 2, subtract 3, subtract 4, subtract 5
9. 34, 40, 46, 52, 58; add 6 each step
10. 205, 1,025, 1,030, 5,150; add 5, multiply by 5, add 5, multiply by 5

CLOCK QUIZ 1 page 79

1. 3:00 p.m.
2. 8:40 p.m.
3. 3:15 a.m.
4. 11:15 p.m.

TWO COMMON LETTERS 1 page 80

1. ji
2. pt
3. em
4. gh
5. pu
6. ew
7. lv
8. di
9. ka
10. rr

HOW MANY WORDS? 1   page 81

The answers in these lists are not exhaustive.

1. **Idiosyncratic**: idiot, dictionary, indicator, syndicator, rancid, crayon, dystonic, acidity, cystoid, scant, candy, acid, corn, crony, sync, city, coy, icy, cry, can, cod, in

2. **Scramble**: marble, calm, cable, blame, ramble, lamb, camel, clams, balm, carb, crab, scab, beam, lab, be, me

ALLITERATION – CELEBRITIES   page 82

There is no one correct answer. As long as every word starts with the same letter you got it right.

TWO DEFINITIONS 2   page 83

1. Rare
2. Polka
3. Range
4. Over
5. Row
6. Saw
7. Coast
8. Fly

A BID ON WORDS   page 84

1. Abide
2. Morbid
3. Forbid
4. Libido
5. Rabid
6. Counterbid

IMAGES MEMORY 1   pages 85–86

Shell, Towel, Umbrella, Starfish, Shovel, Flip-flops

WHAT IS THIS LOCATION?   page 87

1. Cape Canaveral
2. Mount Everest
3. Dover
4. China
5. New Orleans
6. Antarctica
7. Cambodia
8. Rome
9. Ben Nevis
10. Pacific Ocean
11. San Francisco Bay
12. Pearl Harbour
13. Nevada
14. Dubai
15. Moscow

COMPLETE THE WORD SEARCH 1   pages 88–89

1. Egg
2. Irony
3. Essential
4. Tab
5. Pisa
6. Candid
7. Swift
8. Ponytail
9. Vest
10. Net

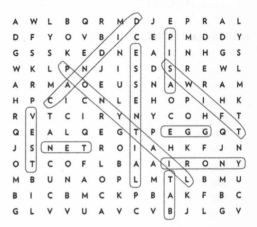

LETTER-NUMBER SUBSTITUTION CODE 1   page 90

1. Landmark
2. Camaraderie
3. Marionette
4. Outsmart
5. Marathon
6. Demarcate
7. Customary
8. Marginal
9. Grammar
10. Premarital

MISSPELLED WORDS 1   page 91

weigh, calendar, library, column, conscience, exceed, foreign, discipline, intelligence, address, noticeable, balance, until, weather, argument, believe

LOGIC WORD PROBLEMS 2   page 92

1. Helen – Chocolate
   Frank – Coconut
   Eddy – Custard
   Joyce – Raspberry
   Emma – Apple
2. Lou – Red bike
   Connie – Yellow car
   Stuart – Silver bus

WHAT'S THE CATEGORY? 2   page 93

1. **Sporting goods:** baseball, boots, fishing net, cricket helmet, sweatshirts, umbrellas
2. **Mechanic:** brake light, grease, overalls, wrench, jack, seat cover
3. **Electronics:** headphones, camera, wire cable, power cord, book light, adapters

FIRST AND LAST LETTERS 2   page 94

1. Aisle
2. Rise
3. Gasp
4. More
5. Blade
6. Mascot
7. Test
8. Mane
9. Edit
10. Stir
11. Dear
12. Idea

ORDERED LETTERS 1   page 95

1. d
2. c
3. a
4. d
5. c
6. b
7. d
8. c

SHARED FOOD LETTERS   page 96

1. soup
2. beef
3. cake
4. salad
5. bread
6. raisin
7. cookie
8. cream
9. fish
10. pie

SHAPE ADDITION   page 97

1. c
2. b
3. d
4. b
5. c
6. a
7. c
8. d

PURCHASING PROBLEMS   pages 98–99

1. Remote control car and colouring book
2. Skillet, boiling pot, and serving dish
3. Cheese, deli meat, and crackers
4. Calculator and pencils
5. Beef, broccoli, and rice
6. Couch, armchair, and end table

DECIPHER THE LETTER CODE 4   page 100

Message: I always wanted to be somebody, but now I realise I should have been more specific.

COUNT THE VOWELS   page 101

There are 120 vowels.

AGING WORDS 4   page 102

1. Pageant
2. Rummage
3. Wager
4. Agenda
5. Image
6. Garage
7. Agent
8. Pages

DOMINO ORDER 4 page 103

Here is one possible order:

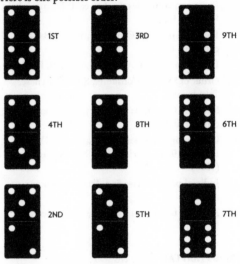

1ST   3RD   9TH

4TH   8TH   6TH

2ND   5TH   7TH

VENN DIAGRAM – TRANSPORTATION page 104

1. 408 people
2. Train
3. 204 people
4. 170 people
5. 102 people
6. 102 people

NAME SOMETHING 1 page 105

The answers listed are not exhaustive.

1. P professions: physician, publicist, psychologist, photographer, pharmacist
2. S professions: surgeon, scientist, social worker, surveyor, statistician
3. M books/movies: *Moby Dick, Macbeth, Madame Bovary, Malcolm X, Miracle on 34th Street*

LETTERS-TO-WORD MATCH 3 page 106

Absurd, Botany, Gravel, Hornet, Injure, Jockey, Kindle, Longer, Mobile, Pardon

WHAT'S NEXT? 1 page 107

1. c
2. b
3. a
4. b
5. a
6. c
7. b

CALCULATION WORD PROBLEMS 2 page 108

1. 34 total items; 18 flowers and 16 apples
2. 0 feet 5 inches
3. 5 pies
4. 4 gallons will last 16 days
5. 16 feet
6. 10 times

ACCOMPLISH THIS TASK 1 page 109

Here are two possible answers for each task

Keep papers together: staple them; put them in clear plastic wallets
Join two pieces of wood: use hanner and nails; bind them together with rope
Make a blanket: hand sew squares together; learn how to knit or crochet
Climb a hill: run up; ask for a lift
Travel across the country: hitchhike; join a long-distance cycling group
Clean the car: visit a drive-through carwash; get a bucket of soapy water and handwash it
Cook an egg breakfast: a quick scramble; make an omelette loaded with healthy ingredients
Catch up on current events: read the newspaper; see what's trending online

BAD WORDS page 110

1. Badge
2. Forbade
3. Badminton
4. Badger
5. Badmouth
6. Troubadour

MATCH THE PARTS 1 page 111

1. dancer
   accuse
   leader
   formal
   botany
   parade
   canary
   reason

2. enlist
   cavity
   images
   invent
   linear
   sodium
   active
   frolic

TWO COMMON LETTERS 2 page 112

1. fa
2. eb
3. ra
4. un
5. ct
6. pa
7. sc
8. ir
9. ey
10. rl

DISCOVER THE PATTERN 2   page 113

1. **14, 18, 22, 26**; add 4 each step
2. **80, 160, 320, 640**; multiply by 2 each step
3. **5, 7, 6, 8, 7**; add 2, subtract 1, add 2, subtract 1
4. **16, 14, 18, 16, 20**; add 4, subtract 2, add 4, subtract 2
5. **32, 128, 64, 256, 128**; multiply by 4, divide by 2, multiply by 4, divide by 2
6. **45, 42, 126, 123, 369**; multiply by 3, subtract 3, multiply by 3, subtract 3
7. **20, 20, 25, 25, 30**; add 5, multiply by 1, add 5, multiply by 1
8. **18, 23, 22, 28, 27**; add 2, subtract 1, add 3, subtract 1, add 4, subtract 1, add 5, subtract 1
9. **4, 20, 4, 24, 4, 28**; multiply by 2, divide by 2, multiply by 3, divide by 3, multiply by 4, divide by 4
10. **144, 720, 4,320, 30,240**; multiply by 1, multiply by 2, multiply by 3, multiply by 4

COMPOUND WORDS 1   page 114

The answers listed are not exhaustive.

1. become, became, because, behold, beheld, begrudge, behead, belittle, befit, befriend, belabour, bemoan, beloved, beside, betaken, belong, begot, bebop, beset
2. inside, inward, into, inmate, inland, infield, income, indoors, infuse, inhale, insert, install, invest
3. outcome, outgrow, outside, outlaw, outrun, outfit, outback, outcast, outbid, outcry, outdone, outlook, outreach, outsource, outwit, outward

SYMBOL CODING 3   page 115

Go back and check yourself, or have a friend check your answers.

SEQUENCING ITEMS 2   pages 116–117

The answers listed can go in either direction.

1. **Writing process:** Outline, Rough draft, Editing, Final copy
2. **Water cycle:** Evaporation, Condensation, Precipitation, Accumulation
3. **Food chain:** Plankton, Fish, Bird, Cat
4. **Smallest to largest:** Paragraph, Flyer, Pamphlet, Novel
5. **Lowest to highest:** Foundation, Basement, Attic, Roof

6. **Chronological order:** Kennedy, Ford, Reagan, Bush
7. **European countries west to east:** Portugal, Italy, Hungary, Bulgaria
8. **Electoral process:** Campaign, Voting, Ballot counting, Election
9. **Lowest to highest:** Ankle, Thigh, Waist, Forehead
10. **Order of buying:** Consumer, Store, Purchase, Take home
11. **Smallest to largest:** Blueberry, Mushroom, Avocado, Cantaloupe
12. **Chronological order:** Rosa Parks (1955), The Beatles (1964), *Apollo 11* (1969), Nixon resigns (1974)
13. **Judicial process:** Hearing, Trial, Sentencing, Appeal
14. **Smallest to largest:** Electron, Atom, Molecule, Element

WORDS THAT CAN   page 118

1. Vacant
2. Scandal
3. Canoe
4. Candid
5. Pecan
6. Candle
7. Cancel
8. Canvas

FAMILY TREE GAME 2   page 119

1. Ida
2. Nellie
3. His great-grandfather Gerald
4. Victor and Sam
5. Allie
6. Paul

MATCHING CLUES 3   page 120

1. Locket, mock, napkin, peak
2. Packet, task, prank, silken

WHAT'S THE CATEGORY? 3   page 121

1. **Closet:** zippers, hooks, hangers, photo albums, mothballs, hat box
2. **Science lab:** slides, eyewash kit, tubes, element chart, goggles, funnels
3. **Bank:** change, loans, interest, cheques, vault, tellers

ORDERED LETTERS 2   page 122

1. C	4. C	7. B
2. B	5. A	8. B
3. D	6. D	

WHAT'S THE ITEM? 2   page 123

1. Dust
2. Clothes pegs
3. Straw
4. Button
5. Sponges

CLOCK QUIZ 2   page 124

1. 3:38 p.m

2. 6:30 a.m.

3. 9:20 p.m.

4. 5:30 a.m.

DECIPHER THE LETTER CODE 5   page 125

Message: A computer once beat me at chess, but it was no match for me at kickboxing.

COUNT THE CONSONANTS   page 126

There are 244 consonants.

WORDS FULL OF AWE   page 127

1. Declaw
2. Awestruck
3. Drawer
4. Flawed
5. Gnawed
6. Outlawed
7. Seaweed
8. Thawed

DOT COPY 2   page 128

Go back and check yourself, or have a friend check your copied design.

NAME SOMETHING 2   page 129

The answers listed are not exhaustive.

1. C countries: Canada, Chile, Costa Rica, Chad, Cambodia
2. G drinks: Gatorade, Gin, Ginger Ale, Grape juice, Grenadine
3. Y things: Yard, Yacht, Yarn, Yoke, Yo-Yo

LOGIC WORD PROBLEMS 3   pages 130–131

1. Sarah – second
   Walter – third
   Abby – fourth
   Neal – first
   Mallory – fifth
2. Lori danced the Lindy Hop with Leo.
   Amy danced the Jitterbug with Brian.
   Hank danced the Swing with Jane.
   Randy danced the Salsa with Natalie.

TWO DEFINITIONS 3   page 132

1. Leaves	5. File
2. Left	6. Ball
3. Nail	7. Pound
4. Fast	8. Mean

EDIT THE WORD 1   page 133

There could be several correct answers

1. Sable, Tale
2. Hunt, Hut
3. Lace, Ace
4. Sail, Ail
5. Fume, Use
6. Swan, Can
7. Barn, Bar
8. Bank, Tan

ACCOMPLISH THIS TASK 2   pages 134–135

Here are two possible answers for each task:

Dial a phone: phone number, something to say to the other person
Make coffee: coffeemaker, water
Grocery shop: shopping list, cart
Wrap a gift: money to buy the gift, someone to give it to
Go on a date: a plan, a location
Take a photo: camera, an interesting subject
Play a game: board game pieces, players

Feed your pet: pet food, bowl
Take a nap: bed, quiet
Play an instrument: talent, practice
Use a flashlight: batteries, dark
Write a cheque: money in the bank, signature
Wash your hair: shampoo, water
Keep a secret: a secret, strength of character
Ride a bike: a destination, inflated tires
Hem a dress: thread, needle
Go swimming: pool, swimsuit
Bake a cake: recipe, oven
Put out a fire: towel to cover over a small fire, baking soda to smother it
Replace a light bulb: light switch turned off, a new light bulb
Make ice: water, freezer
Walk around the block: sneakers, motivation
Tell a joke: a punch line, sense of humor

LETTER TRANSFER 3   pages 136–137

1. Florence
2. Navy
3. Heart
4. Texas
5. Darwin
6. Swung

Final message: The road to success is always under construction.

A CUP OF WORDS   page 138

1. Occupation
2. Recuperate
3. Cupboard
4. Cupid
5. Hiccup
6. Occupy
7. Porcupine

CODING – OCCUPATIONS   page 139

1. Physician
2. Teacher
3. Accountant
4. Electrician
5. Pilot

LOGIC WORD PROBLEMS 4   pages 140–141

1. Sally – Jack of Hearts
   Rick – Ace of Spades
   Jay – King of Diamonds
   Beverly – Queen of Clubs

2. Harry – Lawn chair
   Emma – Scissors
   Joanne – Hammer
   Leo – Door hinge
   Diane – Wrench

ORDERED NUMBERS 1   page 142

1. c
2. a
3. d
4. b
5. d
6. d
7. a
8. c

MATCHING CLUES 4   page 143

1. Sketch
   Shiver
   Spark
   Think
2. Slick
   Yank
   Wicker
   Yoke

START HERE – END THERE   pages 144–145

There are many correct answers. For each answer just one example of an answer is given. You can check your answers with a calculator.

1. $2 + 18 - 5 = 15$; $2 \times 3 + 9 = 15$; $2 / 2 + 14 = 15$

2. $3 + 15 - 1 = 17$; $3 \times 3 + 8 = 17$; $3 / 1 + 14 = 17$

3. $4 + 20 - 2 = 22$; $4 \times 3 + 10 = 22$; $4 / 2 \times 11 = 22$

4. $5 + 50 - 7 = 48$; $5 \times 8 + 8 = 48$; $5 \times 30 / 3 - 2 = 48$

5. $6 + 70 - 2 = 74$; $6 \times 6 \times 2 + 2 = 74$; $6 \times 25 / 2 - 1 = 74$

6. $7 + 82 - 1 = 88$; $7 \times 11 + 11 = 88$; $7 \times 20 / 2 + 18 = 88$

7. $8 + 30 - 8 = 30$; $8 \times 5 - 10 = 30$; $8 \times 10 / 2 - 10 = 30$

8. $9 + 20 - 4 = 25$; $9 \times 3 - 2 = 25$;
$9 \times 4 / 2 + 7 = 25$

9. $10+40-2=48$; $10 \times 4+8=48$; $10/ 2 \times 9+3 = 48$

10. $12 \times 6 - 10 = 62$; $12 / 2 \times 10 + 2 = 62$;
$12 + 50 = 62$

11. $15 \times 6 - 4 = 86$; $15 / 2 \times 12 - 4 = 86$;
$15 \times 4 + 26 = 86$

12. $24 \times 3 + 20 = 92$; $24 / 2 \times 8 - 4 = 92$;
$24 \times 4 - 4 = 92$

WORDS THAT FIT   page 146

1. Benefit
2. Misfit
3. Outfit
4. Profit
5. Retrofit
6. Graffiti
7. Befitting
8. Fitness

LETTERS-TO-WORD MATCH 4   page 147

Anchor, Attach, Cactus, Charge, Palace, Launch, Orchid, Scenic, Secret, Tickle

SYMBOL CODING 4   page 148

Go back and check yourself, or have a friend check your answers.

SUNNY WORDS   page 149

1. Sundae
2. Sunken
3. Sunbathe
4. Unsung
5. Sundress
6. Sunscreen or sunblock
7. Tsunami
8. Sundial

CALENDAR QUIZ 3   pages 150–151

1. Sunday the 14th
2. Saturday the 6th
3. Wednesday the 24th
4. Wednesday the 10th

TWO COMMON LETTERS 3   page 152

1. eg
2. lo
3. in
4. ru
5. ft
6. sr
7. ia
8. bl
9. tr
10. ic

CLOCK QUIZ 3   page 153

1. 9:45 p.m.

2. 4:00 a.m.

3. 7:05 a.m.

4. 12:50 p.m.

HOW MANY WORDS? 2   page 154

The answers in these lists are not exhaustive.

1. **Accoutrement:** accruement, accrue, counteract, recontact, contact, utterance, accent, contract, concrete, create, account, centrum, romance, concert, acumen, concur, cancer, accent, menace, occur, cameo, cream, came, coma, can, cue.
2. **Gardening:** danger, gander, anger, enrage, grading, ranging, grinned, edging, dagger, grand, gang, dang, aged, egg, gig, dig, in.

FURRY WORDS   page 155

1. Sulfur
2. Unfurl
3. Furnace
4. Furious
5. Refurbish
6. Furniture
7. Furrow

MIDDLE LETTERS 2   page 156

1. Smile
2. Hen
3. Echo
4. Utensil
5. Deli
6. Emotion
7. Aches
8. Seasons
9. Path
10. Salute
11. Chat
12. Speed

MEMORY CROSSWORD 1   pages 157–158

Near, Amuse, Battle, Repair, Sender, Casino

IMAGES MEMORY 2   pages 159–160

Visor, Passport, Suitcase, Toothbrush, Compass, Wallet

DOT COPY 3   page 161

Go back and check yourself, or have a friend check your copied design.

"D" WORDS   pages 162–163

1. Dot
2. Date
3. Detail
4. Dial
5. Direct
6. Dissolve
7. Domestic
8. Down
9. Draw
10. Drop
11. Drive
12. Dust
13. Decline
14. Depress
15. Dull
16. Dive
17. Dose
18. Deck

WORD MAZE – PATRIOTIC   pages 164–165

1. Citizenship
2. Freedom
3. Independence
4. Nation
5. Democratic
6. Justice
7. Flag
8. Veteran

BETTING WORDS   page 166

1. Better
2. Betray
3. Sorbet
4. Between
5. Betrothal
6. Alphabet
7. Diabetes

SHAPE MATCH 2   page 167

1. 4th and 7th shapes match
2. 2nd and 5th shapes match
3. 1st and 7th shapes match
4. 4th and 7th shapes match
5. 4th and 7th shapes match
6. 2nd and 4th shapes match
7. 1st and 5th shapes match
8. 5th and 7th shapes match

TRUE OR FALSE FACTS 2   pages 168–169

1. False
2. True
3. True
4. False
5. True
6. False
7. False
8. False
9. True
10. False
11. True
12. False
13. False
14. True
15. False
16. False
17. True
18. True
19. True
20. True
21. False
22. False
23. True
24. False

MISMATCH 2   pages 170–172

1. A Jet Ski is not for land transportation.
2. Mix is not a way to cut meat.
3. Ham is not a type of beef steak.
4. A fountain is not a form of water.
5. Waves are not a water mass.
6. A stream is not something you walk on.
7. A sheep is not a baby animal.
8. A report might not be based on facts/truth.
9. Reality is not made up or invented.
10. A manuscript is not a publicly distributed document.
11. An answer is not an emotional reaction or feeling.
12. Branch is not a family word.
13. Ocean is not an object you take to the beach.
14. Bowler is not a soccer position.
15. Armour is not a weapon.
16. Sydney is not a capital city.
17. Microscope is not an adjective.

WORDS FULL OF FUN   page 173

1. Function
2. Fund
3. Fungus
4. Funnel
5. Refund
6. Funeral
7. Malfunction

WHAT'S THE CATEGORY? 4   page 174

1. **Ocean:** sand, shells, coral, tide, wreckage, divers
2. **Hospital:** bandages, needles, insurance, medications, sheets, elevator
3. **Restaurant:** menu, cashier, spices, booths, utensils, oil

WHAT'S NEXT? 2   page 175

1. a
2. c
3. a
4. b
5. c
6. b
7. c

CALCULATIONS   pages 176–177

1. Ages are 2, 4, 6, 8, 10, 12, 14, 16, 18, 20
2. 80 seats
3. £200 per month
4. 3 yards
5. 6 sweets each
6. 30 planks of wood
7. 4 hours
8. 5 large tables and 2 small tables
9. 1 coat

HOW MANY WORDS? 3   page 178

The answers in these lists are not exhaustive.

1. **Prestidigitation:** Rest, Digit, Dig, It, On, Tad, Opt, Date, Diet, Drag, Den, Drip, Gate, Oat, Pie, Pig, Pin, Pine, Pear, Pare, Rap, Reap, Rid, Ride, Rat, Rise, Risen, Sit, Sip, Sir, Stir, Stand, Snap, Side, Sedation, Sedan, Tie, Tip, Tan, Trip, Tide, Tired, Riptide, Edition
2. **Mellow:** Meow, Low, Elm, Mole, Well, Moe, Owe, Owl, Woe

WORDS FULL OF INK   page 179

1. Think
2. Link
3. Sink
4. Stink
5. Drink
6. Tinker
7. Shrink
8. Wrinkle

TWO-LETTER PLACEMENT 2   pages 180–181

1. canine
2. actual
3. disco
4. allow
5. inland
6. calm
7. faint
8. factor
9. gossip
10. floral

11. labour
12. crispy
13. inside
14. kindle
15. fossil
16. local
17. sign
18. issue
19. dialogue
20. blank
21. desire
22. legal
23. local
24. enact
25. cousin
26. saliva
27. scarf
28. raise
29. plaque
30. grain
31. linear
32. fiscal
33. react
34. wise

ORDERED NUMBERS 2   page 182

1. b
2. c
3. d
4. a
5. c
6. d
7. d
8. b

ORDERED SYMBOLS 1   page 183

1. c
2. d
3. b
4. c
5. a
6. b
7. d
8. d

THREE-LETTER PLACEMENT 2   pages 184–185

1. endear
2. tartar
3. spouse
4. walker
5. brand or beard
6. clear
7. house
8. altar
9. enormous
10. bearing
11. errand
12. callous
13. seeker
14. start
15. north or earth
16. orange
17. weary
18. furious
19. kernel
20. heart
21. snore or stare
22. cued
23. grand
24. rescue
25. serious
26. earth or north
27. bakers
28. starch
29. barbecue
30. rocker
31. unlearn
32. lousy
33. cranky
34. stars

ASKING WORDS   page 186

1. Mask
2. Flask
3. Task
4. Askew
5. Basket
6. Gasket

MATCHING CLUES 5   page 187

1. Cable, absorb, abrupt, ballad
2. Badger, ballet, barely, double

SHARED NATURE LETTERS   page 188

1. tree
2. beach
3. wind
4. leaves
5. lake
6. flower
7. mountain
8. breeze
9. rain

WORDS FULL OF AIR 1   page 189

1. Éclair
2. Despair
3. Chairman
4. Airbrush
5. Prairie
6. Solitaire
7. Impair
8. Millionaire

CALCULATION WORD PROBLEMS 3   page 190

1. 10:30
2. Yes
3. 19 adults
4. 33 flowers
5. 16 sodas
6. 640 copies of the flyer

"G" WORDS   page 191

1. Goal
2. Glad
3. Game
4. Grace
5. Guest
6. Groom
7. Graph
8. Grill
9. Guard
10. Gross

MATCH THE PARTS 2 page 192

1. behave
   gotten
   locket
   rumour
   sparse
   motive
   parody
   colour

2. theory
   worker
   bundle
   devour
   funnel
   injure
   nuance
   humble

OUR WORDS page 193

1. Tourism
2. Glamour
3. Source
4. Journey
5. Court
6. Savour
7. Adjourn
8. Courier
9. Gourmet or gourmand

PLACEMENT OF LETTERS 2 pages 194–195

1. change
   agency
   region
   tongue
   finger
   magnet
   voyage
   golden

2. dialogue
   higher
   signal
   ignore
   vigour
   assign
   wagons
   mingle

3. gallop
   belong
   orange
   crunch
   during
   slogan
   growth
   legend

4. engine
   timing
   gentle
   harbour
   bright
   origin
   racing
   loving

SOLUTIONS TO A PROBLEM page 196

Here are two possible solutions for each problem:

Feeling stressed out: pause and concentrate on your breathing; call a friend for support

Car won't start: call a mechanic or roadside assistance; choose an alternative mode of transport

Can't find keys: retrace your steps and try to find them; use a spare set for now – the location will come back to you

Have a headache: take aspirin; have a nap

Electricity goes out: check the mains breaker switch; light some candles

Burn your hand: run it under cool water for 20 minutes; cover the burn with a strip of cling film

A fly in the kitchen: open door and coax it out; sit down and observe the fly for a while

Neighbour's dog won't stop barking: speak to your neighbour about it; concentrate on an activity to distract you

Double-booked appointments: call one party to reschedule and apologise; arrange your time to accommodate both

Fallen out with an old friend: Write them a letter of conciliation; mention to a mutual acquaintance that you wish you could mend things

Shrunk a knit in the wash: rewash and stretch; give it to a friend's child

ORDERED SYMBOLS 2 page 197

1. c
2. b
3. d
4. a
5. c
6. d
7. d
8. b

WORDS THAT HAM IT UP 1 page 198

1. Chameleon
2. Thames
3. Hammer
4. Sham
5. Hamper
6. Shampoo
7. Chamber
8. Hammock

COMPOUND WORDS 2 page 199

The answers listed are not exhaustive.

1. bedside, bedtime, bedrock
2. newspaper, newsstand, newsclip
3. ladybird, ladylove, ladyfinger
4. pigsty, pigpen, pigtail

5. handcuff, handshake, handbag

6. lifeless, lifesaver, lifelong

7. sandbag, sandbox, sandpaper

8. fireworks, fireman, fireplace

9. eyelet, eyebrow, eyeball

10. backbone, background, backlog

11. rainfall, rainbow, raindrop

12. moonlight, moonshine, moonbeam

13. buttercup, butterfly, butterball

14. bookworm, bookshelf, bookcase

15. doorbell, doorstop, doormat

16. headlight, headache, headstrong

SEQUENCING ITEMS 3   pages 200–201

The answers listed can go in either direction.

1. **Order of maths education:** Algebra, Geometry, Trigonometry, Calculus

2. **Chronological order:** *Casablanca*, 1942; *Ben-Hur*, 1959; *The Sound of Music*, 1965; *Chariots of Fire*, 1981

3. **Chronological order:** Amelia Earhart, 1932; United Nations founded, 1945; Moon landing, 1969: Berlin Wall, torn down 1989

4. **Lightest to darkest colour:** Yellow, Orange, Blue, Black

5. **Shortest to longest time commitment:** Dialing a phone number, Reading a brochure, Running a marathon, Writing a novel

6. **Process of mailing a letter:** Write letter, Address envelope, Stamp, Put in mailbox

7. **Process of starting a campfire:** Dig hole, Gather kindling, Stack firewood, Light match

8. **Process of getting dressed:** Trousers, Belt, Socks, Shoes (It can be any order you prefer as long as trousers come before belt and shoes, and socks comes before shoes).

9. **Process of planting:** Dig hole, Place seed, Cover with dirt, Water

10. **Process of building:** Planning, Designing, Buying supplies, Constructing

11. **Slowest to fastest:** Walking, Jogging, Running, Sprinting

12. **Process to marry:** Courting, Vows, Reception, Anniversary

13. **Across Europe East to West:** Serbia, Slovenia, Switzerland, Spain

14. **Order of holidays during a year:** Valentine's Day, Easter, Halloween, Christmas Day

15. **Process of purchasing an item:** Choose, Pay, Change, Receipt

MISSPELLED WORDS 2   page 202

acceptable, liaison, exhilarate, receipt, grateful, licence or license, jewellery, rhyme or rhythm, accommodate, guarantee, sergeant, threshold, humorous, ignorance, millennium

TWO COMMON LETTERS 4   page 203

1. gh
2. lm
3. sk
4. fr
5. ab
6. bu
7. is
8. bl
9. he
10. ju

BLANK CROSSWORD   page 204

Have a friend check your answers.

MATCHING CLUES 6   page 205

1. Before
   Belong
   Edible
   Humble
2. Labour
   Marble
   Obtain
   Ribbon

WORDS WITH OUT   page 206

1. Routine
2. Sprout
3. Shout
4. Route
5. Snout

6. Youth
7. Payout
8. Scout
9. Boutique

PARTS OF A WHAT? 1   page 207
1. **Camera:** lens, flash, shutter, aperture
2. **Phone:** speaker, keypad, cord, receiver
3. **Car:** window, ignition, wheel, hood
4. **Boat:** deck, rudder, masthead, tiller

WHAT'S THAT PHRASE? 2   pages 208–209
1. Every cloud has a silver lining
2. Fish out of water
3. Go for broke
4. Go out on a limb
5. Goody Two-Shoes
6. Happy as a clam
7. Hard pill to swallow
8. Head over heels
9. In a pickle
10. Jack-of-all-trades
11. Jump the gun
12. Keep on truckin'
13. Knock your socks off
14. A mountain out of a molehill
15. My cup of tea
16. On cloud nine
17. Rain on your parade

LETTER TRANSFER 4   pages 210–211
1. Ivory
2. Diamond
3. Aldrin
4. Arizona
5. Peanuts
6. Jamaica
7. Golf

Final message: Age is a question of mind over matter:
If you don't mind, age don't matter.

COMPLETE THE WORD SEARCH 2   pages 212–213
1. Elope
2. Hay

3. Donate
4. Entrance
5. Genes
6. Ignore
7. Tame
8. Cent
9. Ladle
10. Robes

```
A  W  L  B  Q  R  M  T  H  E  P  R  A  L
D  F  Y  O  G  B  K  L  A  D  L  E  Q  Y
T  S  S  K  E  L  N  O  J  E  N  H  G  S
W  A  L  F  N  L  I  S  D  S  R  E  W  L
A  R  M  T  E  R  O  B  E  S  E  R  A  M
H  P  K  E  S  P  L  P  H  O  N  D  H  K
L  L  T  C  S  T  U  E  E  C  T  H  L  T
Q  H  A  Y  N  E  T  G  P  E  R  B  E  A
J  A  N  E  L  A  O  C  T  R  A  R  J  N
O  V  C  T  N  T  B  N  A  S  N  O  O  C
M  B  U  O  A  N  P  S  M  N  C  B  M  U
B  I  D  B  M  I  G  N  O  R  E  F  B  C
G  L  V  V  U  C  E  I  Y  K  J  L  G  V
```

UPSIDE DOWN   page 214
1. C
2. B
3. D
4. C

HOT WORDS   page 215
1. Photo
2. Hotel
3. Shot
4. Hotline
5. Slingshot
6. Orthotics
7. Psychotic
8. Dichotomy

LETTER-NUMBER SUBSTITUTION CODE 2   pages 216-217
1. Applicable
2. Practice
3. Eradicate
4. Replicate
5. Despicable
6. Predictable
7. Education
8. Allocate
9. Revocable
10. Cabinet

TWO DEFINITIONS 4   page 218
1. Deck
2. Light
3. Rock
4. Staff
5. Marks
6. Note
7. Difference
8. Scale

FIRST AND LAST LETTERS 3   page 219
1. Tantrum
2. Solar
3. Atlas
4. Lead
5. Heard
6. Reign
7. Above
8. Satin
9. Line
10. Wish
11. Stain
12. Drop

CALENDAR QUIZ 4   pages 220–221
1. Sunday the 28th
2. Friday the 26th
3. Saturday the 13th
4. Tuesday the 30th

RAPPING WORDS   page 222
1. Trap
2. Wrap
3. Strap
4. Rapid
5. Drape
6. Scrape
7. Entrap
8. Graphic

ONE COMMON LETTER 1   page 223
1. P
2. D
3. U
4. M
5. L
6. C
7. Y
8. K
9. H
10. F

MIDDLE LETTERS 3   page 224
1. Plea
2. Nice
3. Tent
4. Inner
5. Apple

6. Mimic
7. Negate
8. Lure
9. These
10. Crawl
11. Pedal
12. Toad

MEMORY CROSSWORD 2   pages 225–226

Marker, Accrue, Amoeba, Detail, Bushel, Sing

IMAGES MEMORY 3   pages 227–228

Swing, Pool, Fence, Lawn chair, Spatula, Barbecue grill

CALCULATION WORD PROBLEMS 4   page 229
1. A. £8.78
   B. £16.22 profit each
   C. £243.30 total profit
2. 96 strawberries
3. 257 people
4. 321 people
5. Yes

WORDS FULL OF AIR 2   page 230
1. Stairs
2. Hair
3. Fairy
4. Unfair
5. Dairy
6. Pair
7. Affair
8. Repair

MATCHING CLUES 7   page 231
1. Parade
   Patent
   Level
   Entree
2. Basket
   Erase
   Note
   Ideal

EDIT THE WORD 2   page 232

There could be several correct answers.

1. Rusty, Duty
2. Firm, Far
3. Fear, Ear